THE GRAND PEREGRINATION

THE GRAND PEREGRINATION

being
the life and adventures
of
Fernão Mendes Pinto

by
MAURICE COLLIS

CARCANET
in association with the
CALOUSTE GULBENKIAN FOUNDATION

This book is the third in a series *Aspects of Portugal* published
in Great Britain by Carcanet Press in association with
the Calouste Gulbenkian Foundation and with collaboration
from the Anglo-Portuguese Foundation.

Series Editors: Eugenio Lisboa, Michael Schmidt, L. C. Taylor

First published in 1949
New edition 1990 by
Carcanet Press Limited
208–212 Corn Exchange Buildings
Manchester M4 3BQ

British Library Cataloguing in Publication Data

Collis, Maurice
　　The grand peregrination. — (Aspects of Portugal).
　　1. Asia. Description & travel. Pinto, Fernao Mendes, 1510–1583
　　I. Title　II. Series
　　915'.043'0924

　　ISBN 0-85635-850-9

Printed in England by SRP Ltd., Exeter

Introduction

Maurice Collis had an unusual apprenticeship. Born and brought up in Ireland, he joined the Indian Civil Service in 1912, being posted to Burma. He had chosen his career in a youthful spirit of adventure and romance. Also, the pay was good. His literary inclinations at that date were vague and indecisive: he wrote a short book on the Napoleonic legend as developed by nineteenth century poets and could not find a publisher for it.

On closer acquaintance, the Orient turned out to be both more and less exciting than he had expected. He suffered much from the loneliness of country stations where he might be the only educated person for a hundred miles. He was a sociable man: congenial company and conversation after a day's work were essential for his happiness. Then again, his mind was always hungry and it was difficult to obtain sufficient books and magazines to occupy the long, dark evenings, to overcome a feeling of being cast away in jungles and mangrove swamps. He wrote melancholy poems, in Spencerian mode, full of Celtic Twilight and Druids. These did not express his real personality which was fundamentally optimistic, energetic and much given to laughter, though there were storms.

By 1922 he felt a great longing to leave the civil service and settle in London. His dream was to become a writer and to take part in the efflorescence of intellectual and artistic life which characterized the twenties and early thirties in Europe. He was on home at the time, spending part of it in Paris in a daze of excitement at the new ballet, the new theatre, the new exhibitions, buying the latest novelists and poets, the literary magazines, getting married. But he could not find any suitable job and although he managed to get his poems published, the lack of public interest and the cruel things the critics said were most debilitating.

Introduction

In spite of his dissatisfactions, the Orient had enchanted him. The stream of books ordered from London included many on the art, history, literature and philosophy of Asia. He devoured all these works with the greatest enthusiasm, becoming widely and variously learned. He observed Burmese village life, its customs and festivals, the elaborate traditional dramas played by travelling bands of actors. He had his horoscope drawn on a palm leaf by one of the last survivors of the royal astrologers of the court of Mandalay.

By the late twenties Maurice had risen to the position of magistrate in Rangoon and his feeling that he was in the wrong career was strongly reinforced by his superiors. He passed the same sentence, for instance, on a European who ran over some Burmese as would have been inflicted on a Burmese who damaged Europeans. He gave a nominal sentence to an Indian political agitator on the grounds of lack of proper evidence. These rulings could not be challenged in law, which made matters worse. He became far more friendly with prominent Burmese and Chinese residents of Rangoon than social custom allowed. He published humorous stories in local newspapers. Although these activities earned him a special place in popular opinion, they resulted in his next posting being to a country station, far to the south of the capital, on the borders of Siam, a considerable demotion.

Yet it was here, in the remote port of Mergui, that he finally was able to embark on his true vocation as a writer. The place had been a noted pirate stronghold in the seventeenth century, the chief figure being Samuel White, a renegade from the East India Company. Maurice discovered many relics of those times, such as, cannon, wine bottles, candlesticks, kitchen utensils and Mrs White's grave, complete with inscription. He read all the contemporary accounts of White's adventures which had culminated in a furious engagement with an East India Company flotilla and a simultaneous massacre of his followers by the Burmese. Maurice was tremendously excited by all this. Wherever he went, he was treading in the footsteps of Samuel White. His house was on the site of White's headquarters. Three of White's cannon were outside his door and ceremonially fired on the Burmese new year. He was told that the town was pestered with ghosts who could not be propitiated by any Buddhist prayer because they were aliens, the relict of some great battle in a fabulous past.

As he gathered more and more information, it dawned on Maurice that this official banishment was to be his salvation. He had spent twenty years turning himself into an orientalist and, at last, he had found the subject for his first book. He resolved to write it during his next long leave and, if he could get it published, to leave the civil service and begin the literary career he had so long desired. He saw that Spencerian poems and amusing short stories were a mistake; that the history of Asia provided an infinity of possible subjects, untouched by other modern authors. As he stood on the wharf receiving a farewell address from the local people, he knew that the long time of uncertainty was over; that at the age of forty five he was going to begin an entirely new life in which the haunting presence of the East would become a memory and a peaceful inspiration.

Once arrived in London, he set to work with characteristic energy and singlemindedness to turn the dream into reality. At times, he was troubled by difficult questions such as, what if it doesn't work out? Will it bring in enough to keep the family going? Suppose it's another false start? He banished such thoughts. And he was right. *Siamese White* was published in 1936 to a chorus of praise from the right critics. The publishers begged him to hurry up with his next book. He could hardly believe it.

He set to work to consolidate his position, writing book after book with the accumulated energy of frustrated years. *The Grand Peregrination* (1949) was his seventeenth volume. He chose the subject simply for its appeal to his romantic temperament and wrote with enthusiasm. This book is among his best: full of curious adventures, curious learning, beautiful prose and a fast narrative pace. Now read on.

Louise Collis

To
CHARLES BOXER

Acknowledgments

Before beginning this book I sought guidance on the Portuguese and German commentary which has grown up round the text of Fernão Mendes Pinto's *Peregrinaçam* and is chiefly scattered in learned publications. As a first step I called on Professor Edgar Prestage, the doyen of Portuguese scholarship in England. He received me with much kindness and advised me to make the acquaintance of Mr. Armando Cortesão and Professor C. R. Boxer. Following his advice, I went to see Mr. Cortesão, who gave me much useful preliminary information and lent me publications of his own which bore on the subject. My next step was to call on Professor Boxer. He is well known for the extraordinary generosity of his character and to say that he laid himself out to help me more than he has helped many others would probably be to minimise his good nature. But I am bound to declare that I seemed to be the especial object of his bounty, since the amount of time he gave me and trouble he took to provide me with information and eradicate my errors was more than anyone could habitually dispense. So high a view of their duty to make a present of their learning to those who ask for it, is, in my experience, far from common among scholars. In declaring my profound indebtedness to Professor Boxer, I do not, however, wish to place him in the invidious position of being held responsible either for the way I have presented my matter or the conclusions I have drawn from it.

In addition to the paramount assistance afforded me by Professor Boxer, I was fortunate in finding others who made my task easier and wish to thank Colonel H. H. Wade for his help in deciphering some old Portuguese documents, Mr. Stephen Freud for his rendering of a tough German commentary, and Mrs. Helen

Acknowledgments

Parry Eden for drawing my attention to what was a valuable embellishment for my narrative.

February, 1949   Maurice Collis

Contents

Contents

CHAPTER ONE

Pinto leaves Portugal to make his fortune

———————————————

The object of the present book is to present Fernão Mendes Pinto to the British public. He has long been regarded as the most extraordinary of all Portuguese adventurers of the sixteenth century, but no biography of him exists in English, though he has particular interest for us, inasmuch as he anticipated by a generation all our great Elizabethans, and visited those countries afterwards to be incorporated in our empire, long before any of our pioneers reached them. He was not merely an adventurer, one who, as he says, was shipwrecked five times and thirteen times sold as a slave, but was a man of mind and sensibility. His vision of the Portuguese empire of the Indies, the Eastern dominion preceding our own, was wide, and embraced every aspect of its life. Living in an epoch of extreme religious bigotry, he was no bigot; at a period of narrow views, he was a liberal; born in cruel and vainglorious times, he was kind and considerate, without vanity and essentially humble. What makes him, however, unique among the startling figures of the sixteenth century is that, after his return home from twenty years' wandering, he wrote the *Peregrination*, a book which the Portuguese rightly regard as one of their classics, for it is not only an account of his travels but a work of art, which is at once a picture of Asia, a relation of what he did and saw, a summing up on the Portuguese empire, a vast gallery of portraits, and an encyclopedia of adventure, both in the sphere of action and of the spirit. We possess no translation of it, except the old one that Henry Cogan gave us long ago in the Cromwellian period. That is an abridgement, for among other omissions it does not give the most dramatic episode in the whole, the strange encounter between Pinto and Francis Xavier, the Apostle of the Indies. What I have sought to do is to found a narrative on the text of the *Peregrination*, just as a biographer does upon any cardinal document, and to utilize as I go along the commentary which subsequent scholarship has heaped up. The difficulty is to define at each stage what precisely Pinto is conveying. Is a given episode a report of fact or is it an impression? Is he recording what he saw or heard, or is it a synthesis or an invention? My endeavour has been, however, not to overwhelm the reader at once with all the questions which might be asked. I seek to lead him from episode to episode, inviting him to enjoy an unusual story, and gradually enabling him to arrive at a true judgment of what he has been reading. My aim is double—to entertain, and to present an estimate of an enigmatic personality, whose experiences in Asia are the prototype of so much that followed, and serve to illuminate by comparison our own peregrinations over the East.

Fernão Mendes Pinto was born about 1509 at Montemor-o-Vehlo, a town at the mouth of the Mondego river, which is halfway between Oporto and Lisbon, his father being a poor nobleman. Our Henry VIII came to the throne in the same year, and the great Tudor period began in which were destined to appear seventy years later Drake and Raleigh and the other adventurers who laid the foundations of the British empire. But by 1509 Portugal had already founded an empire. The Portuguese were navigators long before we took to sailing overseas. They began to explore down the African coast in the fourteen-thirties. By 1469 they were in Benin, by 1482 on the Congo, by 1488 round the Cape of Good Hope, and by 1498 Vasco da Gama had reached India. In 1510, when Pinto was a year old, they took Goa by force from its Hindu ruler and began to build there the most beautiful city which any Europeans have ever built in India, and in 1511 they seized Malacca from the Malays, a position of the same strategic importance as the future Singapore and which gave them command of the route to China, the main sea route for merchandise in Asia. In those lands they were able to buy very cheaply goods

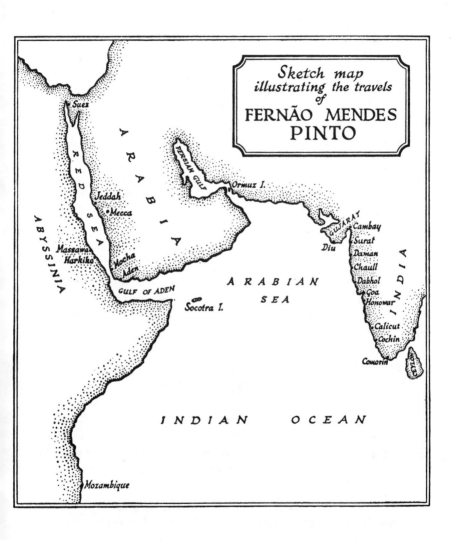

Sketch map illustrating the travels of **FERNÃO MENDES PINTO**

Suez

ARABIA

RED SEA

PERSIAN GULF

Ormuz I.

Jeddah

Mecca

ABYSSINIA

Massawa
Harkiko

Mocha

Aden

GULF OF ADEN

Socotra I.

GUJARAT

Diu

Cambay

Surat

Daman

Chaull

Dabhol

Goa

Honowar

Calicut

Cochin

INDIA

ARABIAN SEA

Comorin

INDIAN OCEAN

Mozambique

which were enormously in demand in Portugal. For instance, an amount of pepper, bought in India for two cruzados, i.e. about five pounds, sold at first in Portugal for about two hundred pounds. The share of the Crown in the oriental trade amounted to four times the internal revenue of the country. It was estimated that a Portuguese adventurer who went East could make more in a day than he could at home in a year by working his land. The population of Portugal at this time is said to have been about a million and a quarter, and most of it was extremely poor. Every young man, brave enough to face the dangers and privations of the voyage to Goa, sought to get there and make his fortune.

Pinto's family lived in wretched circumstances, though he says that his mother spoiled him. He remained at home in Montemor-o-Vehlo until he was twelve. At that time an uncle of his came from Lisbon. Liking the boy, he offered to take him off his father's hands: there was no future for him at Montemor, but at the capital he would have opportunities. Pinto returned with him to Lisbon. It was 1521, the year that John III was crowned King of Portugal, of whom the historian Herculano said: 'Without believing that John III was an idiot, we suppose his intelligence to have been below mediocrity.' Pinto declares that the most vivid memory of his childhood was the funeral of Dom Manuel, the previous King, which he watched soon after his arrival at Lisbon. His uncle now got him the appointment of page to a lady of title. But after eighteen months in this noblewoman's household he did something which he does not specify, except to say that it put him in such imminent danger of severe punishment or mortal revenge, that he was terrified and ran away. He found a small ship in the Tagus estuary, laden with horses and ready to sail for Setubal, a port near-by to the southward, where King John at the moment was holding his court, because the plague was bad in the capital. He offered his services and was taken on board.

This was a prelude to his later adventures, for the ship, after rounding Cape Espichel near Sezimbra and when only fifteen miles from Setubal, was attacked by a French pirate and taken. French pirates had enormously increased on the Portuguese coast,

attracted by the rich merchantmen that were now arriving in
numbers from Goa. The Frenchmen made their seizure without
having to fight, ferociously leaping upon the Portuguese un-
awares; they looted the cargo and scuttled the vessel. Pinto was
bound hand and foot and thrown into a hold aboard the pirate.
The intention was to sell him and his shipmates to Moslem slavers
on the Barbary coast, whither the pirate was bound with a cargo
of arms. To break the spirit of the captives, they were beaten continually. After thirteen days of this, another Portuguese ship
was sighted. The pirate gave chase and, closing in, gave her a
broadside. In this case the Portuguese fought hard, but were overcome. The cargo of slaves and sugar was worth twenty thousand
pounds. This booty was so considerable that the Frenchmen decided to give up the idea of the Barbary Coast, and return home.
Keeping some of the more able-bodied Portuguese to help them
in their navigation, they put the rest ashore, including Pinto.
'We were landed at night,' he says, 'in a road called Melides,
miserably naked, our bodies covered only with the marks of the
lashes which they had inflicted on us so cruelly during the preceding days.' A lady, Donna Beatrice, daughter of the Earl of
Villanova, happened to be residing near-by at the time. She was
very kind to Pinto and his companions, clothing and nursing
them back to health, for their sores were festering and they had
fever. When he was able to travel, Pinto walked the distance to
Setubal, the place to which his ship had originally been bound.
He arrived destitute, but was lucky enough to obtain a post in
the household of a gentleman of the Faria family. There he
worked four years, when he was taken as valet by the bastard son
of John II, the much beloved Dom Jorge, Grand Commander of
the Order of Santiago and once heir to the throne of Portugal,
though at the last moment Dom Manuel had been preferred.

Time went on; Pinto grew up in the service of this personage of
royal blood, his position being that of Gentleman-in-waiting. It
may be assumed that his education was not neglected and that his
attainments grew to include some knowledge of literature, an
acquaintance with the etiquette and manners of society, and the

practice of arms. But the pay given to the gentlemen of a noble household was small; unless they had private means, it hardly sufficed. Being without these, Pinto found that he could not live on his salary. He began to think of the East and of the fortunes that many he knew had made there. It was not adventure or glory that attracted him; for them he would not leave the amenities of Dom Jorge's palace. Money alone it was that he wanted; with money he could revive the name of his family. He need not stay in the East for long. If he were lucky, three years would see him home again. As he had no capital, he could not fit out a merchant ship or even buy a share in one; a pity, for a single round voyage of that sort meant a fortune. He would have to go as a soldier, engaged to defend a ship on the way to India and on arrival to enter the Viceroy's army. But he would not have to remain in the army. There were ways by which a soldier could become a man of business. He had education; he was a gentleman. Once out there he should be able to attach himself to some merchant, as assistant or agent, his salary a percentage on the profits. Having saved some money he could finance a venture of his own. And one successful venture was enough.

But he had not forgotten the alarming experience of his childhood when he narrowly escaped being sold to the Moors of Africa. The seas were full of pirates; he might be captured again. And there were shipwrecks, disease, death at the hands of savage islanders, every kind of grievous hardship. When he thought of these perils, he was less eager to go. It would be better, perhaps, to stay where he was. He was poor, but at least he was safe and well. There was no hurry to make up his mind. In fact, he let the years slip by. Not until 1537, when he was twenty-eight, did he decide to ask his master for leave to go. The permission was given, but he was disappointed that Dom Jorge, though he secured him a passage as soldier on one of three ships that belonged to King John III, did not accommodate him with as liberal a present as he expected in consideration of his lengthy service as Gentleman-in-waiting.

He embarked on 11 March of that year, 'meanly accommodated,' as he says, 'and submitting myself to whatsoever fortune should arrive in those far distant countries, either good or bad.' His fortune was to be often bad and his sojourn was to be long. Perils and privations and unimaginable escapes were to be his lot for twenty years. He was to visit every country on the vast littoral of Asia, see many Kings, great splendours and cruelties, be merchant, ambassador, slave, and pirate, meet a great saint and see a great light.

CHAPTER TWO

Pinto arrives in India and goes to Abyssinia

The fleet with which Pinto sailed consisted of the three ships belonging to the King and two others owned by private merchants. Some of the Captains bore notable names, one being a son of the great da Gama; and the ships, too, were some of them notable, as for example *The Flower of the Sea*.[1] The voyage to the Cape was without incident and, coasting up the east side of Africa, they all came safely to Mozambique. This was part of the Portuguese empire, which, unlike the future British empire, was not territory but may be compared to dots on the immense littoral of Africa, India, Malaya and the Islands. The dots were strong points, castles which served as trade emporiums in this dominion of the seas. Mozambique was one of them.

Its Captain, whose name was Pegado, had received orders from the Viceroy or Governor of the Indies, as was called the head of the imperial administration at Goa, that all ships for India that year should make their landfall, not at Goa, but at Diu, a fortress at the top of the west coast of India. On arrival there they were to reinforce the garrison with their soldiers, because a Turkish attack was believed to be imminent. These orders he conveyed to the Captains of the fleet.

An explanation of what signified this Turkish attack will enable the reader to understand at once the general situation in those waters as it existed at the time of Pinto's coming East. Alexander the Great had opened communications between the Mediterranean and India, and his successors, the Greek Seleucid Kings,

[1]Because it was called after Albuquerque's ship, which foundered with all his treasure off the north coast of Sumatra in December 1511.

had kept them open until the Romans entered and took up the task. The successors of the Romans, the Byzantine Caesars, maintained the connection until the time of the Arab prophet, Mohammed, in the seventh century A.D. The Arabs, by conquering Persia and Egypt, terminated the thousand years of direct intercourse. After the Arabs had civilized themselves, they studied the records of Greek culture, being particularly interested in the scientific side of it. In due course they overran the greater part of Spain and Portugal and founded universities there. It was ultimately from this source that the Portuguese learnt their science of navigation, without which Henry the Navigator in the fourteen-twenties could not have undertaken the explorations which culminated in finding a sea way to India. The Arabian power, with its seat in Persia, was overcome in A.D. 1256 by the Tartars. The Tartars reopened the route between Europe and Asia, and it was during the time of their hegemony that Marco Polo made his famous journey. But this did not last. Soon after 1300 the Tartar power began to crumble and the Turks, a steppe people who had become Mohammedans, established their independence in a corner of Asia Minor. Their martial prowess was such that from this obscure beginning they grew, by the sixteenth century, to be the strongest military nation in the world, their taking of Constantinople in 1453 being only one of their many triumphs. Pinto was eleven years old when their Sultan, Suleiman the Magnificent, came to the throne. Caliph of the Faithful, head of the whole Mohammedan world, his dominions included Egypt, Syria, Arabia, Asia Minor, Mesopotamia, with the Balkans up to the borders of Hungary. Raids were often made beyond that, as in 1498, the year da Gama reached India, when the Turks devastated Poland. It was the Eastern trade which enabled them to finance these exploits. They had an absolute monopoly of it since all oriental commodities entered Europe via the Persian Gulf and the Red Sea, which were patrolled, as was the Indian Ocean, by Turkish fleets.

Given its proper setting in this way, the Portuguese feat of arms in wresting an oriental empire from the most formidable military power of the time can be seen to have been extraordinary, a much more spectacular feat than England's subsequent conquest of India. And, indeed, it inspired the epic of Camoens, who immortalized the great navigators, while ours have found no sacred bard. The most striking feature of the Portuguese capture of the Turks' trade route was the rapidity with which it was made. Da Gama reached India in 1498; in the next dozen years the Portuguese established themselves from Ormuz on the Persian Gulf to Malacca and the Islands. The Turkish fleets which should have prevented this were defeated and driven off the seas.

There is no need to give details, but the main reasons why the Portuguese beat the Turks should be stated if what follows is to be fully understood. These were: the Portuguese were better seamen; their gunnery was better; their science of navigation was better; and they had a better leader, because Albuquerque, who was chiefly responsible for the conquest, was a man of genius.

To return now to the sailing instructions given to the fleet at Mozambique: that it should go to Diu and reinforce the garrison against a threatened Turkish siege. The explanation is that, though by 1537 the Portuguese were strongly set in their empire of the Indies, the Turks were still counter-attacking. They had lost the Eastern trade; it was a matter of vital importance to regain it. In fact, they never regained it; the decline of Turkish power began from the date of its loss. But they sent fleet after fleet, and their corsairs and adventurers, leagued with the native Mohammedans of India, Malay and Sumatra, preyed on Portuguese shipping and did all the harm they could. Nevertheless, the Portuguese always beat them, even when they sent men from that picked corps, the Janissaries, the Turkish foot-guards.

Obeying their instructions, the King's three ships—it was they that had the soldiers on board—went to Diu, where they arrived in September 1538. The Captain of the Fortress, Antonio da Silveira, was delighted at the reinforcement, which amounted to seven hundred men. He kept open table for them, gave them presents in addition to their pay and had the sick nursed back to health. After Pinto had been there something over a fortnight, a certain Captain, a great friend of his, who had been ordered to command with another Captain a reconnoitring expedition to the Red Sea in order to find out what precisely were the Turkish plans against Diu, asked him to join it. There was a chance of making money, he said, by loot or by the capture of a Turkish ship. Pinto agreed, and they set out in two foists, small galleys propelled by oars and sails. It was a risky expedition, for though the Portuguese could water on Socotra Island by the approaches to the Red Sea, they had not taken Aden at its mouth, nor had they a castle inside it. The Red Sea remained a Mohammedan lake. A certain fraction of the old trade still flowed up it, for though the Portuguese had diverted the main stream to the Cape route, they could not cut off every Turkish ship. But Pinto did not realize the dangers he was running. As he says: 'Implicitly believing the Captain's promise that I should soon be a wealthy man, the thing in all the world I most desired, I fondly pictured myself already rich, without reflecting on the uncertainty of men's promises and that the voyage was full of peril.'

Being caught in the tail of the monsoon, they had a rough crossing of the Indian Ocean, but arrived safely at Socotra and took on water. Now came the moment when they had to enter the Red Sea. Pinto's friend, the Captain, had instructions how he was to get the information about the Turks: he should inquire in Abyssinia. This opens a very curious sidelight on oriental history. As I have said, East and West were in touch until the Arabs severed the connection in the seventh century. Europe at the time was barbarous and ill-informed, but it was dimly realized that various Christian communities had been cut off in the East. Men vaguely recollected that the Abyssinians were Christians. But they had forgotten where the Abyssinians lived, for all the ancient maps had disappeared. At the time of the Crusades, when Europe was counter-attacking the Moslem block, not for trade but for religious reasons, the belief that a Christian kingdom existed somewhere in the Moslem rear had military importance. This interest in the Abyssinians called forth the famous forged letter of 1165, purporting to be written by the Emperor of Abyssinia to the Byzantine Emperor. In it he describes himself as King of Kings, inasmuch as seventy Kings paid him tribute. His army, he said, consisted of forty corps, each of one hundred thousand foot and forty thousand horse. His dining-table was an enormous emerald, at which thirty thousand persons daily sat down to dinner. At his right were ranged twelve Archbishops, and twenty Bishops sat on his left. He signed himself Prester John, but does not seem to have given his address.

Europe's critical acumen was so low at the time that the letter was believed to be genuine. It gave substance to the legend of Prester John, an enormously wealthy Christian potentate, residing somewhere in the East and, if he could be found, ready to join forces with Western Christendom against the common enemy, the Moors. The thing was to find him. Marco Polo, when he started on his journey across Asia in 1271, expected to find him somewhere in Tartary. In 1316, however, some Dominican missionaries stumbled upon Abyssinia and people began to argue that its King must be Prester John, though it was a great disappointment to find him so poor a ruler in comparison with the fabulous signatory of the letter. Moreover, he was a schismatic, because his Church, the Coptic, preached heresies. Others did not believe it was he. The visiting Dominicans, who were quite ignorant men and had no maps, were not able to describe clearly where Abyssinia was; in the maps of the middle of the fourteenth century, though Prester John is transferred from Tartary to Africa, he is placed variously on the upper Nile, in the south-east corner, and on the Guinea coast. As Africa was shown to have a shape very different from what it, in fact, possessed, the sum was that no one knew where Prester John lived. In the fifteenth century, when the Portuguese were working their way down the African coast, they looked out for Prester John at Benin. Not finding him there, they concluded that they would come to his kingdom after rounding the continent. Though not as powerful as had been thought, he would be a useful ally against the Turks (as would also be the Indians, whom they believed had been taught Christianity by the Apostle St. Thomas). Eleven years before da Gama reached India,

Pinto arrives in India and goes to Abyssinia

John II sent Pero de Covilham to find Prester John once and for all. This traveller, a prototype of Richard Burton, knew Arabic, and among other feats entered Mecca disguised as a Moslem. Eventually he reached Abyssinia in 1493 and settled down there for the rest of his life. But once the Portuguese were in India and had begun their operations against the Turks, they found it was a naval war and that the Emperor of Abyssinia could be of little assistance. Nevertheless, they played with the idea of land operations; for instance, Albuquerque made a plan to raid Mecca, seize the body of Mohammed and ransom it for Jerusalem, a crusading notion quite outside the commercial policy. Abyssinia would have had a part in this plan. Saner councils prevailing, the Portuguese gave it up. But they kept in close touch with Abyssinia, whose position inside the Red Sea gave them a forward observation post. When Covilham died, they sent other agents and some soldiers to act as bodyguards and teach gunnery. It was from these people that Pinto's friend, the Captain, was to get information, and he carried a letter addressed to a certain Henry Barbosa.

The strait at the entrance to the Red Sea was not efficiently patrolled by the Turks, for the two foists had no difficulty in entering; with a following wind they sailed in the burning heat of that desert gulf for three hundred miles, the mountains of Abyssinia towering on their left. When they were opposite Massawa, a port on its east coast, they saw at sunset a dhow, an Arab sailing vessel of some two hundred tons, and followed her to ask news of her crew. Before dark they closed with her and called out to her Captain, demanding to know whether the Turkish fleet had left Suez and if so where it now was. But no answer was received, or rather the Arabs answered with a sudden discharge of ordnance. Looking down at the foists, which were much smaller than their dhow, they shouted in triumphant high spirits, brandishing swords, waving flags and streamers, and called upon the Portuguese to give themselves up. This bravado had some effect; the foists lay off and the two Captains called a council. It was decided that such a piece of impertinence could not be tolerated; they must accept the challenge and fight it out. Accordingly they began to batter the dhow with their artillery, a tactic that never failed if the odds were reasonable, so superior were the Portuguese as gunners. It was already dark when they opened fire, and all night they hung close to the dhow, their balls passing clean through her hull. When the sun rose she was a shattered hulk. Sixty-four of her men were dead, and when the Portuguese came alongside and flung fire-pots on deck, a sort of incendiary bomb, as was then often done before boarding, the rest of the Arabs jumped into the sea, except five who were too badly wounded. Of these, one was the Captain, who appeared to be a European.

The Portuguese interrogated him, asking as before about the Turkish fleet, but he was a stubborn man and would answer nothing. Under torture, however, he gave the information that the Turkish fleet had sailed from Suez and was in the Red Sea, though not, he believed, bound for Diu, but for Aden, which was to be strengthened as a base for a future attack on the Indian coast. In the course of his torments he confessed that he was a renegade Christian, a native of Majorca, who had abjured his faith for love of a Moslem girl, with whom he was living in Jeddah, the port of Mecca. This deeply shocked the Portuguese. They begged him to give up his abominable belief. Now that he was again in Christian company, let him save his soul from certain damnation. Though they spoke gently, urging him with tears to recant, he would not, but with brutish obstinacy, as it seemed to them, gloried in his errors, as if he had been born a Moslem. Horrified by his wickedness they tied a stone round his neck and, bound as he was, threw him into the sea. Keeping the other four Arab prisoners, they sank the dhow with its cargo, which was nothing but packs of old stained cloth, a great disappointment.

After this sea-fight, very insignificant compared with those in which Pinto was afterwards to be involved, the foists put into a port five miles south of Massawa, called Harkiko, which was in the territory of the Emperor of Abyssinia. Here they met the agent of Henry Barbosa, the man to whom the Commander of Diu's letter was addressed. He had been sent to wait at Harkiko on the chance of seeing a Portuguese vessel, because the Portuguese in Abyssinia, nervous over the recent Turkish moves, wanted to be reinforced. The agent had a letter to this effect and said he would take the Captains to a town some distance inland, where Barbosa was stationed as Commander of the Queen-Mother's bodyguard, a force composed of Portuguese. The Captains, however, decided to send Pinto and three others; they should carry the letter from the Captain of Diu, get Barbosa's answer and return, since it was impossible to comply with his request for help. Meanwhile, the foists could be careened.

Next day Pinto set out with his three companions, mounted on mules, accompanied by Barbosa's agent and by some Abyssinian guards. In his narration of this journey we begin to notice his manner as a writer. He shows himself full of curiosity; he tends to admire what he sees and to present it in a pleasing light. His tone is optimistic; he is in no way prejudiced against native inhabitants, nor does he feel superior to them. Though a Catholic of the sixteenth century, he is a liberal Catholic, indeed a Catholic of quite exceptionally wide outlook. He is essentially humane; in the episode just described of the renegade Christian, one perceives that he thought the man's torture and death over cruel. Though he will frequently record such doings, they always seem to move him to pity. He likes to dwell on what is admirable. A gentleman, whatever colour he may be, is always a gentleman. A noble action excites him. Women in particular have his respect. In the course of the *Peregrination* there are many striking portraits of oriental women. He makes his characters talk at length, and though we must suppose that their speeches are invented, as those in the Greek and Latin historians, they ring true to anyone acquainted with the East and certainly represent the heart of what was said.

So he sets out on his mule along the coast belt that lies below the high tablelands of central Abyssinia, for Harkiko was in what we call Eritrea and was five hundred miles from Addis Ababa, the capital. They travelled for a week or so at the rate of fifteen miles a day and, though they left the plain and entered the foothills, they did not penetrate far into Abyssinia proper. Pinto gives various names, which cannot now be identified, a characteristic of his book, where he is composing a scene rather than relating an actual experience. One cannot say for sure whether unidentifiable names are invented, or are copyists' errors or misprints, or due to forgetfulness or incorrect information. But they are probably an indication that the passage where they occur is not a piece of reporting, though presented as such for literary reasons. As the book goes on, frequent comments will be made on this point, until eventually it is possible to formulate an explanation. With this warning, I continue the relation.

Pinto and his companions stopped each night at a monastery and were kindly entertained by the Coptic monks. At the second place, soon after their arrival there came riding to them on horseback a young Abyssinian nobleman, only seventeen years old, with his bodyguard on mules. They noticed that his horse had harness in Portuguese style; the saddle-cloth was of purple velvet trimmed with a gold fringe. It turned out that the Governor of the Indies had sent him those accoutrements by the hand of one, Lopez Chanoco, who on his return journey was captured by the Turks in the Red Sea and taken as a slave to Cairo. On hearing of this the young nobleman sent an Addis Ababa Jew to redeem him, but Chanoco died before the Jew could reach Cairo. Deeply concerned that the man who had carried a present which he valued so much had lost his life, he had a splendid requiem mass sung and, hearing that Chanoco had three young daughters at Goa, now left destitute, he sent them a sum of money equivalent to seven thousand pounds, 'a liberality truly royal,' exclaims Pinto, 'and which I relate here as well to testify to the nobility of this prince as to serve as an example of charity to others.'

This prince provided the four Portuguese with horses in place of their mules, and sent servants with them, who were able to make the journey far more comfortable, having authority to demand the best food and lodging. In this way they arrived at the place where Barbosa and his forty Portuguese guardsmen were stationed. These men, though living an easy life and provided with everything they fancied, were miserably homesick in their remote outpost, and welcomed Pinto and his companions with tears of joy.

It was too late that night to call on the Queen-Mother. Next morning, however, after a hearty breakfast they all went to her palace. It happened to be a Sunday, and she was hearing mass in her chapel. Presently, being told of their arrival, she called them into her presence. They knelt and kissed the fan she held in her hand. She smiled and said: 'You cannot imagine how glad I am to see you, Christians from the outer world.' And she made them sit on mats closer to her than was usual and addressed them in a tone of great good humour. What is the name of the Pope, how many kingdoms are there in Europe, have any of you been to Jerusalem? These were some of the questions she put them. And she complained that the ruin of the Turk was not being accomplished with the speed she would like.

They spent nine days there and every day waited upon the Queen and tried to satisfy her thirst for news. The last day, when they came to say good-bye, she seemed upset and urged them to stay on. When Pinto told her they must get back to the foists with Barbosa's reply to the Commander of Diu's letter, she sighed and said: 'I am sorry that you are going so soon, but since it cannot be helped, I wish you a safe and profitable voyage home.' Before they left next morning, she sent them each a present of one hundred and twenty pounds in gold, a sum which at that date would have sufficed to start Pinto on the commercial career he wanted. She had already provided them with food, horses and a guard. This Queen belonged to a type of Eastern lady, dignified, religious, generous and emotional, which Pinto often describes.

When the four Portuguese were back in Harkiko, they helped their companions to finish the careening, and nine days later they all set sail for India. But now their luck turned. The Queen's good wishes, uttered with such warmth, were to be signally falsified. They had weighed anchor an hour before dawn and with a following wind were gliding southwards along the coast when, in the early afternoon, as they passed one of those treeless islands, utterly barren and burnt like a brick, which abound in that region, they discerned three vessels on the other side of it. Prudence demanded that they should get out of the Red Sea as soon as possible. But the sight of the vessels tempted them. If they could make prizes of them, their voyage would be truly worth while. Here was their chance. Course was altered. As the wind had fallen, the oars were got out. After two hours they were round the island and could see the vessels clearly. Only then the truth dawned on them. They were not Arab trading dhows, as they had seemed, but Turkish men-of-war galleys, scouting ahead of the main fleet, and far larger and more heavily armed than the little foists. There was nothing to do but run for it, and the foists were turned back towards the land. But they had been detected by the Turks, who hoisted more sail and, favoured by a breeze springing up behind them, gave chase. Though the Portuguese rowed madly in the blinding heat, they were overhauled and soon the Turkish balls began to reach them. In these first discharges nine men were killed and twenty-six wounded. The foists were badly holed at the waterline and to lighten them some of the stores had to be thrown out. The Turkish galleys drew closer, until they ranged alongside, the soldiers on them shouting, gesticulating, firing, and so near that they could even reach the Portuguese with their pikes. A running fight of this sort must end in disaster, for the Turkish ordnance was heavier than theirs.· The only course was to stand and board one of the galleys, and by a sudden dash overwhelm her crew by superior valour. The Portuguese had forty-four men left. A chance offered because the principal galley had drawn ahead of the others and for the moment the two foists could concentrate upon her. They attacked from both sides. A lodgment was made on board, a ferocious hand-to-hand fight ensued, and twenty-seven of her soldiers were killed, huge men reputed to be Janissaries. But the other two galleys caught up and threw reinforcements on board. The Portuguese could not press their initial advantage. Wearied and overcome by superior numbers they were fought to a standstill. Only eleven were left alive and they were made prisoners.

Pinto arrives in India and goes to Abyssinia

After this desperate sea-fight Pinto, who was unwounded, found himself being carried by the Turks down the Red Sea. He says that aboard the large galley was an important officer, an Admiral of the Fleet, whose father-in-law was Governor of Mocha, a town on the Arabian shore of the straits. It was for Mocha they were making. Their arrival there caused a stir. The Governor and all the inhabitants hastened to the waterfront. On landing, the Admiral was given an ovation. His eleven Portuguese prisoners, each attached by the neck to a long chain, were led in triumph through the town. A howling brutal mob encompassed them. In the background was a Moslem priest, a Hajji who had just returned from a pilgrimage to Mecca. He was seated in a cart with a silk embroidered awning, and raising his hands he blessed the mob, enjoining them to thank the Prophet for the victory which the Admiral had won. As he spoke, he became carried away by his fervour, and, livid with fanaticism, incited the crowd to strike the Portuguese, screaming that the Prophet would have it so; the harder they struck, the greater their reward would be in Paradise. Roused to frenzy by his words, the people set on the prisoners, beating them so cruelly that Pinto did not think that he could come through it alive. They were paraded all over the town to the sound of music, the object of every kind of insult and humiliation. Even purdah women came out to shout abuse, and children and ancient men threw slops over them from windows and balconies.

They survived, however, because the soldiers who had taken them saw to it that they were not irretrievably damaged, as it was intended to sell them for slaves. After the parade through the town they were thrown into a dungeon, still chained together. Two of their number, however, were so badly hurt that they died in the night. Next morning, when the jailer saw the dead bodies, he reported to the magistrate, who had them loosed from the chain and dragged by the feet round the town. The populace, given a free hand as the bodies were worthless, battered them to pieces and threw them into the sea.

After some days the surviving nine Portuguese were led into

the market place and put up for auction. Pinto says he was the first to be offered. As the auctioneer was calling for bids, the Hajji arrived in his cart, accompanied by ten other priests, his subordinates. Interrupting the sale, he addressed himself to the Governor of the town, who was presiding, and demanded that the Portuguese should be given to him to take to Mecca, where he would offer them to the Prophet as slaves for his tomb. At that time a number of captured Portuguese were mosque slaves in Mecca. The Governor, however, replied that since they were the property of his son-in-law, the Admiral, the Hajji should prefer his request in that quarter, and added, to smooth his refusal: 'I am sure the Admiral will raise no objection to a course that conforms so well with our faith.'

The Hajji replied: 'Your Honour is Governor here and can give any order you like. If the bequest of the slaves to the Prophet's tomb is made through the Admiral, the Prophet will be under an obligation to him, while you will get no credit at all. Besides, there is no need to consult the Admiral, because the Prophet, anyhow, has a right to the slaves, since the Admiral could never have won the victory, no matter how brave his soldiers, had not the Prophet given it to him.'

In venturing to say this, the Hajji committed a grave indiscretion, for it reflected upon the valour of the Turkish navy. Immediately a Janissary, Captain of one of the three galleys, advanced towards him with a menacing scowl. This man had a great reputation for bravery and was nettled that a mere Arab, albeit a priest and a Hajji, should insinuate that without the Prophet's intervention, as by an angel flying to their help from the sky, he and his men could not have taken a handful of infidels. He glared, and while Pinto, tattered, filthy and covered with weals, waited in front of the auctioneer, he harangued the Hajji with crushing sarcasm: 'If, as I suppose, you want to assure for your soul a happy salvation, you would be better advised to distribute among my poor soldiers some of your own money, said to be far more than a priest should possess, than to attempt to rob them of their slaves by a specious argument. No one would think to see you standing so neat and trim in your robe that you were only a common trickster. But you shall not take me in; if you want to make an offering at Mecca and gain the good graces of the Dean of the Tomb, you shall not do it at the expense of my soldiers and me.'

The Hajji, who had never been spoken to before so rudely, and was surrounded by a crowd of devoted Arabs with no liking for the Turkish soldiery, reproved the Captain in the most bitter terms for daring to insult a holy priest, and called his soldiers many ill names. This was too much. The Turk, commanding his men to draw their swords, set on him and his supporters. A violent commotion arose, involving the whole town of Mocha. The Governor, with the magistrates, strove all they could to restore peace. But they were powerless before the passions of the contestants. A sanguinary battle was fought in the market place, with heavy casualties on both sides. The Turks were greatly outnumbered, but discipline and experience told in the end. They drove their opponents back, killed the Hajji, and in their rage broke into his house, dragged out his wives and children, hacked them to pieces, and looted the house. Then, quite out of hand, they started to pillage the town, dispatching everyone they suspected of siding with the Hajji. The Portuguese, defenceless in the middle of the square, and the bone of contention between the two parties, were in imminent danger. Choosing a moment when the fighting swayed to one side, they crept back to the dungeon, begging the jailer to lock them up, which he did, to their immense relief.

The Admiral managed at length to control his men. But the inhabitants were in a dark mood, and it took all the tact he possessed to pacify them. Three days later, when quiet was quite restored, Pinto and his companions were again led into the market place to be sold along with the stores and cannon which had been taken from the foists. Pinto, as we shall see, was an unlucky man, though in spite of the misfortunes that continually befell him, he did not lose his life, as he might well have done and as did many of his comrades in adversity. Now he was bought by the last person he would have chosen, a Greek renegade, in itself a disconcerting fate, and made far worse because the fellow was a brute. Pinto very seldom denounces a man; nor did he easily lose heart. But of this Greek he says: 'Miserable that I was and the most wretched of all, fortune, my sworn enemy, made me fall into his hands. I shall detest him as long as I live. During the months I was with him, he used me so cruelly that I got desperate, for I could not bear the evil things he did to me. Seven or eight times I was on the point of poisoning myself, which, had I done so, would have given me at least the satisfaction of feeling that I was defrauding him of what he had paid for me, a loss he would have felt, for he was the meanest man who ever lived.'

After three months, a neighbour, seeing from Pinto's face that he would commit suicide, and being sorry for him, advised the Greek to sell him while he could, a sufficient hint, for on the mere suspicion that he might lose his slave, he sold him to a visiting Jew for about two pounds' worth of dates.

The Jew was travelling with other merchants and left Mocha shortly afterwards. Pinto does not say precisely what route he took nor any information about this journey, except that at the end of it they arrived at Ormuz, the island at the mouth of the Persian Gulf which the Portuguese had taken from the Turks and fortified. There the Jew offered him to the Captain of the fortress, Dom Fernandez da Lima, who ransomed him for thirty pounds, some of it his own money and some raised by subscription in the town. The Jew was pleased at the profit, but not so pleased as was Pinto to be a free man again.

This chapter of the *Peregrination* gives a vivid glimpse of the Moslem world. Even for to-day, as anyone who has been to the Red Sea ports will testify, it remains characteristic. The historical facts upon which it rests are unimpeachable. That Pinto went to the Red Sea is probable. Nevertheless, one wonders whether the story, as related, is not his way of describing the situation in the Indian Ocean as it existed when he arrived. For the proper understanding of the vast picture he was about to paint of the whole East, it was essential to begin with a reference to the Turks. His method is always to convey information, not directly by a bald

Pinto arrives in India and goes to Abyssinia

summary of events, but indirectly by representing himself as taking part in them. But I beseech the reader not to worry himself at this stage. The problem will continually be posited and, before the book is ended, he will be led by degrees to find its solution.

CHAPTER THREE

Pinto returns to India and is employed as a soldier

Free, though in tatters and without effects, Pinto left Ormuz a fortnight later on a Portuguese ship with a cargo of horses. Their destination was Goa, but a stop would be made at Diu for water. The wind favoured, and in seventeen days they were across the Arabian Sea and, coasting down Kathiawar, were approaching Diu. The night before they were to enter the port, they saw through the darkness many fires and heard the roll of cannon. What was happening on shore? Pinto's information was that the Turks were consolidating their fleet at Aden. Could it be that they were already attacking Diu? Sail was shortened so as to avoid entering the roadstead before dawn. With daylight a great many ships were descried in front of the fortress, but were too far off to be clearly identified. Perhaps the Governor of the Indies was making an inspection, or the Infant, John III's brother, who was expected from Portugal on a visit. Pinto, however, was convinced it was the Turks. As they hesitated what to do, five galleys were seen leaving the port and making towards them, great ships, covered with flags and streamers so long that the ends dipped into the water. Their lavish bunting proclaimed them; they were Turkish men-of-war. Much alarmed, the Portuguese clapped on all sail and steered for the open sea. Pinto, who so shortly had escaped from Turkish slavery, saw the same fate closing on him again. All day the Turks pursued, but failing to catch up, turned back at nightfall.

The Portuguese continued their course, and two days later put into Chaul, one of their own fortresses, which lay a little south of the present Bombay. There they were told by its Captain that the

Pinto returns to India and is employed as a soldier

Turks had been investing Diu for the last three weeks. 'By the grace of God you have had a wonderful escape,' said he. 'The Turkish fleet, under Suliman Pasha, the Viceroy of Egypt, is a huge one; it has fifty-eight galleys and reserves of men in eight transports.'

After one day at Chaul, the Portuguese left for Goa. About sixty miles north of that city, they met near the mouth of the river Kharepatan three foists commanded by a certain Fernão de Moraes. 'The Viceroy,' he said, 'has ordered me to go to Dabul and capture a Turkish supply ship in that port. But he sent me away at such short notice that I could not collect enough men.' And he begged for the loan of fifteen of theirs.

This was an awkward request. No one wanted to go fighting at Dabul. Eventually twelve men were given him, 'of which number I was one, as being always the least respected,' says Pinto. The three foists made for Dabul, which is seventy-five miles back up the coast. But the Turkish ship had left and de Moraes turned and made for Goa, one hundred and fifty miles to the south.

In my *The Land of the Great Image* I have given a full description of Golden Goa as it was a hundred years later. At the time of Pinto's arrival the more splendid baroque buildings, for which it became famous, were not yet built. The town was little different in appearance from what it had been under Indian rule. Life was rough; murders were frequent, and great licence of manners prevailed. There were few churches, no Jesuits or Augustinians, no Inquisition; it was less a capital than a fortified outpost. Pinto, though his intention was to get into trade, was obliged by his necessitous state to take any job that offered immediately. It happened that the Viceroy was on the point of sending five foists to Honowar, eighty miles to the south, to demand from its Queen a Turkish galley which a contrary wind had driven into her port. One of the Captains of the five foists was a friend of Pinto's. Seeing him so poor and shabby, he offered to enlist him for the expedition. Pinto agreed to go, hoping it might lead to something better, and was very glad to accept an advance of pay amounting to two pounds, ten shillings. 'The Captain and soldiers, pitying the case I was in, gave me what spare clothes they had, by which means I was reasonably well pieced up again,' he says.

There followed the affair of Honowar, which throws light on the relations between the Portuguese empire and the local sovereigns. It is important to note that the Moghuls had been Emperors in India for only twelve years and had not yet extended their dominion to the west coast, which was ruled by independent Kings, some being Mohammedan and some Hindu. The Mohammedans were in alliance with their co-religionists, the Turks, but the Hindus favoured the Portuguese. The ruler of Honowar was a Hindu woman, styled Queen, though she was a feudatory of the King of Kanara, in whose dominions Honowar lay.

The Portuguese made known their arrival in the roadstead by a peal of ordnance, a roll of drums, a blare of trumpets and by martial tunes, to impress the Queen and let her see that they were not afraid of the Turkish ship. After anchoring, Vaz Coutinho, the Captain-in-chief of the five foists, sent an envoy ashore to the Queen with a letter. 'How is it that you, an ally of the King of Portugal, allow a Turkish ship to stay in your port?' Such was the substance of what he wrote to her.

A reply from her came quickly back: 'You and your ships are most welcome,' she said. 'Though a devoted ally of the King of Portugal, my forces were not strong enough to drive away a Turkish man-of-war. But count now on my full support.' And she added: 'If together we can win a victory, I shall be as pleased as though the King of Kanara, my sovereign, were to invite me to dinner and place me next his wife.'

Vaz Coutinho did not believe that, in fact, she would do anything to help him, but he dissembled from prudence. Calling a council of his men, who were more like free-lances than pressed soldiers, he laid his plans before them, urging that an attack should be made on the man-of-war. All signed a paper agreeing to this. Whereupon he entered the river and, after going two cannon-shot, dropped anchor. Hardly was he there when a rowing-boat was seen approaching from the town. In it was a Brahmin, who spoke good Portuguese, no doubt one of the Queen's

Pinto returns to India and is employed as a soldier

ministers. He boarded Coutinho's foist and delivered this message: 'The Queen desires me to say that she begs Your Honour on no account to proceed further. To fight the Turk is much too dangerous. Spies declare he is strongly entrenched beside the place where his galley is moored. Your Honour's forces are wholly inadequate. Her Majesty trembles at the thought of the risks you incur. In the name of God, give up the attempt.'

Coutinho replied: 'I kiss Her Majesty's hands for the extraordinary favour she has done me in conveying such excellent advice. But Portuguese custom precludes me from taking it, for our practice is to welcome superior numbers, since the more there are to fight, the greater their loss and for the same reason the greater our gain.'

With this florid speech he dismissed the Brahmin, giving him a length of green woollen cloth and a hat lined with red satin, a gift which seemed to make him very contented.

But the Queen was right. The Turk was too strong, Coutinho too rash. He had only one hundred and eighty men. Landing with half of these, Pinto being of the number, he marched on the Turkish trench while the foists covered his advance with their artillery. A hand-to-hand fight took place, but after being mown down by grape and blown up by a mine, the Portuguese had to retire to the foists, all their number but two killed or wounded. Among the dead was Coutinho's own son. Pinto was hurt in two places. The foists withdrew to the mouth of the river.

Next morning the Brahmin arrived again, bringing a present of fowl and new-laid eggs. The Queen was very grieved at what had happened, he said. She recommended chicken-broth for the wounded. How she wished His Honour had taken her advice!

But Coutinho, what with his defeat and the death of his son, was in a black mood. 'Take your hens off!' he told the Brahmin roughly. 'Eggs are no substitute for the assistance the Queen should have given me.' And getting angrier 'he could not forbear lashing out some words that were a little harder than was requisite,' as Pinto puts it. 'Tell the Queen,' he said, 'that I will thank her more fully on a later occasion for a present sent to blind me to her treachery! When the Governor of the Indies learns of this, as I swear by the grave of my son that he shall, he will know how to pay her out, I dare say.'

The Brahmin, terrified by these menaces, hastened to the Queen and made his report. 'This accursed Turk's galley will lose me my kingdom!' she exclaimed, and much perturbed, summoned the Council. The advice she got there was to soothe Coutinho. Another Brahmin was sent, more elderly than the first, of more venerable appearance, a close relation of hers. By this time, Coutinho's anger had subsided, and he perceived the need for discretion. The Queen had shown goodwill as far as she dared; to continue to rebuff her would be to risk estranging an ally of Portugal, for which he might incur the Viceroy's displeasure. He therefore received the aged Brahmin with cordiality. After the customary exchange of compliments, the Brahmin said: 'Her Majesty has commanded me earnestly to assure Your Honour that within four days,' and he emphasized the last words, 'her people will burn the galley, which has been the cause of so much ill, and turn the Turks out of the kingdom. That is all she can do, and she promises to do it.'

Coutinho found this too good to be true, but since to make an enemy of the Queen would not further Portuguese interests, he accepted her assurance and told the Brahmin that he believed her to be Portugal's good ally.

After this reconciliation, he sailed at once for Goa to put his wounded into hospital there, or they would have died for want of nursing. The harassed Queen, it seems, made some show of attacking the galley, but that she burnt it is not alleged.

The expedition had been of no advantage to Pinto. Though he had escaped with two wounds which were not serious, he might easily have been killed. But this was the lot of poor soldiers in India—wretched pay, many dangers and no prospects. To better himself it was essential to get into commerce. But how to do this without capital? Such was his dilemma when Coutinho landed him at Goa.

CHAPTER FOUR

Pinto goes to Malacca and visits
Batak in Sumatra

<hr/>

Pinto was discharged from hospital in three weeks. Debating what next to try, he asked the advice of a Friar, probably a Franciscan, with whom he was on friendly terms. This man told him that a certain Pero de Faria had been appointed Captain of Malacca, to which fortress he would shortly be going to take charge. He was recruiting men to bring with him, and the Friar suggested that Pinto should offer his services. True, it was only a soldier's job, but prospects at Malacca were better than in Goa. Lying as it did on the Straits, opposite Sumatra and on the way to China, it was the great entrepôt for the Far Eastern trade. With wider horizons and more freedom of choice, there were chances there of making money, particularly for a man of education.

Pinto was attracted by this suggestion, more especially as he understood that Pero de Faria belonged to the same family as the gentleman whom as a youth he had served for four years before entering the household of the bastard Dom Jorge. He accordingly waited on de Faria, who, on learning that he had worked for the family before, immediately offered him a military post with a scale of pay above that of the other men enlisted. There was, however, one drawback; de Faria, before proceeding to Malacca, was obliged to accompany the Viceroy on an expedition to relieve Diu. That meant more fighting, perhaps desperate fighting. But it was one thing to be an unattached soldier, as Pinto had been so far, at everyone's beck and call, always selected for the least agreeable task, and another to serve under the protection of a nobleman.

Pinto goes to Malacca and visits Batak in Sumatra

The Viceroy had assembled a very large fleet, consisting of two hundred and twenty-five vessels of which eighty-three were of good size, says Pinto, a statement that shows what a strong naval force the Portuguese could muster. But Pinto was not destined to fight at Diu, the siege of which covered the defenders with glory and is accounted in history an heroical exploit among the many accomplished by Portugal in Asia. Frightened by news of the Viceroy's coming with superior numbers, the Turks raised the siege and retreated to the Red Sea. On arrival at Diu the soldiers of the fleet were put to work to repair the fortifications. Pinto, with the rest of Pero de Faria's company, worked for three months on the main bastion facing the sea. This being fully restored, de Faria was ordered to take up his post at Malacca. He returned to Goa, and after provisioning the ships under his charge, sailed East. Pinto gives the date of their arrival at Malacca as 5 June 1539, that is, nine months after his first arrival in India. His dates, as they have come down to us in his *Peregrination*, are in places confused, but this date, which marks the beginning of his experiences in the Straits, may be taken as correct, since it can be checked against the known dates of the failure of the Turks at Diu and of Pero de Faria's appointment to Malacca.

The situation at Malacca will be readily understood because it was an extension of what obtained at Goa. Just as in India the Turks were in alliance with the Moslem rulers of the west coast —at Diu, for instance, the Sultan of Cambay, in which kingdom Diu was situated, invested that city from the land side while the Turks bombarded it from the sea—so in Further India they had their Moslem allies, and planned with their aid to drive out the Portuguese. The Sultan of Achin was the strongest and most warlike of these allies. His kingdom was situated on the northern tip of Sumatra. By reinforcing him with fighting men, munitions and ships, they sought to strengthen him till he could take Malacca.

Sumatra is a thousand miles long and was divided at that period into nineteen independent kingdoms. The rulers of these, some of them Hindu by religion, afraid of the rising power of Achin, which might also turn against them, tended to look for help to the Portuguese. By providing them with arms to counter the arms supplied by the Turks to Achin, the Captain of Malacca aimed at keeping a balance of power. Such was the world of half-civilized Sultans and Hindu Rajahs, to which Pinto had come, a world with which we are surprisingly familiar, because its description in Conrad's novels holds nearly as true for the sixteenth as for the nineteenth century.

As soon as the arrival of the new Captain at Malacca was known, the rulers of those states which were friendly to Portugal sent envoys to congratulate him and renew their treaties of friendship. Among them was the Ambassador of the King of Batak, a Sumatran kingdom south-west of Malacca across the Strait.

He brought Pero de Faria a present of eagle-wood, the famous scented wood of those countries, and a precious resin, then called Benjamon, used for incense. These he presented, as also a letter from the King, which was in the Malay language, written on palm-leaf, as are still some books in Further India. The gist of it was this: 'Will you supply me with cannon-balls and gunpowder for use against the King of Achin, in exchange for pepper, camphor, resin and scented wood, the products of my country? Achin is a tyrant who threatens to take my country. If he does this, he will then attack Malacca.'

Since the Portuguese policy towards Sumatra was to support its various Kings against Achin, and also to open up trade with them, de Faria had no difficulty in giving the Ambassador a favourable reply. After being well entertained for some days, he was dismissed with various munitions of war, such as fire-pots, cannon, grape and gunpowder. These amounted to more than he had asked for, and while he was saying good-bye, he was so overcome with gratitude that he burst into tears.

They gave him a good send-off. About two and a half miles west of the mouth of the Malacca river is an islet called Upeh. Here he was entertained to a farewell dinner by the port authorities. A band played on hautboys, drums, trumpets and cymbals, and a choir sang part-songs, accompanied by a Portuguese orchestra of harps, lutes and viols. The Ambassador was so astonished at this music that he kept on putting his finger in his mouth, an oriental mannerism, denoting stupefaction, which is of great antiquity (among the figures carved on the pedestal for an alms-bowl, Kushan work of the second century A.D., which was in the 1947 Exhibition of Indian Art at Burlington House, was a man with his finger in his mouth as he gazed at the miraculous birth of the Buddha).

After the Ambassador was gone, it occurred to Pero de Faria to take personal advantage of the visit and do some trade with Batak on his own account, for on inquiry he had learnt that commodities there were very cheap. The King, being now under an obligation to him, would no doubt grant every facility. To improve the occasion still more, Pinto should go as his official envoy and flatter the King with further offers of help. A caravel, a variety of light sailing vessel, was loaded with a cargo worth twenty thousand pounds, which, traded for the products of Batak, would yield a great profit. The business side of the venture was entrusted to an agent, a Moslem resident of Malacca, for some Moslems lived as Portuguese subjects. Pinto, besides returning the call of the Ambassador, and presenting a letter and a present, was also to observe carefully what was happening in Sumatra, find out what he could about the strength of Achin, take soundings and plot courses, and particularly make discreet inquiries about a gold-mine which was said to exist in those parts and in which King John III was much interested.

Pinto says that he was not attracted by the prospect. De Faria had said there was money to be made, but how was he to make enough to compensate him for the dangers he was likely to meet when his total capital, a loan, we must assume, was not above two hundred pounds? He thought of excusing himself, but dared not do so in case he offended his chief, who had given him the job out of genuine kindness. So when the caravel was ready he embarked without enthusiasm, and with the Moslem agent set sail for Batak.

Though the kingdom lay across the Strait only some hundred and fifty miles away, it was not possible to enter it from this east side. Here the littoral of Sumatra was a mangrove swamp, behind

which lay a wide flat of jungle, uninhabited, trackless and inter-
sected with creeks. Entrance was therefore always made on the
west or ocean side, where the coastal swamp was not so wide. To
get there entailed rounding the north point of the great island, a
total distance of eight hundred miles.

This voyage was safely accomplished, and in due course Pinto
and the Moslem entered the mouth of a river, perhaps near the
present Sibolga, which led up to the town where the King lived.
The river mouth had the usual appearance of such places in the
tropics. Nothing could be more oppressive than the stretch of
slime on each bank and the overpowering mass of evergreen
jungle behind, steaming in a damp heat of about 80°. (The rain-
fall of Sumatra may reach two hundred inches.) As he passed up
the river through the equatorial forest, Pinto saw the creatures
generally met with there, and was the first European to describe
them. He saw alligators basking on the burnished slime, though
having no name for them he calls them lizards 'which might more
properly be called serpents, because some of them are as big as a
boat, with scales on their back, and mouths two feet wide.' And
he adds that the natives told him, what was quite true, that the
brutes would upset a canoe with a blow of their tails and eat the
occupants as they struggled in the water. He had sight also of
flying foxes, those revolting and giant bats, which are vampires
in all appearance, and was so horrified at them that when he was
informed they hunted apes, pulling them down from the highest
trees, he readily believed it. Cobras he saw too with their hoods, so
venomous, they assured him, and he did not doubt it, 'that if any
living thing came within reach of their breath it died soon afterwards, there being no remedy or antidote against it.' The other
terrible serpent of these jungles he also noted, the python, and he
rightly states that it hangs by its tail from a bough and, seizing the
passer-by in a toil, lifts him into the tree and swallows him. To
this description he adds the vivid detail, characteristic of his style,
that, trailing thus head downwards from the branch, the serpent
lays one of its ears close to the ground, the better to hear footsteps in the stillness of the night. Nor did he miss the strangest

denizen of the woods, the man-ape, the orang-outang, as big as a great mastiff standing on its hind legs, a beast of which the natives were more afraid than of any other, because of the sudden ferocity of its attack. 'I shall not be surprised', adds Pinto, 'if my readers who have not travelled refuse to believe in such creatures, for those who have seen little believe not much.' He was quite right, he was not believed.

After twenty miles they came to higher ground, where men could cultivate and live. Here the capital was situated, which Pinto calls Panaju. As soon as the King heard that a ship had arrived from Malacca with an envoy bearing a letter and a present, he sent notabilities to conduct him to the palace. The notabilities, however, were disappointingly shabby; they seemed such a rough-looking set of men, with their band of noisy bells and drums, that Pinto concluded the country was a backward place and not as rich as believed in Malacca. But on reaching the palace he met with courtiers far better dressed, and with better manners and address. At the door of the inner stockade he was received by an old lady who welcomed him in with a phrase of verse: 'Your coming here is as agreeable to the King as is a shower of rain to the rice in dry weather.' And she added what was hardly to be expected in such a spot, but was the sort of sentiment that Pinto came to feel represented the essential of Eastern religious thought: 'Enter without fear, for the people you see here are human beings in no different case from those of your own country, for they look to the same God as you for salvation.'

Pinto was then introduced into the King's presence, to whom he made a reverence in the style of the country, and rising, gave him the letter and present. The King asking him the object of his visit, he followed his instructions to raise the King's hopes, so as to get his goodwill in the trade, and said that he had been sent to find out about Achin, its strength and the depth of the water in its roadstead, and afterwards to make report to Malacca. For it was the Captain's intention, he explained, to send his fleet against Achin, capture its tyrant and deliver him to Batak.

'The poor King believed every word I said,' writes Pinto, 'and all the more readily because it was exactly what he hoped I would say.' And to have his most ardent wishes met in this way so overwhelmed him with joy that he rose from his throne and, going to an altar above which, on the wall, was fixed a cow's skull, with gilt horns and crowned with flowers, he addressed to it a sweet and beautiful prayer, some kind of an echo of Hinduism[1] or how Pinto sought to represent the same:

'Dear Cow, that nourishes us mortals with milk, though not constrained thereto by course of nature, as a mother is constrained who feeds her son, nor moved to kindly feelings towards us by any participation in our life of cares, be favourable to the heartfelt prayer that now I offer up to you. This I beseech that you, feeding on the meadows of paradise and happy in the rewards you enjoy for the good you have done us here below, will bless and preserve the friendship that the Captain has for me, so that he may do what his envoy here has promised.'

When he had begun to pray, all his lords had fallen on their knees and now intoned: 'We would die happy could we live to see that day.'

As the King rose to sit again on his throne, he wiped his eyes, which—in the words of our seventeenth century translator—'were all be-blubbered with the tears that proceeded from the zeal of the prayer he had made.'

In the conversation that followed, the King said that he was on the point of making a raid into Achin territory with the arms the Captain of Malacca had let him have, and invited Pinto to accompany him. So it was arranged, as this suited well with Pinto's instructions to get what information he could about Achin. Meanwhile the cargo could be sold, explained the King, and he would see to it that the best value was realized, 'which indeed was the thing I most desired,' says Pinto.

It would be tedious to go into details of the raid which fol-

---

[1]Sumatra had come under the influence of Hinduism in the early centuries of our era, at the time when Hindu immigrants founded in those regions an overseas civilization, as the Greeks did in the Near East after Alexander. Moslem influence was felt from the eighth century.

lowed. The Bataks were defeated and had to retreat precipitately. The King, who was a temperamental man, was so downhearted at his failure, that, accompanied only by two or three favourites, he left the palace and went up-river in a small boat to a retreat by a temple in the woods. There he remained a fortnight; on his return to the capital he sent for Pinto and the Moslem trade agent.

'Have you sold the cargo to your advantage?' he inquired.

'Thanks to Your Highness's favour,' replied the agent, 'the goods were rapidly disposed of.'

'Is anything owed you?' asked the King. 'If there is, I will see that it is paid at once.'

The agent assured him that all was settled up. And Pinto, in an effort to cheer him, for he was still very low, repeated the promise, made at the first, that the Captain of Malacca, gratified as he would be by the satisfactory cargo that the caravel was bringing back, would not fail to help him to be revenged upon Achin. But the King no longer seemed to believe this. His mood was far less sanguine than when, weeping with joy, he had prayed to the cow. He had thought over the possibilities and begun to wonder whether, in fact, the Captain was capable of keeping his promise. Now he stood awhile musing with himself, and then said: 'Ah, man of Portugal, you oblige me to speak out, and I will tell you frankly what I think. I am not so ignorant as to believe, nor can you persuade me, that he, who has not been able to revenge himself upon Achin, has the power to help me to do so.' And he cited several instances where the Achinese had taken Portuguese ships and massacred their crews. 'No,' he concluded, 'if Achin attacks me, I shall have to bear the brunt alone. You in Malacca cannot do more than defend yourselves, for your position is not any easier than mine.'

This was a true appreciation of the state of affairs, for the Portuguese, though they had taken Ormuz from the Turks, Goa from the Indians, and Malacca from the Malays, and built a string of fortresses pivoting on these, had not felt strong enough to attack Achin, with its fortifications manned by resolute fighting men and supported by a large and well-armed fleet; nor were they ever strong enough, but Achin attacked them and nearly took Malacca. Indeed, between this time and 1641, when the Portuguese lost Malacca to the Dutch, the King of Achin attacked it ten times, on one occasion (1615) bringing against it five hundred sail, of which two hundred and fifty were galleys, one hundred larger than any then used in Europe. In short, Achin, with its haughty aristocracy claiming descent from Arabian princes, and a population that loved fighting for its own sake, was the only formidable native power whose headquarters was on the trade route to the Far East. Gladly would the Portuguese have destroyed it if they could. But they had not the force. By the time of Iskandar Muda (1607–1636), who claimed that he was descended from Alexander the Great, the Achinese had conquered more than half of Sumatra. It was not until 1873 that Achin was taken by the Dutch, and not till 1901 that the last Pretender and his remaining paladins were decisively routed and obliged to flee the island. Such being the nature of the Achinese, the poor King of Batak had a true intuition, and justly assessed their power and character. Pinto was taken aback by his forcible statement. 'I must needs confess,' he writes, 'that his words, uttered with so much resentment at my hollow promises, made me ashamed, for I knew that all he said was true, and I had not the face to speak to him again of any succour.'

When the cargo was stowed—it included tin and the resin used for incense, both highly valuable commodities—Pinto went to take leave of the King and ask his formal permission to sail. He was not quite sure how he would be received, but found His Majesty as kind and well disposed as ever. 'I was very glad,' he said, 'when my Port Superintendent told me yesterday that you had done good business with the Captain's cargo. But perhaps he only said it to please me. Tell me whether you are really satisfied.'

Pinto assured him that he was.

'I am truly delighted to hear it,' said the King. 'And now I advise you to start back, for the weather is favourable but may not remain so, and should you be cast away on Achin, they would eat you alive there, the tyrant himself taking the first bite! You know the device they have on their crest? "Drinkers of the troublous blood of the Kafirs." You have heard, I suppose, what they say of you? That coming from the end of the world you have seized more kingdoms in India and the Isles than any corsairs who ever lived. Take warning, therefore, and tell the Captain from me when you return that the tyrant of Achin's one ambition (a holy duty laid on him by the Prophet) is to drive the Portuguese out of the Indies. But may God so order it that he fails.'

After saying this, he gave Pinto a letter for Pero de Faria, and also a present for him of javelins tipped with gold, a quantity of scented wood of the best quality, and a tortoise-shell box enriched with gold in which were large seed pearls and sixteen pearls of size and quality. To Pinto, personally, he gave a sum in gold and a sword garnished with the same. His farewell was made 'with as much demonstration of honour as he had always used to me before,' adds our author, as if he were surprised by the King's unchanging warmth and admired him for it.[1]

[1]G. Schurhammer, S. J., doubts whether Pinto ever went to Batak. His *Fernão Mendez Pinto und seine Peregrinaçam* (Asia Major, vol. III, published as a booklet in Leipzig in 1927) is a paper of critical notes on the *Peregrination* from the point of view of an historian. William Marsden in his *History of Sumatra* (1788) and Collet in his *Terres et peuples de Sumatra* (1925) show that the state of Batak was situated on a tableland in the centre of the island and was inhabited by a primitive Malay people who practised a ritual cannibalism. Marsden, however, admits that Pinto shows that he knows more about Sumatra than any other European of the sixteenth century. It is possible, however, that in the sixteenth century Batak extended to the ocean coast. (For this subject see also *Forgotten Kingdoms in Sumatra* by F. M. Schnitger, Leiden, 1939.) The central tableland may have been semi-savage and the rest similar to other coast kingdoms, another of which we shall be introduced to shortly. Even if most of Batak was very primitive, it does not necessarily follow that the King and his Court were at that level. The Courts of small Rajahs were always modelled on those of neighbouring royalties of higher culture. The Shan States are a case in point; in most of them are hill tribes with prehistoric manners and customs, but their Courts and ceremonial are modelled on that of the late Court of Mandalay, which in turn looked to classical Indian precedents.

One little fact difficult to explain, if Pinto invented his journey to Batak, is that he records noticing among the King of Batak's artillery train some guns stamped with the arms of France and declares that the King got them from the wreck of a French ship commanded by a certain Rosado. Now it is known that some nine years previously three ships left Dieppe on a voyage to Sumatra

Pinto goes to Malacca and visits Batak in Sumatra

for the first time in French history, and that one of them was never heard of again. In this connection it is interesting to know that Tomé Pires, a Portuguese who was in Malacca in 1512 and wrote his *Suma Oriental* there, records in that book, when noting on the nineteen Sumatran kingdoms which he lists, that the King of Batak was well off because *The Flower of the Sea*, the ship in which Albuquerque was returning in December 1511 from Malacca to Goa, and which contained all his vast loot and treasure, was wrecked on the Batak coast, and the King 'recovered everything the water did not spoil'. (See Hakluyt edition of the *Suma Oriental*, edited by Armando Cortesão, vol. I, p. 146.)

In sum, Marsden and Collet's observations on Sumatra, written respectively two hundred and three hundred and fifty years after the *Peregrination*, hardly suffice to prove a case against Pinto. But we must remember his plan and method, to describe the whole Asian scene in an autobiographical framework. Sumatra had to be described at this point, if his narrative was to develop clearly, and he had got to go there if his method were to be consistent.

CHAPTER FIVE

Pinto's narrow escape in the Malay state of Kedah

P into frequently repeats that his sole object in scouring the East was to make money, with which to retire in Portugal and relieve his poor family. But there is little about business in the *Peregrination*. It is of the adventures that he met with while on business that it treats. Though these appear to happen in the inconsequent manner that pertains to the normal chances of life, we perceive after a time that all of them have a significance beyond the mere fact that Pinto experienced them. Each amounts to a description of the state of a country, unknown or little known at the time in Europe. Woven into them are history and politics, often issues of great moment that bear on the main course of events in Asia. Sometimes the adventures are bound up with critical happenings inside the kingdoms where they occur. At the least they show us the principal states of the Orient in a characteristic light, and after reading them, we exclaim: 'That is just what would happen in such a place.' Nowadays the journalist or literary traveller on his tour of the world seeks interviews with leading men, discusses policy, and in a direct manner describes scenes and people. If he is lucky enough to have an adventure it is of a casual nature and only loosely connected with what is going on. But this is not the way that the *Peregrination* is constructed. In each country that Pinto visits he has a personal experience of some kind which takes the place of a direct description of leading men and current affairs, because the men and the affairs are part of the adventure. While reading of what happened to him, we read at the same time a statement of what was most significant in the

50

place. In real life personal experiences rarely take that form, but his in the *Peregrination* always do. In this chapter will be narrated an alarming adventure in one of the Malay states. So cleverly is the little drama presented that no one could say where it is an arranged impression and where a plain report of what happened.

Having, as we have seen, bade a warm farewell to the King of Batak, Pinto descended the river to its mouth on the ocean. Thereby was a little island inhabited by poor fishermen, and he remarks that for want of salt they could only cure the roe of the female shads they caught—one of the many authentic touches which add so much to the verisimilitude of his narrative. Steering north-west he sailed up the coast of Sumatra and, rounding the northern point of Achin, took a bearing north-east on which he crossed to the mainland by Junkseylon, the tin island off Siam, one hundred and fifty miles south of the present Victoria Point. With the peninsula on his port, he worked southwards towards Malacca and came in two and a half days to the Malay state of Kedah. There, the wind failing, he anchored at the mouth of the Perlis river, near Alorstar, now an air-station on the Rangoon-Singapore route. While waiting for a breeze, he decided to go ashore with his companion, the Moslem agent, and pay his respects to the King or Sultan of Kedah in the hope of filling the time with a little trade. On reaching the palace compound and sending in the usual present, they found the Sultan engaged in performing the obsequies of his father. There were the usual music, dances, flags and cries of gladness, which in those temperamental countries are used to prevent melancholy turning to madness. The Sultan himself was distributing alms to a crowd of paupers. But Pinto noticed an undercurrent of apprehension and dismay. After inquiring the cause he was told in a whisper that the Sultan had murdered his father to cover an intrigue with his own mother. In short, Pinto had arrived in the thick of a domestic imbroglio of a kind to which oriental Courts are prone, and one especially typical of the Malay states into which then, as now, the peninsula was divided. He was further informed that the Sultan, aware of the shocked state of public feeling, had given orders that anyone overheard murmuring against him would be arrested and put to death. It was said that several nobles had already been executed. Spies were everywhere and the people hardly dared to open their mouths.

When a seafaring man on going ashore walks into such an unpredictable situation, his instinct is to return at once to his ship. This was what Pinto shortly did, but the agent accepted an invitation to dinner. He was a loud sort of man and without tact. Pinto gives his name as Coja Ali and says that he boasted no Malay would dare touch him because he was agent to the Captain of Malacca. The dinner was given by a Mohammedan, who held the appointment of Strangers' Merchant. After the toasts had been well honoured, the company began talking in a noisy manner about the King and his misdeeds, calling him a parricide and a beast. Spies were at hand, under the house or in the garden within earshot, and immediately ran to tell the Sultan. Police were sent to arrest all the diners. The house was surrounded, the police broke in and seized host and guests, seventeen in number. They were dragged before the Sultan and hacked to pieces, a typical example of Malay frenzy.

When the Sultan had calmed down he reflected that the putting to death of the Malacca agent might have awkward consequences when the Captain heard of it. He had some merchandise in Malacca, which would probably be confiscated in reprisal. He therefore decided to send for Pinto and give him his own version of the affair.

It was by now quite late, and Pinto was asleep on the caravel, entirely ignorant of what had happened. He woke up suddenly to find his cabin full of dusky figures. 'The Sultan has ordered us to bring you to him,' they said. Surprised and apprehensive, he got up and was rowed ashore. It was midnight before they reached the outer courtyard of the palace. This was crowded with men in cuirasses, girt with swords and carrying lances. 'I must admit that the sight of these armed men seemed very ominous at that hour, and it occurred to me that treachery was afoot,' Pinto writes, meaning that he suspected the King of a design to seize his ship and massacre its crew, a thing not unheard of in those parts. His conductors, noticing how he looked askance at the armed men, assured him that he need not be alarmed; the guards had only been ordered out to catch a thief. But it looked so sinister, the darkness, the torches flaming, the silence, the inscrutable soldiers, that a sudden panic gripped Pinto, and though he tried to speak he could only utter unintelligible words. As they waited, however, he controlled his fear sufficiently to ask permission to return to the ship. 'I have forgotten my keys,' he told them. 'If you let me go back to the ship to look for them, you shall have forty gold pieces.' To which they replied that not for all the gold in Malacca would they dare to do this, for they would lose their heads.

This answer very much increased his apprehensions, and when twenty of the armed men now moved up and stood round him, he saw himself a prisoner, and though the retainers who had fetched him again declared that he had nothing to fear, he could not believe them, and passed the rest of the night in dreadful suspense, waiting in the courtyard for he knew not what.

At dawn the Sultan ordered him to be brought into his presence. 'I have never felt more frightened in my life,' says Pinto. 'On entering the inner courtyard I saw the King mounted on an elephant, with a hundred retainers in attendance, not counting the guard, which numbered more. When he beheld me coming towards him, pale with agitation and out of breath, he said: "Do not be afraid. Come nearer to me, and I will tell you why I have sent for you." '

When Pinto was close to the elephant, the Sultan made him a sign to look to one side. He did so and, terrified beyond measure to see on the ground the mutilated trunks of a number of men, their limbs and heads scattered about, and pools of blood everywhere, he threw himself by the feet of the elephant and, half out of his wits, implored the King to make a slave of him rather than cause him also to be hacked to death. 'I swear on the faith of a Christian that I have done nothing to deserve death,' he cried. And trying to rouse the Sultan's cupidity, he declared: 'I must tell Your Highness that I am the nephew of the Captain of Malacca.

He will give whatever is demanded for my liberty. And the ship I came in has a rich cargo. Your Highness has only to help yourself.'

'God forbid that I should do such a thing!' exclaimed the Sultan. 'No, no! But you still tremble? Calm yourself. And get up from the ground. When you are quite restored I shall tell you why I put your companion to death.'

It was only then that Pinto knew that Coja Ali was among the pile of dead. The knowledge accorded ill with the Sultan's reassurances. His fears increased, if that were possible. Seeing him thus, parched and sweating, the Sultan told a man to give him water. Of this he drank a large quantity. Then a servant was ordered to fan him, and they let him rest there for a while. Gradually his fears abated, his head cleared, and he found himself able to take in what the Sultan began to say. He appeared to be justifying himself. Though he had put his father to death, he had been obliged to do so in self-defence, because his father, misled by the lies some rascally slaves told him about the relations between his wife and his son, had tried to kill him. 'I had always respected my father and paid him every filial duty. I cannot tell you what a terrible ordeal it was to kill him,' he declared. And he went on to speak of a cruel conspiracy of slander directed against him by malcontent nobles. 'I had to put a stop to it,' he explained, 'and when last night it was reported to me that your companion, whose body you see lying there, used the most outrageous language about me, honour demanded that I should execute him.' And he protested that he was a great friend of the Portuguese, and had no designs on the ship and cargo.

Pinto still considered himself in great danger; if the Sultan thought that he did not believe him and on return to Malacca would create trouble there, he would kill him now. Pinto had to convince him that he thought him justified in executing Coja Ali. How to do this he had no clear idea, but prompted by instinct burst out: 'When I inform the Captain of Malacca what Your Highness has done to his agent, he will be delighted, for at the same time I shall tell him that the fellow had misappropriated part of his merchandise and, guessing that I suspected him, tried to poison me twice.'

He spoke at random, but convinced the Sultan, who replied: 'I can see you are a sensible and honest man, and, what is more, a loyal friend.' And he took out of his belt a kris, a lovely piece of craftsmanship, and gave it to him. On getting leave to withdraw Pinto pretended that he would be staying on at Kedah for ten days, thinking it prudent to cover his real resolve to sail at once, since the Sultan was the kind of tyrant who, if he thought that he was hurrying away, might arrest him again out of caprice.

Pinto got on board his ship as quickly as he could without attracting attention. The moment he was there, he told the sailors to hoist sail, and did not even stay to haul in his anchor, which he left in the sea. 'Up to the last moment I imagined they were coming after me to take me back, so greatly shaken was I by the extreme danger of death in which I had been,' he says.

I have no doubt that Pinto here describes a personal experience. And we must accept that it happened at the declared time and place, because we know nothing to suggest the contrary. Nevertheless, we should not overlook its literary appropriateness. Pinto had recorded a visit to one Sumatran King and was about, as we shall see, to describe a visit to a second. The art of composition demanded that between these two Sumatran episodes there should be inserted a happening of a quite other kind.

CHAPTER SIX

Pinto's mission to the King of Aru in Sumatra

It was about sunset when Pinto was clear of the Perlis river and, making all the speed that he possibly could, sailed down the Malay coast to Malacca. As he came into the road, the town seemed delightful to him, the Portuguese houses rising on the hill with the Church of Our Lady on the highest point, the river in the middle, and the Malay quarter to the left with its cheerful bazaar. 'The first thing I did on disembarking,' he relates, 'was to go to the fortress to salute the Captain, Pero de Faria, and tell him that the voyage had been successful.' He gave him a map of the coast of Sumatra, as he had seen it, with the rivers, the towns, the mountains and with soundings all marked. As for the gold-mine, he told him where rumour said it was situated. De Faria was very pleased and promised to send him on other voyages, in which he would have opportunity of making money.

Three weeks later an Ambassador arrived from the King of Aru with precisely the same request as the Ambassador from Batak had made. Aru was another of the Sumatran kingdoms, and lay east of Batak and so nearer to Malacca; indeed, since it could be entered from the Straits coast, it was quite close. The Ambassador said that an attack from Achin was imminent, and asked the Captain to supply Aru as he had supplied Batak. If anything, the case was stronger, for since Aru was nearer, it would provide Achin, if conquered, with a forward position yet more menacing to Malacca. But Pero de Faria refused aid for reasons which need not be detailed here. The Ambassador departed, much disappointed.

Public opinion, however, was on the Ambassador's side, because his master, the King of Aru, was popular in Malacca. De

56

Pinto's mission to the King of Aru in Sumatra

Faria was persuaded that he had acted wrongly, and changed his mind, though the munitions he decided to send consisted only of a dozen arquebuses and a few cannon-balls and helmets. 'Pinto,' he said, 'will you take these across the Strait. I shall be sending the King also a personal present, a suit of gilt mail lined with red satin, and for his wife and daughters materials for dresses.'

Pinto saw his opportunity and asked for a rise in pay, which de Faria granted, and made further promises, hinting that he would send him next to China, the land where the largest fortunes were made. 'I undertook the mission in an ill hour,' says Pinto, 'in regard to what happened to me thereon, as will presently be seen.' He left for Aru in October 1539, that is, exactly four months after his arrival from Goa.

Some days later he was in the mouth of the Panei river, on which the capital of Aru stood. It happened that the King was near the river-mouth, for he was fortifying it against the attack he feared. Pinto came ashore and was received with great warmth. After he had presented his letter and explained that he brought munitions, the King was so overjoyed that he took him in his arms, exclaiming: 'Last night I dreamed this would be so. With these supplies I shall be able to defend my country.'

And on foot as he was, attended only by six lords, he took Pinto by the hand and led him to the palace, which lay up the bank a few miles away.

Though Aru has long since ceased to be marked on our maps, it is to be found on the old charts, as Daru, and is mentioned as such by Tomé Pires, the Portuguese who first listed these Sumatran ports, though his *Suma Oriental* was lost until Armando Cortesão found the manuscript in 1937, one of those dramatic discoveries which make a scholar's life sometimes so exciting. Since the town was on the Straits coast, which is mostly a mangrove swamp, there must have been some higher ground at that spot. Pinto does not say what it looked like, but we can guess, for all the ports on these coasts that lay a distance up a river, as they generally did rather than on the sea-front, had features in common. The river-mouth itself was always fringed with mangrove, low bushy trees with twisted trunks whose roots are in the silt but seem to grow out of the sea. At the mouth nothing was to be seen except a brown tidal river flowing silently through a solitude. After going in a distance, the banks rose and the mangrove disappeared. Cultivation began and the town came into sight, or rather the place where the town was known to be, for little was visible except palm, banana and durian trees. If it was a fortified town, there was a brick and earth rampart surmounted by a stockade, above which showed the tops of the fruit trees. If it was not fortified or hardly so, one saw a big orchard with thatched roofs peeping through the greenery. But inside the orchard was a teeming life. The King's palace, surrounded by its own stockade, was like the bamboo and thatched houses of the town, but much more spacious, with a large compound, wide verandahs, inner courtyards, a hall of audience and a high ornamental roof, all of wood, carved, painted or gilt.

It was to such a palace and through such a garden city that the King of Aru led Pinto by the hand. When he had entertained him to a lavish dinner, he presented him to the Queen, a woman of temperament and decided character, as will appear in the sequel. This was a special honour, for the King of Aru was a Mohammedan, though allied to Portugal against his co-religionist of Achin.

When the arms sent by de Faria were unpacked and presented and the King saw how meagre they were, his high spirits left him and he began to speak of the danger he was in: 'Achin's strength is not in his people, but in the money he has from trade, which lets him hire foreign mercenaries. But I am too poor a King to buy help. Come with me and I will show you how hateful is poverty.'

Saying this, he took Pinto to his arsenal, an outhouse with a thatched roof, and, having had the door opened, disclosed his paltry store of munitions, forty small cannon, one heavy piece which he had bought from the Portuguese, forty muskets, some bundles of wooden spears with poisoned ends, and some shields and lances. 'These, with twenty elephants and fifty horse-guards, are all I have to resist the might of Achin,' he declared. 'Is it enough to turn back his Janissaries?'

Pinto's mission to the King of Aru in Sumatra

It was certainly not enough, thought Pinto, but in an encouraging tone he replied that he dared say it would keep them busy. The King shook his head and began to complain about the blindness of the Portuguese. 'Your Viceroy and your Captains of the fortresses think only of making a private fortune,' he declared, 'and do not give their mind to public affairs. They have let Achin grow strong and now find it too expensive to put him down.' He spoke angrily and as if hinting at the meanness of de Faria's present of arms. Pinto tried to answer him, but admits he could not. The abuses of the Portuguese administration were notorious; the corruption of their officers passed belief. The King related various foul and enormous malversations which had gone unpunished, and Pinto represents himself as too shamed to reply. The conversation is an example of the indirect method of the *Peregrination*; instead of himself criticizing his fellow countrymen, the author puts the criticism into the mouth of another.

After this talk Pinto was sent to lodge with a merchant. During the succeeding days, rumours of the immediate arrival of the Achinese terrified the inhabitants. The King decided to evacuate all the women to a village in the heart of the jungle. Even the Queen left on her elephant. This alarmed Pinto, who says that though the merchant entertained him well, he would rather have been at some other place with any poor victuals. But he could not leave without the King's permission. The King, however, had no desire to detain him. After five days he sent for him: 'When do you want to go?' he asked.

'At such time as it may please Your Greatness to command me,' replied Pinto, 'though I should be glad were it sooner than later.'

'You are wise,' said the King, and taking two gold bracelets from his arm handed them to him. 'Do not think me mean,' he added, 'because I give you so little. I have always wanted to have much so that I could give much. And here is a letter for the Captain of Malacca, and this diamond too, and you shall say to him that I will not forget the sum I owe him for the munitions he has so kindly sent, and will pay it in person, when I am more at leisure than at this grievous time.'

Pinto's mission to the King of Aru in Sumatra

This touching description of the doomed King of Aru is characteristic of Pinto, who was moved by the King's dignity in his distress and, moreover, thought the Portuguese attitude to small native rulers was cold and ungenerous.

The departure was fixed for the same day at sunset. The galley, with its complement of twenty-eight, descended the river and coasted along with a fresh land breeze. When the next day they began to make the crossing to Malacca, a violent storm struck them from the north-east. It was the first watch of the night. The wind was so sudden that it carried away the mast. The ship was driven back towards the shore and foundered, all the crew being drowned but five. Pinto managed to scramble on to a rock and spent the night there with the four other survivors, Indian seamen, it appears. At dawn their situation was revealed. They were on a reef close to the shore. But the shore was a mangrove swamp behind which lay impenetrable jungle, 'a wood so thick,' says Pinto, 'that a bird, were she never so little, could hardly make way through the branches of it.' To land seemed useless, as they could not walk in the swamp nor force a way through the forest. Perhaps a boat would pass and pick them up. In this hope they remained three days on the reef, suffering dreadfully from hunger and thirst. Unable to endure the misery longer, they swam ashore and tried to walk along the coast. Knee-deep in the ooze, sometimes sinking to the belt, they toiled a little distance and at sunset came to a river. By this time they were much exhausted and feared to try to swim across. Darkness descended and the tide came in. They passed a horrible night, part of it with the water up to their chins and exposed to the mosquitoes and sandflies, which swarmed out of the jungle and bit them. Dawn came at last, but it did not seem that they could hold out much longer. Their one hope had been to fall in with some inhabitant. But was it possible to suppose that human beings could exist in such a place? Pinto had put this question to his companions more than once. Now in their desperate plight he asked it again. Was there a chance of coming across anybody? The eldest of the seamen was an old Mohammedan, who lived in Malacca and had a wife there.

Pinto's mission to the King of Aru in Sumatra

He was thinking of her and, not able to restrain his tears, sighed: 'Alas! there is no chance. Nothing remains but to resign ourselves to death.' And then, standing as they were in the mangrove by the muddy river, he began to say that from what he had heard in Malacca one could be certain of saving one's soul by the mere fact of being a Christian. He was not sure that the Prophet could save his soul and therefore, since death was near, he begged Pinto to make him a Christian immediately. After saying these words, and while his arms were about Pinto's neck, for he had embraced him, weeping, he suddenly died, overcome by exhaustion and because he had received during the wreck of the galley a severe head wound, which had turned septic from dirt and flies.

Thus Pinto, himself half-dead from tiredness and loss of blood, for he, too, had received deep cuts, was left holding in his arms the body of a Mohammedan whose soul had taken flight before there had been time to save it from damnation. In this predicament he sank down fainting. The three other seamen came to his aid and, as best they could, buried the corpse in the ooze.

Debating now what to do, they resolved to swim over the river, for on the other side they perceived some great trees; if they could climb into them they would be safe from snakes and crocodiles, and might be able to get a little sleep. Two of the seamen plunged in first, leaving the third to swim with Pinto and, if need be, support him in the water. When the first two had reached the middle of the stream, Pinto waded in up to his waist, the other seaman holding him by the hand, and was on the point of following when he saw the snouts of two crocodiles close to the swimmers. In a moment the reptiles had seized them in their jaws and dragged them under in a swirl of foam and blood. At the dreadful sight, Pinto was so terrified that he could not cry out. 'I do not know how I got out of the water,' he says. For hours he and the seaman remained on the river bank, too stupefied to utter a word. To cross the river was impossible, to go back was useless; there was nothing for it but to die where they were. Towards evening the mosquitoes attacked them again and to cover themselves from their bites they lay down at the margin of the water. In this way they endured all night.

61

Pinto's mission to the King of Aru in Sumatra

What they still dared to hope for now took place; a fishing boat turned into the mouth of the river. Getting out of the water, they knelt in supplication on the bank. The fishermen stopped rowing, and came close to the shore. The remaining seaman told them what had happened and begged them to take him and Pinto aboard. But as soon as the fishermen knew that they had to do with ship-wrecked men, their cupidity was aroused, for those who have escaped the sea are always believed to carry valuables, their most precious possessions, such as gold pieces or jewels, which they hide in the mouth or even swallow. The head fisherman, therefore, replied to their plea for rescue by demanding that they should first give up their money, though he justified himself by declaring that he was a poor man and could not afford to feed them otherwise, particularly as they were so weak and wasted as to be useless as oarsmen. Pinto and his companion, however, had been overwhelmed too suddenly by the tempest to gather up their valuables and were obliged to declare their utter destitution. The fishermen did not believe them, and made a show of pulling away, but Pinto urgently told the seaman to shout out that he would fetch a good price as a slave or in ransom money, for he had rich friends in Malacca. Hearing this, the fishermen returned and took them off, four of them carrying Pinto and the seaman on board, as both were too weak to manage it by themselves. But when they had them aboard, convinced there were valuables hidden somewhere about them, they tied them to the mast and began to beat them. When this torture effected nothing, they concluded the valuables were in their stomachs, and compounded an emetic, which they gave to the seaman only, for Pinto after the beating was in a state of collapse. The emetic was of so violent a kind that the seaman vomited blood for an hour, when he died of exhaustion. As no gold was found in what he brought up, the fishermen concluded that Pinto likewise had none and, as if in regret for their brutality, they washed the cuts they had inflicted on his back, though with a mixture of lime which gave him great pain.

After visiting fish-traps in the river, the fishermen returned to their village, which was on the Siac river, some distance further east along the coast. Since they wanted to make Pinto into a saleable slave, they looked after him well. But when he had recovered from his hurts and exhaustion, they could find no buyer for him. Three times he was put up to auction without a bid being made. It seems that the villagers thought that he would be more a hindrance than a help. His owners, in no mind to continue feeding him, turned him out of doors to shift for himself by begging. As the inhabitants were extremely poor, he was hardly able to keep alive. The village was exactly opposite Malacca across the Straits, which here are about a hundred miles broad, and Pinto reckoned that sooner or later a ship would put in. One day as he was lying in the sun by the sea, watching the horizon and profoundly miserable, a Mohammedan happened to pass, a small merchant from Palembang, a town at the eastern end of Sumatra. He had had dealings with the Portuguese in Malacca and was astonished to see a man of that nation lying half-naked on the beach.

'Are you really Portuguese?' he asked. 'How do you come to be here in such a state?'

Pinto assured him that he was Portuguese and, a sudden hope springing up that the Mohammedan might rescue him, declared that if the man would take him to Malacca he would be well rewarded by the Captain. The merchant at first refused to help, but Pinto pleaded so earnestly with him, declaring that the Captain would pay ten times more than what it would cost to buy him from the fishermen, that eventually the merchant agreed. To prevent the price from being run up, however, he did not go directly to the fishermen with an offer to buy, but employed a local man to bargain with them, who managed to secure Pinto for seventeen and sixpence, as in truth his owners were very tired of him.

The merchant was a dealer in salted roes, which he bought from the fishermen along the coast. His ship, one of the kind that had oars and sails, was at a village fifteen miles away. Pinto was taken there, and after the vessel had been loaded with more barrels of roes, they crossed the Straits to Malacca. On landing the merchant took Pinto to de Faria. This was the second time within a year that Pinto had been brought to the Captain of a fortress as a slave.

Pinto's mission to the King of Aru in Sumatra

'Pero de Faria was so astonished to see me in such lamentable plight,' he says, 'that the tears stood in his eyes. "Is it really you, Mendes Pinto?" he exclaimed. "Your face is so wasted that I can hardly recognize you." '

When the news got about, people flocked into the fortress to see Pinto; and as he recounted his misadventures, some left silently, some shrugged their shoulders and others crossed themselves. So sorry for him were they, that a fund was got up for his benefit, which made him better off, as he declares, than when he set out on his unlucky journey. De Faria was generous to the fish-roe merchant, giving him over a hundred pounds in ransom money, besides freeing him from all customs dues and making him a personal present of two good pieces of Chinese damask. Pinto, who was far from well, was lodged with the Customs Registrar, whose wife put him to bed at once and nursed him back to health.

Before proceeding with the relation of his adventures, Pinto inserts here an account of what happened to the King of Aru. The Achinese made their expected attack and in the course of the fighting the King was killed by an arquebus-ball. The town of Aru was taken and remained occupied by an enemy detachment after the main body returned to Achin. The Queen from her hiding-place in the woods harried the Achinese garrison by frequent raids, but lacking supplies, was obliged to give up the struggle and flee to Malacca. When Pero de Faria was informed that her prahus were in the port, he sent his son to welcome her. On her arrival at the castle she was given a salute of guns and de Faria received her with a good deal of state. Afterwards he provided her with a house to live in and accommodated her following in tents outside the town. Encouraged by this reception, the Queen asked him to send an expedition to retake Aru, revenge her husband, and drive the Achinese out of the kingdom. De Faria led her to believe at first that he would help her, though in fact his resources were quite inadequate. She kept on bothering him to act, but he continued to put her off, until eventually he declined to see her when she called. Refusing to take the hint, and being desperate, she waylaid him one Sunday at the gate of the castle, when she knew he would be going to the Church for mass. As he came out with his gentlemen, she approached with her ladies, and he was obliged to stop and give her his attention. After the usual exchange of compliments she said with much feeling: 'I request the gallant Captain out of his generosity to spare me a few moments of his time. Though I am a Mohammedan and therefore ignorant of his religion, nevertheless I am a woman and have been a Queen, and he ought to treat me with respect.'

A crowd had now collected and de Faria felt much embarrassed. He could not think of anything to say; by taking off his cap and making a low bow he hoped to quiet the Queen, so that he could pass. But she was not to be got rid of. It seems that the Church of Our Lady was close by, for she bowed to the Church gate, as if by implication calling Christendom to witness the justice of her plea, and let fall a flood of supplication: 'My greatest desire is to avenge my husband, but as a woman I am too weak to effect it alone. I came first to you, because the Portuguese have long been our allies and have a common interest with us to stop Achin. In the presence of many noblemen you promised to aid me in my adversity, but have done nothing. I know your excuse; you have written to the Viceroy and await his orders. But a great expedition of that kind is unnecessary. With a hundred well-armed Portuguese, supported as they will be by my own people, who are excitedly waiting for my return, I can retake Aru. Yet when speed is required, you have procrastinated for months. Help me now, I beseech you, or be frank and say clearly that you will not.'

So spoke the desolate Queen, and Pero de Faria, with a shame-faced air, for his conscience, says Pinto, was not clear, could only mutter that he expected shortly to hear from the Viceroy, when doubtless some reinforcement would be sent to Malacca, if the other pressing affairs of the Indies permitted.

The Queen replied that she had grave doubts about help from that quarter. This caused de Faria to lose his temper. 'You accuse me of telling you a lie!' he cried, and, as Pinto phrases it, 'lashed out some words that were more rude than was fit.'

Pinto's mission to the King of Aru in Sumatra

The Queen burst into tears, and fixing her eyes again on the Church gate at which they had arrived, for in an attempt to shake her off de Faria had moved on some paces, she exclaimed through her sobs, which nearly choked her: 'My poor husband made a great mistake in ever trusting the Portuguese nation. The more we do for you, the less you regard us. Single-handed we tried to hold off the Achinese attack, and thereby sought to shield you. We should have done better to have allied ourselves with them and let you suffer the consequences. If you had neither the will nor the power to succour me, why did you beguile me, a poor lonely widow, with your fine promises?'

Having said this, and more, with increasing indignation and grief, she turned her back on the Captain and, without listening to what he said in reply, immediately went back to her house, summoned her chief men, ordered her prahus to be got ready and the very next day left Malacca. Of her subsequent history Pinto relates that she sailed to Kampar, a Sumatran state eastward of Aru, and married its King on condition that he retook Aru; that the said King did retake Aru; that the Tyrant of Achin, as Pinto always calls him, was so angry with the officers he had left in charge of the town that he caused them to shave their beards, on pain of being sawn in two, and to go dressed as women and playing cymbals through the villages, with the further injunction that should they at any time require to make an asseveration, there should be substituted for 'so help me God' the words 'so may God bring me back to my husband again' or in alternative 'so may I have joy in the children of my womb'—a punishment which they found so scandalous that 'some fled the country and others made away with themselves, some with poison, some with halters and some with the sword.' Of this astonishing example of royal humour Pinto remarks: 'A relation altogether true without any addition of mine;' and, indeed, we may accept it as such, for not the most resourceful romancer could have invented it.

The Sultan of Achin eventually reconquered Aru, but though he frequently, as has been stated, attacked Malacca, he was never able to take it nor to close the Straits to Portuguese commerce.

CHAPTER SEVEN

Pinto's disastrous venture at Patani

With Pinto's return from Aru the theatre and the nature of his adventures change. From acting as an emissary to the petty sovereigns of Sumatra, he begins his travels in the great kingdoms of Further Asia and comes in contact with Portuguese who are not in the employ or under the control of the Viceroy, but are adventurers at large. A career of wider opportunities opens, but beset with its own alarming perils. He will acquire knowledge of vast territories known at the time to but few Europeans, and will participate in events of increasingly great historical importance.

Some months after the events described in the last chapter, probably at the beginning of 1540, he was sent for by Pero de Faria, who told him of a job likely to put him in the way of making money. The Captain, who like all Portuguese in government employ engaged in private trade, had an agent in Pahang, the Malay state on the east side of the peninsula, about a hundred miles north of the present Singapore. He wanted Pinto now to take a consignment of goods to this man, whose name was Tomé Lobo. When at Pahang, he should be able to do a little trading on his own account. And he could go on to Patani, a port further up the same coast and a centre to which came the ships of traders from the China seas. Chances of all kinds were to be found in such an entrepôt.

This seemed to Pinto like real business at last. So promising was the venture that he was able to borrow two hundred and fifty pounds from his friends. A cargo boat was placed under his charge and, accompanied by four other Portuguese, he left Malacca, passed through the Singapore Strait and steered northward to Pahang. When in the neighbourhood of Tuman Island they picked out of the water twenty-three persons from a Portuguese ship which had sunk near that spot on the way back from the Moluccas. On the eighth day they reached Pahang river and rowed up it to the town of that name. Tomé Lobo was there, and Pinto made over to him de Faria's goods.

After some days Pinto told Tomé Lobo that he proposed to go on to Patani as de Faria had advised. But Lobo begged him not to go: 'My life is in danger,' he said, 'for a leading man of the town, who has a grudge against me, swears to burn down my house and murder me.' This alarmed Pinto, for if Tomé Lobo were assassinated, he himself could hardly escape, and he became the more anxious to start for Patani. 'Pero de Faria would not be pleased were you to leave me alone at this time,' protested Lobo. Pinto compromised; he would wait fifteen more days; let Lobo quickly change de Faria's merchandise into gold and go with him to Patani out of harm's way. This was agreed and Lobo hastened to sell his goods for gold and diamonds. But the day before they had arranged to sail for Patani a disastrous event took place, not precisely what Lobo had anticipated, but what amounted almost to the same thing.

An Ambassador from some state in Borneo, who had been resident in Pahang for three or four years, discovered that the Sultan of Pahang had become his wife's lover and had him assassinated by hired bravos. The town was convulsed by this event and, during the disorders that ensued, Tomé Lobo's enemy surrounded his house with a band of retainers. Pinto was there, and when the ruffians broke in he escaped with Lobo to his ship in the river. But they were unable to take anything with them; the gold and diamonds had to be left behind, to the value of over twenty-five thousand pounds. Indeed, they only just got away with their lives, for Lobo had six sword-cuts, one of which laid open his right cheek, a flap of which hung down on to his shoulder.

The riots and fighting continuing on land, and their situation in the river being most alarming, they rowed down to the mouth.

Pinto's disastrous venture at Patani

But, reluctant to return to Malacca with such a disastrous story to report, they resolved to go on to Patani, where there was hope of getting aid, as many Portuguese lived there. It lay three hundred miles north, and was the seat of a Malay Sultan. In the sixteenth century the Malay Sultans of the whole peninsula were feudatories of the King of Siam, to whom they paid homage every three years, either going with presents to Ayudhia, the capital, or to Ligor, a port town one hundred and fifty miles north of Patani, where the King of Siam kept a Viceroy as his representative.

It took Pinto and Tomé Lobo six days to reach Patani. They were well received by the Portuguese residents, to whom they recounted what had happened at Pahang. 'No need to worry,' they were told. 'We Portuguese here are on good terms with the Sultan. When he hears that the Captain of Malacca, his friend, has been robbed of his property in Pahang, he will give us leave to take reprisals.'

In due course the Sultan granted them audience. When they asked to be allowed to seize goods belonging to Pahang merchants in Patani up to the value of de Faria's loss, he immediately agreed. 'It is reasonable that you should do to them what they have done to you,' he said affably.

Armed with this permission, they looked about for Pahang merchandise. Some days later, they heard that three junks, owned by foreign Mohammedan residents of Pahang, were lying in Kelantan river-mouth sixty miles to the south, where they had put in owing to bad weather on their return from a voyage to China; they were reputed to be very richly laden. It was decided to capture them, and with that object eighty Portuguese set out in three vessels under the command of Fernandez Dabreu, a gentleman whose father had a post at Court in Lisbon. Arriving at the Kelantan river, they took the junks by surprise and, after a stiff fight, captured all three, which they carried back with them to Patani. On arrival there, the Sultan, in spite of protests from the Mohammedan community, allowed the Portuguese to take from the junks goods equal in value to those stolen at Pahang, and accepted the statement that the value of the latter was twenty-

five thousand pounds. This was regarded by all except Mohammedans as very reasonable and, indeed, generous on the part of
the Portuguese, for the value of the silver ingots on the junks, not
counting the rest of the cargo, was estimated at one hundred and
fifty thousand pounds. Tomé Lobo and Pinto were also reim-
bursed for what they had personally lost, and so Pinto was again
in possesssion of the two hundred and fifty pounds which he had
borrowed in Malacca.

During the next three weeks Lobo and Pinto were engaged in
selling the Chinese goods allotted to them. One day a Portuguese
ship anchored in the river. On board was an emissary sent by
Pero de Faria to the Sultan of Patani to discuss a trade agreement.
This emissary's name was Antonio de Faria da Sousa, a relation
of Pero de Faria's and a man with whom afterwards Pinto was
to have much to do. To avoid confusion he will be referred to
from this onwards as Antonio.

While engaged in his diplomatic talks with the Sultan, this
Antonio also traded on his own account and tried to sell a quantity of Indian cotton which he had with him. But the market for
these goods was very sticky and he was advised to send them for
sale to Ligor, the big town on the coast one hundred and fifty
miles further north, where the Siamese Viceroy lived. It happened to be about the time when the Malay Sultans would be
going to pay their respects to the King of Siam in the person of
this Viceroy. The occasion was always marked by free trade, all
customs dues being taken off. In consequence, the town would be
crowded with merchants from all parts of the East, and Antonio
was assured that his cottons would go off quickly. He therefore
directed his agent, Borralho, a clever dealer with long experience
of the country, to take the goods there. Pinto, on being told that
he might hope for a profit of six hundred per cent, asked permission to accompany him, a request to which Antonio readily
agreed.

On arrival at the mouth of the river leading to Ligor, the ship
anchored, for the wind and tide were unfavourable. As usual, the
banks were an uninhabited mangrove swamp. It was ten o'clock

in the morning and they were on the point of sitting down to a meal, when suddenly a junk came round the bend, far larger than the little vessel they were in. It approached on the ebb and, when level with their bow, dropped anchor and swung till it lay on their starboard. Instantly grappling-irons were thrown on their deck and they were dragged alongside it. So quickly was the grappling done, and such was their surprise, that no attempt was made to throw out the irons. As soon as their vessel was secured, there burst out of the other's deck-house and from under the awnings a body of armed men, Mohammedans among whom were some Turks, who with ferocious shouts hurled stones, darts, and javelins among the Portuguese and their crew. The missiles killed or severely wounded most of them, and as the pirates leaped down with drawn swords, Pinto, himself wounded, plunged into the water. With two others he reached the bank and struggled through the mud till the mangrove trees hid them. From there he saw the pirates kill the wounded, carry the cargo of cottons on to the junk, sink his vessel and, in their hurry to be gone before they were discovered, cut their cable and clap on all sail.

The whole affair had lasted only half an hour, and Pinto, staring at the empty river and at his two companions, found it hard to believe that the catastrophe was not an hallucination. There followed the same sort of experience which he had suffered a few months back on the Sumatran shore, for these mangrove swamps are all alike; there is no way of getting out of them on foot. One of his companions died of his wounds, and he with the other, who happened to be Borralho, the dealer, waited as best they might for a boat to pass. At sunset, a salt-boat was seen entering the river. When it was within hail, they called again and again to the crew to rescue them. Their frantic cries were heard by the owner, an elderly woman, who emerged from her cabin, stick in hand. When she saw the two Portuguese in the mud, she struck her slaves for not having stopped, and ordered them peremptorily to bring her boat to the bank. Four of her men were then landed and carried Pinto and Borralho on board.

The woman, a Malay lady of quality, as it turned out, who had

come down in the world, treated them with the utmost consideration and kindness; took their shirts and trousers to have them
washed; lent them Malay clothes to put on; and called them to
have a meal with her in the cabin. Borralho, of course, knew
Malay well, and so the conversation went easily. 'Eat, eat,' she
said, pressing the food on them as she served them herself. 'And
don't let your misfortunes make you despair. I have suffered far
worse.' And she gave them to understand that her husband, a
Malay of high position, had been involved in a rebellion against
the King of Siam, for at the time there was a movement among
the Malays towards complete independence. When the rising
failed, he and his sons were put to death. 'With these eyes I saw
them torn to pieces by the elephants,' she said, weeping. 'All our
estate was confiscated, and I was reduced to the condition of a
slave. But I will not weary you with the long tale of my misfortunes, nor of how I came to be mistress of this salt-boat. Long ago
I have been resigned to my lot. It was not God's doing but my
own sins that were the cause of my sufferings.'

To this Pinto and Borralho replied that they, too, made no
complaint against God, but ascribed solely to their evil conduct
what had befallen them.

'Tell me,' said she, as the boat glided up the river, 'the whole
course of your disaster.'

They did so, and asked whether she could inform them who
the pirate was. At this, one of her people interposed: 'From the
description of the junk, it must have been Koja Achem, an Indian
of Gujarat, whom we know left this morning with a cargo of
scented wood for the island of Hainan in the Gulf of Tongking.'

'That's it!' exclaimed the old lady, striking her breast. 'Why, I
know the man, and I have heard him publicly boast of the number
of Portuguese he has killed.'

They asked why Koja Achem was so set against the Portuguese.
For answer she said that his father and two brothers had been
killed off Jeddah in the Red Sea by a Portuguese Captain during a
sea-fight. Thereafter, he had avenged himself on their nation
whenever he could. He was trader, and pirate, and champion of

72

Islam, one of the worst freebooters in the China Seas, infested as they were with formidable corsairs. Pinto and Borralho thanked the lady for the information. She took them on up to Ligor and shortly afterwards sent them back to Patani in the ship of a merchant who was a relation of hers. There they found Antonio waiting for them, and reported to him the total loss of his cotton goods.

CHAPTER EIGHT

The pursuit of the pirate Koja Achem begins

━━━━◆━━━━

To understand what follows one should bear in mind that Malacca was the Captaincy that lay furthest east on the mainland of Asia. Later, in 1557, the Portuguese were to get the lease of Macao in China and turn it into an important Governorship. But in 1540, the year at which this narrative has now arrived, the Viceroy of Goa made no appointments beyond Malacca.[1] This, however, is not to say that the Portuguese as individuals did not venture eastward of the Straits. We have met them already at Pahang and Patani on the China side of the Malay peninsula. But these men were bold traders who dared to go beyond the waters where the Portuguese fleets were master of the trade routes. They were to be found also settled in small communities still further east, particularly at Ningpo, a port in China in the region of Shanghai. They lived and voyaged in those distant seas at their own risk. The ruler in whose territory they were settled might at any time turn on them, and there would be no redress. Afloat in their ships, their survival depended upon their arms, for the seas were very dangerous—not on account of storms and uncharted rocks, for such were the lot of all seamen everywhere at that time, though perhaps the sudden typhoons and unknown shores of Further Asia made sailing there particularly hazardous—but because of piracy. None of the sovereign states policed the sea, not even the great empire of China. If a ship's captain were strong enough and it were convenient, he

[1]The Portuguese had settlements among the islands, cf. in the Moluccas their fortress of St. John the Baptist on Ternate (founded 1521), and the smaller settlements at Tidore and Amboina. In general charge was the Captain of the Moluccas.

would seize and rob whom he met. Every ship was not a potential pirate, for to be able to do violence arms and fighting men were necessary, items that cost money. Nor was it in the long run sound business for a merchant to act as a pirate, because he spoiled his market by alienating the people. But in seas where no law runs, violence and robberies of all kinds are common. In the Far Eastern seas there were pirates de carrière; marauders, free-booters, corsairs and buccaneers, who also traded; and merchants, armed to protect themselves from such thieves, who themselves on occasion did some thieving. The small traders and fishermen kept close inshore. One can understand why such minor traffickers, when they came upon distressed mariners from vessels of the bigger sort, felt little sympathy and took what they could from them.

Inside the official part of their empire, the Portuguese ships observed the rules of civilized navigation and only attacked their Mohammedan opponents. But outside it the adventurers who traded in the China seas were restrained only by their conscience as Christians. Some of them became professional pirates; some buccaneered on occasion; some, whose business was wholly trade, were high-handed when it suited them. But their reputation in general was such that the Chinese government was inclined to class them all as pirates. (These Portuguese adventurers had also another profession, that of mercenaries in the kingdoms of Siam and Burma, as will be disclosed in the later chapters of this book.)

With this explanation in mind, the reader is briefed to understand the course which Antonio took, when he heard the news that the corsair Koja Achem had robbed him of his cottons.

'On first being told,' says Pinto, 'he was so upset that it was half an hour before he could utter a word.' The news soon got round of what had happened, and all those who had had a share in his venture came crowding to the house. Their losses added up to ten thousand pounds, and they were in a state of consternation. Antonio's cottons were mostly bought on borrowed money, and he declared that he dared not return to Malacca and face his creditors. 'They would take an action against me,' he said, 'and that would be ruin, for I have no reserves.' And he went on: 'Instead of miserably presenting myself before those who accommodated me, the right course is to go after the man who has robbed me.'

His resolution was well received by the other losers, who wanted to know how he would carry it out. At that, he called for a Testament and swore on it that he would leave Patani forthwith and follow Koja Achem till he found him. 'And then I shall force him to disgorge ten times more than he has taken,' he declared. 'Besides, the ruffian killed on my ship thirteen Portuguese and thirty-six others, a villainy which, if it is let pass, he will commit again and as often as he pleases.'

Those present took his point about the national honour, and several immediately volunteered to go with him. The whole Portuguese community at Patani rallied to his support, and by their generosity he was able to equip a vessel and enlist fifty-five soldiers. Pinto was one of those who volunteered. He explains: 'I had no option. To return penniless to Malacca was out of the question. What could I have done when I got there? No one would have lent me anything again. How could I have faced the friends who had lent me money, with nothing to show but a wretched carcass, and that had three javelin holes in it, and a head all swollen from the blow of a stone, wounds that had brought me thrice to the article of death and been the cause of an operation and the removal of a bone?'

Antonio left Patani on 9 May 1540, intending to make straight for the isle of Hainan, whither Koja Achem was said to have gone. First steering across the mouth of the Gulf of Siam, he came to the delta of the Mekong river, a region between the kingdoms of Cambodia and Champa, both of which were tributary at that time to Siam. This was the usual route to China, which the Portuguese had been using for at least twenty-five years, but they knew nothing of the country inland. Pinto had never seen a river as large as the Mekong, and wondered where its source might be. The people he met at the mouth told him a fanciful story. The geography of inner Asia was as much a mystery in those days as was that of central Africa three centuries later.

The pursuit of the pirate Koja Achem begins

Leaving the region of the Mekong, they coasted up the shores of what are now Cochin-China and Annam, but then was Champa, the seat of a Hindu civilization which had been as remarkable as that of the Khmer in Cambodia and whose sculpture of playful monsters French savants of recent years have enabled us to enjoy at the Musée Guimet. The Chams, however, had some seventy years before ceased to be an independent people and the jungle was beginning to swallow their great temples. Of their tragic fall, Pinto gathered nothing. From the deck of his ship he saw only mouths of unknown rivers, an immense stretch of jungle covering flat and mountain, and occasionally, when near the shore, the roofs of thatched houses in a haze of sunlight.

They were already in pirate seas. To this day one group of islands on this coast is called the Pirate Isles on our maps. One morning they anchored at the mouth of a river. After they had been riding there awhile, in debate whether to enter the river and look for supplies at a town which, as they surmised, lay a distance up it, a large sailing vessel came in from the high sea. As it passed them, they saluted by hanging out pennons and flags. The crew of the vessel, however, did not return their salute, but crowded the bulwarks, abusing and gesticulating, blowing trumpets and conch-shells, and beating drums in a hostile and contemptuous manner. Pinto adds the touch, so true of that part of the world, that a Negro, standing on the top of the poop, showed them his backside in derision. The crew was a mixed one of Achinese, Turks, Chinese, and other nationalities, a villainous-looking collection of men.

Incensed by their behaviour, Antonio gave them a broadside, to see whether that would teach them better manners. They replied with a fusillade from the small cannon they carried, but passed on and disappeared round the bend of the river. Antonio did not think it prudent to follow and remained at anchor where he was.

After nightfall a careful watch was kept and at two o'clock in the morning three black objects were seen moving on the surface of the water. It was impossible to make out what they were and a man went to wake Antonio, who was asleep on deck on top of the hen-coop. 'We pointed out to him the black things,

77

which were now not far off. "Those are boats!" he cried, "get your arms quickly!" Sure enough, they were boats, and we rushed for our weapons.'

Antonio ordered them to take up their stations and all waited, watching intently. Everyone was now certain that the night prowlers were from the vessel that had passed. 'I dare say they do not guess that we have fifty armed Portuguese aboard or they would not be so bold,' observed Antonio. 'Keep down out of sight,' he ordered, 'and don't let them see the light of your matches. Let them think we are asleep. And have your grenades ready.'

When the boats were an arrow-shot away, their crews seemed to take counsel together. The biggest boat then went to the starboard side and the two smaller ones to the stern. The Portuguese let forty men climb aboard without showing sign. Then suddenly Antonio issued from the deck-house at the head of his soldiers and, invoking the help of St. James, flung himself on the pirates. Taken utterly by surprise, the fellows were cut down to a man. Antonio then ordered hand-grenades to be flung into the boats. The men in them threw themselves overboard. Five were taken out of the water, among them the Captain of the vessel and the Negro who had shown his backside.

Antonio had two Achinese put to the question, in order to find out what their vessel was and where it had come from. But nothing could be wrung from them but obscenities and curses. 'Let us see if we can get the Negro to speak,' said he then. 'Hoist him up and start work on him.'

'At this the Negro started to cry, begging us not to hurt him,' says Pinto, 'and protesting that he was a Christian like us and ready to answer whatever we asked. Antonio ordered him to be unbound, and gave him a biscuit and a glass of wine.' In response to this kind treatment, he began to speak: 'I am not as I seem. They made me show my backside. My name is Sebastian, and once I was the slave of a man you well know, Gaspar de Mello.'

'Gaspar de Mello?' they echoed. 'The noted Captain! He was killed by pirates.'

'Yes, he was killed,' said the Negro. 'And who killed him?

78

The pursuit of the pirate Koja Achem begins

That man there, Similau, the Captain of the pirates who were foolish enough to attack you.'

Antonio gave a gasp of astonishment: 'So this Similau is the dog who killed Gaspar de Mello!'

'Yes, it was he,' continued the Negro. 'I was on his ship when the pirates took it two years ago near Ningpo in China. On that occasion, Similau slaughtered twenty-five Portuguese. And his intention, thinking you few, was to have slaughtered you this night, squeezing your brains out of your heads by the torture of the twisted forehead-cord, as he did in my sight to de Mello, my good master, and to the others with him. May God grant that he now pays the penalty!'

Antonio then took Similau, bound as he was, and fastening a cord round his head, twisted it with a stick until the pirate's skull split and his brains burst out, and he did the like to his surviving companions. Then, embarking his men in boats at the turn of the tide, he went up-river to the pirate vessel which, the Negro told him, had only Chinese boatmen in charge. Creeping silently in, the Portuguese climbed on to the poop and saw the Chinese below, asleep on the deck. Four grenades were enough to cause them to jump into the water. Some were drowned and the rest Antonio took up and made slaves of, for he needed them to sail and row the pirate vessel, which was junk-built, and large and high. At dawn he drew up an inventory of the cargo. There were found thirty-six thousand ounces of silver, besides other valuable goods, which he did not stay to list at that time, because his seizure of the junk had alarmed the inhabitants of a little town on the bank at this place, who could be seen hurrying about and signalling with fires as if to summon help. Fearing that they were in league with the pirate and would attack him, he hoisted the junk's sails and, setting the Chinese to row, got out of the river as fast as he could.

This story of a fight with pirates is the first of its kind in European literature. In much else, too, the *Peregrination* anticipates modern romance. At the time of its publication, it was an extremely original book.

CHAPTER NINE

The pursuit continues

Accompanied by the junk, Antonio sailed northward along the coast of Champa. Near Cape Varela they put into a river-mouth to make inquiries about Koja Achem. Canoes with fruit and fish came out from a little village near-by. Pinto tells us what these fishermen said among themselves, when they came aboard. The passage is an example of how he puts his criticism of the Portuguese into the mouths of others. It is as if he were unpleasantly aware that he and his companions, roving the seas in an armed ship and making private war on pirates, were themselves little better than pirates, at least in the eyes of the local inhabitants.

One of the fishermen says: 'Here is a great novelty, with which it has pleased God to visit us.'

'Let us pray Him,' says another, 'that He ordain out of His infinite goodness that these bearded men are not connected with those who in the guise of merchants spy out a land and afterwards pillage it like bandits.'

'It might be better,' says a third, 'to retire to the shelter of the jungle in case the sparks from their torches should burn our homes and crops.'

A fourth puts in: 'In any case, our best course will be to give them no hint that we suspect them. Let us speak politely, find out all we can, and send in a report to the Governor.'

When this was repeated to Antonio by the interpreter, he did not let the fishermen see that he knew what they had said, but received them kindly, bought the provisions they offered and paid the price they asked. They seemed pleased, and inquired where he came from and what brought him to their coast. As they had never seen any Europeans before, they accepted his assurance that he and his men lived in Tenasserim as foreign subjects of the King of Siam, and that in his capacity as merchant he was on his way to trade as far as the Lu-chu islands.[1] He had put into their river, he said, because he was on the look-out for a friend of his called Koja Achem. Had they seen him? They had not. He also told them he had merchandise to sell (the contents of the pirate junk). But they assured him that there was nothing in their village except nets and fishing boats and that they were much too poor to buy goods. If he went up the river, however, he would come to a town where he could sell his cargo ten times over to merchants who went with elephant caravans to the Laos hill country. But Antonio replied that he was in too great a hurry, bade them farewell and sailed on.

Pursuing his way north to a point as far as the present town of Tourane, he bore north-east across the entrance to the Gulf of Tong-king and after one hundred and sixty miles reached the great island of Hainan, within the administration of the then Emperor of China, Chia Ching of the great Ming. Coming towards evening to a river-mouth, he sent his ship up to explore under Borralho, his man of business, while he stood off in the junk with most of his fighting men. Borralho reported on his return that the river was full of Chinese junks and that at the bar a solitary junk was riding, which perhaps was Koja Achem's, as it looked like a pirate ship.

When Antonio heard this, he became convinced that he had found his enemy. 'My heart tells me so,' he cried. Changing back into his own ship with his men, he set out there and then, it being the middle of the night, to attack the junk.

He was mistaken, however. It was not Koja, but another pirate who had also done to death a noted Portuguese Captain. What

[1]The Lu-chu are the string of islands stretching from southern Japan to Formosa, the chief of which is Okinawa where the Americans fought their last terrible battle in the Japanese war before they dropped the atom bomb. In the sixteenth century Lu-chu had a King who was a feudatory of China. Lu-chu junks occasionally visited Malacca (see Pires, *Suma Oriental*, vol. I, p. 130 —Hakluyt edition).

The pursuit continues

Pinto relates of the seizure of this second pirate is a double of the story he has just told about Similau, with certain ingenious new details added. After the capture of the junk the pirate Captain is found hiding in a scuttle. He has taken the name of Sardinha out of bravado, having killed the real Captain Sardinha at Singapore. As before, the pirates are put to the question. A boy is about to be tortured, when his father, in appearance an old Mohammedan, intervenes and says that he is a Christian Armenian who was serving under Captain Sardinha when he was killed. In a hold of the pirate ship they discover nine young Portuguese children 'chained together by the hands and feet, and so thin that every bone in their bodies could be counted'. An inventory being made of the cargo, it was found to include much property stolen from the Portuguese, such as three trunks full of silk quilts and suits of clothes; a silver-gilt basin and ewer, with a salt-cellar and twenty-two spoons; three candlesticks and five gilt cups. The story is told with dramatic force and the variations are skilfully introduced. It may well be substantially true, but placed so soon after the other it sounds artificial. One may suppose that during his travels in the China seas, at this time and later, Pinto met with some, and heard tell of many, pirates, and that in his account of the cruise with Antonio he takes the liberty of collecting them together into a sequence. By this device the meeting at last with Koja Achem becomes a climax to which the other fights gradually lead up. Altogether one feels that this is no log of a voyage into pirate waters, but a carefully constructed picture. The facts are true, but the setting is arranged. Nevertheless, it is not clear how far this is so, for the stories hinge into each other and are relevant to the whole panorama of the *Peregrination*.

As the result of the capture of the two pirate ships, Antonio and his companions had become enormously rich, for the value of their two cargoes was estimated at over one hundred thousand pounds. As Pinto often repeats, his sole object in coming East was to make his fortune. But he had intended to make it by legitimate means. To go out and fight pirates who had despoiled the Portuguese was all very well if their loot were to be returned to the proper owners or their heirs, or credited to the public funds. But Antonio regarded the loot as his own property. Pinto, writing long afterwards and looking back on these events with the eyes of a man who, as will be seen, underwent at a later date a spiritual reformation, is not easy in his conscience about these episodes in his career. For instance, in the matter of the second pirate he makes the old Armenian say to Antonio: 'The course you hold is in no way conformable to the Christian law which you professed in your baptism,' a remark which, he says, so confused Antonio that he did not know what to answer.

But, the reader will exclaim, if Pinto felt that his adventures with Antonio were on the whole questionable, surely that is the strongest argument for their truth? When a man writes his autobiography he does not invent actions which show him in a light of which he is ashamed. If he puts in episodes which he hints were to his discredit, it can only be because they were true and that by confessing them he eases his conscience. We are, however, still left with the impression that the cruise with Antonio has been arranged in some degree. And this feeling is strengthened when, one after another, more pirates are brought on the scene, each one a species that differs from the last, as if Pinto were enumerating examples of the various types to be met with in those seas.

But before introducing his next pirate, he inserts a little scene where an old pearl-fisher is the chief character. Antonio with his ship and the two captured junks had anchored in a bay further along the Hainan coast. The water was dotted with small pearling craft and divers were coming up with oyster shells. Said one of Antonio's seamen: 'Here is a chance. Why not take the pearls?'

In this way Pinto's insinuation that they were little better than pirates is taken a step further; they openly contemplate piracy.

Antonio refuses, but Pinto gives for his reason, not that robbing pearl-fishers on the high seas was a crime, but that it was unsafe. 'The sounder course,' he is made to say, 'will be to barter our loot for pearls. We cannot drag all our present stuff about with us. Change it into valuables that take up no room—that is the obvious thing to do.'

The pursuit continues

So they anchored near the pearl-divers, and ran up a flag that was known in those parts as an invitation to trade. At that, boats put out from the shore with provisions. On one of them was an old Chinaman, some sort of a Headman of the pearl-fishers. He went on board the junk where Antonio was. Having never seen a European before, he was much astonished at the sight of the Portuguese and wanted to know who they were. Antonio gave the same answer as to the Champa fishermen, that they were of Siam, and said they wanted to exchange their merchandise for pearls.

To this the old man replied that the pearls were not for sale, because it was the Emperor of China's private fishery. 'What is more,' he went on, 'you are trespassing here. No ships are allowed to anchor in this bay. There are some Chinese warships not far off. If they catch you here, they will burn your vessels.' And he convinced Antonio that it would be prudent to move on.

As he spoke, he let his eyes wander round the junk and noticed the Portuguese sitting in groups, throwing dice on the deck. They were dressed in finery, suits of clothes which were their share of the loot, as were the silks that they staked in their gambling. He smiled and observed caustically: 'I have never seen such smart young fellows on a merchant ship before. Evidently in your country silks are dirt cheap. I have been watching your men stake and lose a piece of damask at one throw.' It was impossible to mistake his meaning. The insinuation was that the silks were stolen.

Antonio tried to parry by saying that the young gamblers were the sons of rich merchants and had no idea of the value of money. But though the Chinaman hastened to agree, one saw that he did not believe a word. 'Tell those fellows to stop and put the silks out of sight,' Antonio whispered to one of his mates, and in an effort to convince the Chinaman that they all were really merchants, for he did not want him to spread rumours on shore, he had the hatches taken off a hold which was full of the pirate's pepper. This time the Chinaman seemed more convinced. And to remove his suspicions altogether, Antonio made much of him, presenting him with two cakes of wax, a bag of pepper and an elephant's tusk. The old man was much delighted and gave Antonio in return a tortoise-shell box of seed pearls, along with twelve large pearls. Before going, he said: 'I will tell you where you can sell your goods,' and he named a place further up, which seems to have been the present Tan-chow. 'But don't trust the Chinese,' he said confidentially. 'They are all liars, though you can trust me, for I am a rich man and can afford to speak the truth. Be careful. Never let the lead out of your hands; there are banks everywhere along this coast. And when you get to port don't land your cargo. If you do, they will begin to squeeze you. It is far better to sell from the ships.'

And the old man climbed down into his boat after many compliments and promises, 'of which they are never sparing in these parts', comments Pinto with a dry humour that he often uses.

CHAPTER TEN

The rape of the bride

———◆———

The third pirate is now introduced. On reaching the bar of the river leading to Tan-chow, Antonio tried to enter, but had difficulties owing to the current. He had been striving thus for some time, when two high junks came out of the river. They were chained together, a device sometimes used when attacking on the tide, and as soon as they were in range, fired without warning from twenty-six small guns. The direction of their course made it plain that they aimed at enveloping the Portuguese junks with the chain. To avoid this, Antonio retired. The pirates then unchained themselves, the better to manœuvre, and quickly overhauled him. As soon as they were close, they poured in a rain of arrows and darts. The Portuguese, sheltering under the half-deck, replied with volleys from their arquebuses. At length, forty of the pirates, who were Chinese, leapt on to the poop of Antonio's junk, and a desperate hand-to-hand fight ensued. After half an hour they were driven off, and Antonio counter-attacked and captured their ship. But Borralho, who was in charge of the second Portuguese junk, and had also been boarded, was hard pressed. Antonio went to his aid and the pirates threw themselves into the sea. Both the Chinese vessels were thus taken.

And now they heard crying from one of the holds: 'Jesus have mercy! Jesus have mercy!' Quickly they opened the hatch and peered into the darkness. They could see nothing, but heard Portuguese voices calling for help: 'Lord Jesus save us!' Antonio sent men down and soon one by one were brought on deck two Portuguese with five small children and ten servants, a pitiable crowd, chained hand and foot, naked and famished.

The rape of the bride

'How did you fall into the hands of the pirate?' Antonio asked of one of the Portuguese, for the other was too far gone to speak. A long story was the reply, in the course of which it transpired that their captor had been baptized in Malacca under the name of Francisco da Saa, but had relapsed to paganism and taken to piracy.

'Can you pick out the body of the renegade dog?' cried Antonio.

When the man said that he could, Antonio took him by the hand and they went from corpse to corpse, turning them over if need was to see their faces, and found the pirate captain at last with a great cut over his head and thrust quite through the body. 'That is certainly he,' said the man. And he pointed, as a proof, to the massive gold chain on his neck, attached to which was a dragon, the tail and paws enamelled in green and black. Antonio ordered them to drag the corpse to the prow, to cut off the head and fling all in the sea.

An inventory of the goods on the two captured junks was made, and the value estimated at forty thousand ounces of silver. Since he had not enough men to navigate both junks, Antonio burnt one and added the other to his existing force of two junks and his original small ship. With this fleet he was about to go up the river to Tan-chow, when some fishermen advised against it; he would be unable to sell a thing there, for the resident magistrate was in a great rage, having been in partnership with the pirate, who was in the habit of giving him a third of all booty in return for protection against the authorities, a corrupt practice not uncommon in China then and in the following centuries. 'If you go up,' continued the fishermen, 'not only will you be refused trade, but you will be in great danger. We hear that His Honour has made fire-rafts, piled with pitch in barrels and other combustibles, ready to be loosed on the ebb against you.'

As trade was clearly impossible in such conditions, Antonio made off along the coast eastwards, looking for a place to sell his booty. One evening, when he was anchored not far from shore, four small decked boats came rowing into sight. Presently was heard the sound of music. He was not sure what sort of boats they might be and put himself in a posture of defence. But on their getting near they were seen to contain a gay party. Actually, it was a girl accompanied by her people on the way to meet a suitor belonging to some other village. The rendezvous was the very place where the Portuguese were anchored. Seeing the junks, the girl and her family assumed that the suitor and his friends were on them. They approached in high spirits and, after waving flags in salutation, withdrew a distance and anchored close inshore, expecting that the suitor would presently call, as had been arranged through third parties that he should.

Antonio, who of course did not know these facts, remained puzzled by the behaviour of the occupants of the boats. They looked like a party celebrating an occasion, but, it occurred to him, they might be spies, sent out to watch him by officials on shore. When dark fell he therefore kept a sharp watch.

On her side, the bride-to-be was surprised that her lover did not come to call. She expected any minute to see lights as he left the junks and rowed towards her. At last, too impatient to wait any more and wondering what it was that delayed him, she sent her uncle with a letter of gentle remonstrance.

Pinto gives the letter verbatim. His object in this invention (for to suppose it were not such would be fanciful) was to engage his readers' sympathy for the girl. The episode, as will appear, was discreditable to the Portuguese. He relates it for that reason. He desires it to be known that their behaviour beyond the limits of their official empire was that of masterless adventurers, that they were prowlers of the sea, despoilers and slavers, and his argument is that these sins called down the divine wrath on them, and on him, too, as one of them. But his presentation is indirect, as, indeed, was necessary, since to have published in the Portugal of the sixteenth century any direct exposure would have been impossible. It may well be that his conduct, and his companions', was worse than he describes; that there were debauches, cruelties, rapes, treacheries, which he does not mention, but the memory of which worried him afterwards. As will gradually become evident, the *Peregrination* is in some sort a pilgrim's progress. Even with this clue, however, it remains a very puzzling book.

The rape of the bride

The girl's letter is too long to transcribe, but its pith was that she reproached her lover for his unpunctuality, which she ascribed to his sweet laziness, and begs him to call without further delay. 'If you fail to come to-night, you will not find me alive when you come to-morrow morning,' she writes passionately.

The uncle with this letter in his hand arrives alongside Antonio's junk. He is invited on board, the Portuguese keeping out of sight, and on his inquiry for the lover is laid hold of and put under hatches with his followers. This arrest, says our author, was attended with some scuffling, but the seamen in the uncle's boat were drunk and noticed nothing. It was therefore a simple matter to fasten a rope to the top of their mast, which was level with the junk's poop, and prevent them from getting away. A few fire-grenades were dropped on their deck, and they surrendered without showing fight. Having secured them also in the hold, Antonio embarked on their boat and rowed to where the girl was anchored. He boarded her boat and kidnapped her, along with her two young brothers, six respectable elderly men who were her relatives, her crew and a troupe of old female entertainers. Her other two boats fled 'as if the devil had been after them'.

It was midnight before Antonio was back on his junk. The prisoners were placed with the uncle under hatches. Next morning they were paraded on deck. The uncle and the other respectable relatives looked so old and miserable, and fit for nothing, that Antonio put them on shore. The crews of the two boats he kept because he was short of men to sail his junks; the girl and her two brothers because they were young, white and good-looking.

Later in the day the Portuguese weighed anchor and continued along the coast. After rounding a headland they met five small sailing boats whose occupants saluted them gaily with flags, streamers and silken banners. It was hardly necessary to inquire who they were: the lover, who had mistaken the date, was on his way to the rendezvous with his friends. He passed with his music, never dreaming that the lady of his heart was being carried off under his eyes by a bearded foreigner from the ends of the earth. 'We played him a dirty trick,' says Pinto.

CHAPTER ELEVEN

The shipwreck on the Island of Thieves

———❖———

It were tedious to follow Pinto in every detail of his cruise with Antonio. He brings on a fourth pirate, whose Portuguese captives are not rescued in time to save their lives; he builds up with deft touches a picture of seas, more stormy and less tropical than the littoral of Sumatra; of river-mouths less swampy and a coast more densely inhabited, with a population richer and far more civilized; and of vistas stretching back towards China, unknown and secret, fabulously wealthy. The picture is generally true, as everyone acquainted with those regions and their history will admit, and it is interesting to reflect that an account of the Far East, so varied and full of colour, was available to European readers at a date before the British began to settle there.

The leader of the cruise into Chinese waters is represented as no ordinary corsair. On the contrary, his motives are high, though in the course of his pursuit of Koja Achem and his fights with other pirates, he yields to temptation and himself begins to prey on defenceless wayfarers. He is the prototype in European literature of the romantic highwayman, the gentlemanly bandit, the God-fearing rover, the honourable buccaneer. He never falls to the level of the disgusting pirates in Esquemeling's *Buccaneers of America*, the book which had such a success in the following century. Nevertheless, Pinto does not approve of his behaviour, which we are led to suspect was also his own behaviour during his early years in the East. Sin, punishment and redemption provide one of the themes in the *Peregrination*. Let us now observe how he describes the divine punishment that overtook Antonio and his crew.

Antonio had reached the summit of his success as a buccaneer.

The shipwreck on the Island of Thieves

His fleet, declared to consist of four ships all told, was augmented by the taking of a further pirate vessel, and his booty now exceeded in value a hundred thousand pounds. So strong did he become in the waters round Hainan, that merchants paid for his protection, and the Viceroy of that island, following Chinese practice, offered him the appointment of Admiral, with the duty of suppressing piracy, an honour he declined, though it carried a large salary.

At last, however, the crews began to murmur. They were impatient to get back to Malacca and spend their shares of the loot. Antonio protested that Koja Achem, the prime reason for their setting out, was still at large and unpunished. But they would not be denied any longer the enjoyments which after so arduous a voyage seemed to them irresistibly tantalizing. They had searched for Koja in every river-mouth, every secluded cove, and behind every island. Not a word was had of him; he was not in that part, must have gone marauding further north. God had vouchsafed them each a fortune, Antonio's share many times his loss. To Him could be left the destruction of Koja. So they argued, and Antonio gave in. It was resolved, however, to go first to Siam, the greatest market in all those seas, and there sell for gold what part of the booty was still in goods. With it all converted into precious metal, division would be simplified. No disputes would arise, for each man by a simple sum could calculate his share.

This decision recorded, and sworn to and signed by each member of the company, they arranged to start as soon as the wind was favourable. The ships rode on the south side of an island, which Pinto calls the Island of Thieves. He has the date, October 1540, six months after they had left Malacca. Then, on the night of the new moon, always a dangerous moment in those regions, they were struck by a typhoon blowing up from the south. It was a horrible situation, for they were on a lee shore. Every anchor they had was put out, but their cables were not in prime condition. As the wind increased, they sought to ease the strain on them by cutting down the masts and as much of the dead wood on the high poops as possible. The waves ran so high that their heavy

The shipwreck on the Island of Thieves

ordnance broke loose and crashed about. Everything was done that could be done, even to the extent of jettisoning part of the cargo. As their peril grew more deadly, they fell to prayer. 'But,' says Pinto, 'since we did not deserve mercy on account of our sins, God ordained that about two hours after midnight we were hit by a fearful gust.' Some of the cables broke, the ships fouled one another, and all were driven upon the shore and broken to pieces in the surf. Of the total company of five hundred and thirty-three Portuguese, native mariners and slaves, only fifty-three persons, of whom twenty-three were Portuguese, reached land.

When the sun rose, the survivors were able to estimate their disaster. Nothing remained of their booty but what had been washed ashore. Corpses lay everywhere among broken bales. They had lost ninety per cent of their company and their whole fortune. Huddled together on the beach, many suffering from severe contusions, they stared at the debris and lamented. Antonio, who was among the saved, now addressed them. He was wearing a red coat which he had taken from a dead body. 'Do not give way to grief,' he exhorted them with a steadfast smile. 'God has punished us for our greater good. Though wrecked on this desolate shore, yet will He save us and give us back all we have lost.' So he spoke, and his companions took heart.

The thieves of the sea were now marooned on the Island of Thieves. The text states that it was the outermost island towards the mouth of the Gulf of Tongking, but it cannot be identified. This is intentional: Pinto had an extraordinary memory, and if he had been to a place he recalled its name with tolerable exactitude. When he gives a nonsensical name, as he does in some passages, or, as here, a name chosen for its dramatic fitness, we know that the episode to be described is an imagined scene, founded on fact, no doubt, but arranged to demonstrate some conception of his. In this case what follows is to show that, corsairs though they were, God's face was not turned away from them. They had sinned, He had punished them; but they were Christians and that was enough for Him to save them. This belief was a cardinal one

The shipwreck on the Island of Thieves

for Pinto, and we shall find him leaning on it again. God will forgive even pirates if they believe and call on Him. To demonstrate this article of faith, it was necessary to describe a deliverance so extraordinary as to be like a miracle. What Pinto now relates should be read in this light.

From boyhood our reading has acquainted us with the situation when Europeans are wrecked on a desert isle. We know that they maintain themselves on what is washed up and scan the horizon for a sail. The day comes when their vigil is rewarded; a ship arrives and takes them off. That is the general pattern of all such tales, and Pinto's, which is a prototype in European literature, is no exception. But in its details it is quite particular. He was concerned, as I have said, to give it a slightly miraculous twist. It would not suffice for a ship merely to rescue the unfortunates; they must feel that God was watching over them. So we see Antonio and his companions first searching the wreckage for food in the usual way. But after a while it went rotten 'and stank so vilely that no one could endure the taste of it in his mouth'. Nevertheless, they had to eat it and some died of the effects. 'But there is no place so remote or desert,' says Pinto, 'where the misery of sinners can be hid from God's infinite mercy, which works in ways beyond imagination and, though it may take a natural form, is in real truth miraculous.'

On the feast of St. Michael and All Angels, when they had almost given up hope, a kite flew over their heads and dropped a mullet which it held in its claws. The fish fell near Antonio. When he saw what it was, he was confounded for a moment, and then, overcome with emotion, knelt down and poured out these words from the depth of his heart: 'Lord Jesus Christ, Eternal Son of God, I believe that you will render us the same aid as you sent to Daniel in the lions' den. By the intercession of the sainted Angel, whose feast is celebrated to-day by your Holy Church, deliver us from this place and take us to a Christian land, where we will ever be faithful to your service.' Having made this prayer, he looked in the direction from which the kite had come and saw other kites flying towards them with more supplies of fresh food. Hastening inland, they found some distance away a stream so full of mullet that the kites had been able to pluck them out. Lying close by was a deer, which a tiger had just killed. This food saved their lives.

A few days later, the second part of the miracle happened: they saw a sail on the horizon. They could hardly believe it at first, but when it was certain that the ship, a small Chinese junk, would stop at the island, an idea entered Antonio's head, much at variance with the prayer which he had breathed with such devotion. He told his companions to conceal themselves in the trees on the edge of the beach. The junk came close inshore, and was anchored fore-and-aft, so that a gangway could be let down on to the land. Thirty persons disembarked and scattered in all directions to collect wood and water. Some washed their clothes and some light-heartedly played games, little thinking that danger was near. When Antonio saw that they were so engaged, he said: 'God has miraculously sent us this ship and we must accept His gift. Let us now take it, His sacred name on our lips.' And pronouncing thrice the name Jesus, he got up from his hiding-place and, followed by his companions, rushed the ship without resistance from the few on board and before those on shore saw what he was doing. In a moment the cables were cut and they were rowing out to sea. As soon as they were well beyond reach of the owners, who lined the shore, shouting and gesticulating, they stopped to eat, for the ship's cook, who had been left behind, had ready a huge cauldron of rice and bacon. After the meal they inspected the cargo, which consisted chiefly of silks, worth about two thousand pounds. The ship, too, was luxuriously provisioned; they found hams, sugar, rice and two hen-houses full of fowls.

Pinto, however, could not feel that God, in answering their prayers and sending a ship, had intended that they should steal it. Not trusting Him to see them safe, they had resorted to their old ways and relapsed into sin. He expresses his thought by the following device. Besides the cook they found on board a boy of thirteen, very white and pretty. When Antonio asked him about the ship, who owned it and where it was going to, he replied:

The shipwreck on the Island of Thieves

'It was my father's. In a few minutes you took away the wealth which it had cost him thirty years' labour to amass.'

He seemed so distraught that Antonio was sorry, telling him not to cry, petting him and promising to treat him like a son. But the boy shrank from him, saying: 'I am not so childish as to think that you who have been cruel to my father will be kind to me. Yet if you would be kind, let me swim ashore, for I would rather die with my father than live with you.'

When some of those present reproved him for speaking so rudely, he retorted: 'I was not rude; I was speaking the truth. I saw you just now when you had finished eating and drinking. You joined your hands in thanks to God without a thought of giving us anything back.'

Antonio was so struck, says Pinto, by the Christian quality of the boy's words, that he asked him whether he would like to become a Christian. 'I do not know what you mean,' he answered.

Antonio as best he could explained to him the message of Christ. But he could get no answer from the boy, who exclaimed at last: 'What a religion, where preaching and robbery go hand in hand!' And he went into a corner and wept.

So Pinto states his view that the behaviour of the Portuguese adventurers could not be justified, for they had come out, not only under their King to make money, but under the Pope to preach the gospel. That they were hypocrites is his charge. This criticism, the great criticism which could fairly be levelled against the Portuguese empire, is not to be found in any other contemporary book. Not only does it make the *Peregrination* a document of importance in the history of thought, but it shows that Pinto earnestly desired it to be known that he was not a hypocrite and that he was well aware of the difference between his profession as a Christian and the life he had led. That such was his mind explains why, when he had become rich, he made the renunciation which, as will be related in its place, forms the climax of his adventures. Moreover, it affords the main reason why he felt it more necessary to disclose his opinions by means of an arranged narrative than to set down a mere chronicle of plain facts. While we must doubt whether the episode of the Chinese boy happened, if at all, in the way that he declares, it remains a profoundly true statement of the times. An ordinary adventurer would never have recorded it, since it would have held no interest for him; nor would the writer of a romance of adventure have inserted it, for its seriousness would have spoilt the heroics of his tale. The *Peregrination*, I must repeat, is not a romance; to call it a book of Christian morals, though certainly much disguised, would be nearer the mark, a disquisition by a man of vast experience and tender conscience, on life and death, suffering and salvation.

CHAPTER TWELVE

Koja Achem is brought to bay

In taking the reader through the *Peregrination* I am obliged, as I want to entertain him, to vary my touch, giving prominence to the remarkable and curtailing what is prolix. On this principle I shall therefore summarize for a while the adventures of Antonio and his men after their escape from the Island of Thieves. The question was where to sail. The crews had wanted to go home when each man had a fortune to spend. Now, having lost their loot and being possessed only of a small ship with a cargo worth a few thousand pounds, there was no call to return. Better to go on, said Antonio, to the China Sea. Portuguese merchants were allowed to trade at Chincheo (Ch'uan-chow, on the Formosa Strait) and at Liampo (Ningpo, in the region of the present Shanghai). They might visit one or both of those places and perhaps get assistance there. En route they should be able to take some small prizes; but until they had a larger ship and more men it was useless to think of fighting Koja Achem. This plan of action pleased the crew, and they sailed northwards. At the entrance of the Formosa Strait, near the island of Namoa in Swatow Bay, they met a Chinese pirate of a new variety. Thinking Antonio's vessel was a native craft, he came down on the wind to attack. But when he was close, men in red caps were seen on his foredeck. This told the Portuguese that the wearers were their own countrymen, for red caps of that shape were worn by no one else. A cordial exchange of visits followed. The pirate had thirty Portuguese fighting men on board. Pinto gives his name as Panian and says that he had recruited them at Patani. Antonio and he took to one another and resolved to go into partnership. Their combined

97

forces would be irresistible. Antonio had made one fortune fighting pirates; he would now make another as a pirate himself. But
it seems that his chief object was still to find Koja Achem.

Sailing into the Formosa Strait in company with Panian he
called at Ch'uan-chow. After making some inquiries from the Portuguese ships in port, he continued northwards and some days
later picked up eight Portuguese who were drifting in an open
boat. The men were in a bad state from exposure, and some were
also wounded. The story they told was the first certain news of
Koja Achem. They said that they belonged to a merchantman,
sailing from Ningpo to Malacca, which had been attacked and
taken by him. He had a fleet of three junks and four small vessels,
with a mixed crew of fifteen hundred, one hundred and fifty being
Mohammedans from India, in coats of mail and buff jerkins. The
place where he had taken their ship was by a small island further
up. They had been lucky enough to escape.

Antonio wept with joy on receiving this news. But before en-
gaging so formidable an opponent, he and Panian decided to lay
in more arms. At a Chinese port in the vicinity, where Panian was
on good terms with the Mandarin in charge, to whom he paid a
monthly bribe, they bought what they wanted, such as gunpowder, bullets, swords, pikes and some marine stores. The port
was the first in China proper that Pinto had seen, and he was much
impressed by the industry of the Chinese and, though it was a
small place, by the enormous quantity of commodities for sale.
'China may boast,' he says, 'that more than any other country in
the world she abounds in everything that man may desire.' But it
was a closed country and full of mystery, for no foreigners were
allowed to go inland.

On leaving this little port, they were a well-equipped force,
and set sail to look for Koja Achem at the island where he had
taken the Portuguese merchantmen. It was thought that he was
likely still to be there, because in the fight he had suffered damage,
which would have to be repaired. Three days took them to the
island, where they were told by fishermen that the pirate ships
were lying up a river. Of the fight that followed, Pinto writes:

Koja Achem is brought to bay

'It was so hot on either side that, though I was present, I confess I cannot describe it as a whole, particularly as it was scarce day when it began.' Some details, however, stuck in his memory. As soon as Antonio's flotilla was sighted in the river, gongs, drums and bells were sounded on Koja's junk to summon those of his men who were on shore. On hearing the alarm, they hastened in boats to row out to his assistance. A gunner on Panian's junk was ordered to sink them. But he was in such a state of nervousness that he could not aim properly. Seeing this, a certain Diogo Meyralez shouted in a passion: 'Get out of the way, you fool,' and pushed him so violently that he fell down a scuttle. Meyralez then aimed the gun by means of its wedges, which he knew very well how to manipulate, and, touching it off, sank the leading boat and killed most of the men in the boat behind.

Besides this episode, Pinto also caught a glimpse of Koja Achem at a later part of the battle. The famous pirate was wearing a coat of mail lined with crimson satin and edged with a golden fringe. His men were faltering and he gave a great shout, roaring the Mohammedan profession of faith: 'La ilaha illa-llahu Muhammad rasūl allahi'[1] (There is no god but Allah. Mohammed is the Apostle of Allah), and upbraided his men: 'Will you let yourselves be vanquished by these Christian slaves who have no more courage than white pullets or bearded women!'

Antonio also found it necessary to encourage his men. He said: 'Christ will never forsake us, however greatly we have sinned, for after all we are His, which these dogs are not.' As we have seen, this thought runs through Pinto's book: after all he was a Christian and in spite of his grievous sins that would suffice to save him.

Finally, Antonio and Koja came face to face. A single combat followed. Antonio fought with a two-handed sword, which he brought down on Koja's head, 'cutting through the cap of mail he wore.' Having felled him with this blow, he maimed him in

---

[1]Pinto gives the Arabic words of the Moslem creed fairly correctly. During his long stay in the East, he had no doubt acquired a smattering of various languages, Arabic and Burmese among them. It seems likely that he knew Malay well.

the legs. That was the end. Their champion mortally wounded, the pirates fled. Some were captured and thrown into a hold, bound hand and foot. But there 'they fairly tore out one another's throats with their teeth for fear of the death they expected'. The body of Koja Achem was dismembered and thrown over the side, where crocodiles, which had already tasted some of the corpses, were waiting round the ship for more.

Arranged though this account clearly is, it was written by a man who knew all about pirates and what it meant to fight them in the sixteenth century in some lonely river on a Chinese island. 'I have not used many words,' Pinto comments, 'for had I tried to recount all the particulars of this bloody battle, besides that I am not able to do it, I should have been forced to make a more ample history than this book is intended to be.' This holds good for his whole work. To have noted every detail of the many extraordinary things he saw would have been impossible; the best he could do was to give a general impression of what life was then like in far-eastern Asia for an adventurer who was also a convinced Catholic.

To wind up the story of Koja Achem, it is related that Antonio found a number of sick and wounded pirates on shore in a village temple. They begged for mercy, but he set fire to the building, and killed those who strove to escape the flames, which was a cruelty, Pinto declares.

The booty was enormous. It consisted of satins, damasks, raw silk, taffetas, musk and fine Ming porcelain, valued at one hundred and thirty thousand ounces of silver. In addition was recovered the Portuguese merchantman which Koja had taken, whose cargo was worth a like amount. Antonio resolved to return this ship to its owners at Ningpo when, as he intended, he reached that port.

CHAPTER THIRTEEN

The sack of Nouday

———◦———

From their present position about three-quarters way up the Formosa Strait, the Portuguese were five hundred miles distant from Ningpo. It and Ch'uan-chow, which was close behind them, were the only two ports in China at that date where their nation was allowed to trade. At Ningpo they had even been allowed to build houses on shore. Antonio anticipated that he would get a very good reception from his countrymen there, since he had killed a pirate who had taken one of their richest ships and was restoring them the ship with its cargo complete. Their goodwill would be a great help in selling his loot. He could also repair his vessels and in the spring of 1541 set out refreshed, and perhaps reinforced, on a lucrative adventure of a new kind. As soon, therefore, as his wounded men were better, he set sail for that port, though the late autumn was not a favourable season for a voyage north, as the winds were liable to be adverse and stormy. His fleet consisted of Panian's junk and his own, two of Koja's junks, the merchantman, and two small galleys. Before starting, he transferred most of the loot to his junk, because it was the most seaworthy vessel.

At the north end of the Formosa Strait they encountered a strong wind, which freshened until it was blowing a gale. They were about opposite Fu-chow and had the China coast in sight. The waves grew so high that the two small galleys could make no progress and turned in for shelter to a river-mouth. Night fell, overcast and very dark, and Antonio's junk ran on a bank. He refused to signal to the other ships for fear that they might also run aground. All through the night they tried to save the junk; the masts were cut down and much cargo thrown overboard, including twelve chests of silver ingots. At dawn the junk was high on the bank and badly holed, but the wind had begun to die down. The merchantman, which had ridden the storm unharmed and turned back to look for the lost junk, was now caught sight of. After being brought as close as was prudent, it was hove to, and rafts, to which ropes were attached, were floated towards the stranded vessel. By this means, though with great difficulty and some loss of life, Antonio and his crew were rescued. But nearly all the booty they had taken from Koja Achem had been either thrown overboard or now had to be abandoned, a misfortune which seemed almost more than could be borne, coming on top of the wreck at the Isle of Thieves.

Contact was made with the other ships during the course of the day. And now a new complication arose. One of the two small galleys that had run for shelter joined the fleet about sunset. Its crew reported that the other had broken her moorings and been blown ashore. They could do nothing at the time to help their comrades, but when the storm was over, they made inquiries and learnt that sixteen survivors, among whom were five Portuguese, had reached land, only to be arrested by the Chinese authorities and thrown into prison at a town in the vicinity called Nouday.

Before receiving this news, Antonio had been in the utmost despondency. Though God had spared his life the previous night, his fortune was lost for the second time. What could he do, since God was so set against him? But the news that his comrades were in a Chinese jail braced him to action and he resolved to rescue them, if he could.

The episode that follows is one of the most vivid in the *Peregrination*. We are given an authentic peep into Ming China. It is true that Nouday is not marked on the maps. Beyond the fact that it is stated to have been a small walled town on the coast somewhere in the region of Fu-chow, we cannot locate it. There are possible explanations—Pinto may have forgotten the name or, as given, it may be a printer's error or the town may since have changed its name. Nevertheless, we cannot dismiss the possibility

The sack of Nouday

that the name is an invention. The story itself, however, reads like a real happening, and one which is likely to have occurred somewhere on the China coast at that date. Indeed, it was episodes of this kind which caused the Ming, and their successors, the Ch'ing dynasty, to regard the Portuguese, and all foreigners, as lawless, dangerous people, barbarians given to piracy and raids, and who, unless they were kept at arm's length, would take possession of coastal territory by force of arms.

Antonio's resolve to rescue his comrades from the clutches of the Chinese authorities was immediately put into operation, and he sailed with his ships into the haven of Nouday, a large landlocked bay of the hilly kind usual on the China coast, with the town of Nouday out of sight up the estuary of a river. It was already dusk when he dropped anchor. To discover the lie of the land and where the captives were detained, he sent out spies in two boats with instructions to take soundings, observe what ships were in port, kidnap some of the local inhabitants and bring them back for examination. The boats left at 2 a.m. and returned at dawn with a small cargo vessel laden with pots and sugar-cane, which they had surprised at the mouth of the river. On board were eight Chinamen, two women and a child. When these people were brought on board the merchantman where Antonio was, they were so terrified, being certain it meant death, that they could not answer the questions put to then. Antonio tried all he could to comfort them, but the only response he got, as they wept and trembled, was: 'We are very poor people. Please don't kill us.' Unable to make any headway, he asked a Chinese woman, one of his own slaves (for the Portuguese always carried oriental women on their ships), to try to reassure them. She took them aside and in an hour had them so tractable that they made a statement. The most senior of them admitted that he had seen the wrecked Portuguese with irons on their legs being taken to the Nouday jail. Antonio asked whether he knew why they had been arrested. 'It was believed,' said the boatman, 'that they were notorious pirates that made a trade of robbing such as they met upon the seas.'

Being convinced by this statement that his countrymen were,

indeed, imprisoned at Nouday, Antonio bargained with the Chinese boatmen to take a letter, smuggle it into the jail and bring back an answer. The boatman chosen for the job made all speed. He managed to get into the jail, no doubt posing as a sugar-cane seller, saw the Portuguese, got a signed paper from them and was back on the junk within six hours. The letter stated that the signatories were in cruel durance and unless they were rescued had every reason to believe that they would be executed. 'When we enlisted under you at Patani,' they wrote to Antonio, 'you promised to take care of us. We were on your business when we were overtaken by this dreadful mishap. We beseech you by the Passion of Our Lord to save us.' And Pinto adds: 'To this they added many other pitiful entreaties as might well come from such poor wretches that were captives under the tyranny of a people as fell and cruel as the Chinese are.' This is the considered opinion of a man who, as will be seen, possessed a great deal of information about the Chinese prison system.

Antonio read this letter aloud to his companions and invited them to suggest a plan of action. Some shrugged their shoulders and said nothing could be done; others urged this, others that. But the general feeling was that a rescue involved too great a risk. Antonio knew that they were not really afraid of anything, and, to give them a jolt, said in a voice he made to seem angry: 'I have sworn not to leave these poor soldiers, my comrades, in the lurch, and risk or not I am going to fetch them. To abandon them would be not only dishonourable, but also a sin that would put my soul in danger.'

This little speech pleased the company. You are right, they said. We shall not stand between you and your conscience; on the contrary, you can count on us to the death.

So Antonio won his crew over to what was certainly a dangerous undertaking, since it meant breaking into a walled town on the mainland of China. With his hat in his hand he embraced them. 'I shall not forget how you have backed me up,' he declared, tears in his eyes.

But before resorting to extreme measures, he resolved to try what could be done by negotiation. After all, most Mandarins were open to a bribe. The Magistrate of Nouday would be no exception. If a good sum were offered, he would release the prisoners. Accordingly a petition was written in proper form and the eldest boatman was sent to present it with a bribe worth a couple of hundred pounds. Next day the man returned with an order scribbled on the back of the petition to the effect that the petitioner should have presented it in person. The words that conveyed this order were in the high and mighty style always used by Chinese authority when addressing foreigners. Pinto tries to give an impression of it by rendering the words thus: 'Let your mouth come and present itself at my feet, and after I have heard you, I will do justice,' which, as those conversant with such Chinese official papers will not deny, hits off their manner sufficiently well.

Antonio now tried another tack. He assumed that the Magistrate thought the bribe too small, but in sending a second one ten times as large he accompanied it with a letter, worded less like a petition than the former, and containing a veiled threat that he would not leave the port until the prisoners were given up. The Magistrate would have, he calculated, two good reasons for complying, his own interest and his fear of the consequences if he did not. But the letter contained a phrase so distasteful to him, that it outweighed these considerations.

The boatman who took the letter was cruelly beaten and sent back with a dirty piece of torn paper, on which was written: 'Having desired your abject petition to be read and being about to condescend to consider favourably its prayer and even to accept your miserable present, my ears were stunned by the disrespectful claim that your obscure King was a brother of the Son of Heaven, who is Lord of the World, and at whose feet all Kings kneel and offer their crowns. For such an unheard-of impertinence your petition has been burnt and I order you to leave Nouday immediately.'

This is one of the earliest mentions of the Chinese objection to the diplomatic claim of brotherhood between a foreign sovereign and the Emperor of China. The English were to receive many missives of the kind. Antonio was angry, and when he declared that arguing with Mandarins was useless and that, as he had conceived at the first, the captives would have to be rescued by force, everyone supported him with acclamation. An attack on the town was prepared. Some large fishing boats had been seized, and it was proposed to use them to land a party consisting of forty Portuguese, one hundred and eighty arquebusiers, and eighty slaves and mariners armed with spears, drawn both from Antonio's and Panian's followers. Some pieces of light ordnance were also to be taken. The operation began the next morning before dawn. First the fleet moved from the haven into the river-mouth and anchored in six fathoms close to the walls of the town. Before launching the attack from the boats, it was decided to give the Magistrate one more chance, in case the sight of the ships had weakened his resolution. A third Chinese messenger was forced to go with the same demand and the same offer of money. But the Magistrate, an obstinate man of fanatical virtue, convinced of his own power and blindly contemptuous of theirs, had him executed on the wall as a renegade and his mutilated corpse displayed to the fleet.

This treatment of the messenger so incensed the Portuguese men-at-arms that they demanded to be led ashore immediately. Antonio accordingly embarked them in the boats and, leaving instructions that the ships' batteries should open fire on the town to cover the assault when it began in earnest, led them to a spot a cannon-shot below the roadstead, where a landing was made without opposition. Forming a column, he marched along the bank towards the town walls, before which at this place was an open field. On the battlements were seen Chinese soldiers taking position under standards, and beating drums and ringing bells. They hooted at the small body of foreigners below them and, waving their caps, invited them contemptuously to come on. When the Portuguese were within musket-shot, the gate was opened and a thousand men sallied out over the moat-bridge, some hundred and twenty of them mounted on horses, 'or to say better,' as our Commonwealth translator has it, 'on lean carrion tits that were nothing but skin and bone.' This cavalry began to course up and down the field in a skirmishing manner, wheeling round the Portuguese, though without making any attack, their idea apparently being that the mere sight of them and their military evolutions would daunt the invaders and suffice to drive them back. But the effect was droll rather than intimidating, for their drill was so bad that they ran into each other, and several fell off and sprawled on the ground. It was evident that they were not trained soldiers, but some kind of local levy, probably coolies who had been put into uniform. The sight of their ineptitude cheered the Portuguese, who, drawn up in battle array with the arquebusiers in front, confidently stood their ground. When the Chinese perceived that galloping and wheeling had not caused the invaders to turn tail, they came together into a compact body, though more like a huddled mob than a regiment in its ranks, and seemed to wait to be attacked. Up till this Antonio had withheld his fire, and now ordered his arquebusiers to pour in a volley since the target was so good. The discharge killed some of the Chinese horsemen, and the rest threw themselves on the ground, seemingly terrified by this unexpected blow. This was the moment to press the attack, and the Portuguese advanced, leaving the arquebusiers to reload. The Chinese did not wait for them, but turned and ran for the bridge over the moat, where they arrived in such disorder that they stuck half-way, unable to go forward or backward. Meanwhile, the arquebusiers had reloaded and, coming up, fired another volley into the struggling mass. This time their balls took more deadly effect, and three hundred Chinese fell wounded or dead, 'a pitiful sight,' says Pinto, 'because not one of them had had the heart so much as to draw his sword.'

The Portuguese now pressed on hotly and ran over the bridge to the gateway. There the Magistrate awaited them at the head of six hundred men. He was mounted on a horse and was wearing a Portuguese cuirass lined with purple velvet and having studs of an older fashion. This had belonged, as it turned out, to Tomé

The sack of Nouday

Pires, the author of the *Suma Oriental* already mentioned, who in 1516, twenty-four years before, had led a disastrous embassy to the Emperor of China and died a prisoner in that country. When the Portuguese reached the gateway, a stiff fight took place, for the Magistrate's men were better trained than the ridiculous mob that had been routed. But one of the arquebusiers managed to shoot the Magistrate in the breast, and he fell to the ground, a dead man. At the sight of this, his party lost their nerve, turned their backs, and fled into the town. Their confusion and haste was such that nobody thought of shutting the gate. The Portuguese pursued them into a street that led through the town to a gate on the opposite side, where they escaped into the fields. Antonio closed the gate after them, thereby becoming master of the town, for there were no other troops in it. In the excitement of victory his men, forgetting the object of the attack, were on the point of dispersing to plunder, but he managed to re-form them and, declaring that their first duty was to their comrades, marched at once to the town jail. On getting to the door, they battered upon it, demanding of the jailers immediate entry. Their comrades within, who had been hoping against hope for rescue, guessed it had come and their shouts could be heard. The door was broken down and the Portuguese rushed in, embraced the captives and struck their irons off.

This done, the troops demanded leave to plunder. Antonio gave them half an hour for it. He thought it imprudent to stay longer, not knowing what reinforcements might appear. Moreover, if given no time limit, his men would become totally demoralized. He himself went straight to the Magistrate's house. There he found eight thousand ounces of silver and eight large jars full of musk, which he reserved for himself; the silks and porcelains he left to his servants. Meanwhile his soldiers were very busy ransacking the houses and loading the boats, which made as many as four trips to the junks. When a couple of hours had passed in this way, Antonio became anxious and ordered his men to stop looting, but they were out of hand and paid no attention. The gentlemen of quality were the worst offenders. But since

The sack of Nouday

darkness was approaching, something had to be done, and Antonio took the drastic course of setting fire to the town. It went up in a blaze, for all the houses were of wood. This told the men better than any orders that it was time to finish and return to the ships. Laughing and singing, they began to withdraw, dragging with them some handsome girls, who were tied together in groups of four or five with the cords used as matches by the arquebusiers. They were screaming with terror. Pinto was sorry for them.

So ended the sack of Nouday. As stated previously, the Viceroy had no way of controlling his countrymen when they sailed beyond Malacca. Piracy and the sacking of small ports were typical of these masterless men. Pinto's relation of Antonio de Faria da Sousa's voyage is the best detailed account of what they were like. It helps us to conjure up the other pirates mentioned by historians, such as Gonçalves Tibau, who made himself King of Sandwip island in the Bay of Bengal, and Damião Bernaldes, Antonio's contemporary, who also operated in that bay.[1] Indeed, it holds good for the English pirates who prowled Eastern seas in the seventeenth century, like John Hand, killed when leaping ashore to sack a town in Sumatra in 1684. The last scene in Conrad's *Lord Jim* is also of this kind and is pitched in the nineteenth century.

[1] See Fernão Lopes de Castanheda, viii, 46 (1561).

CHAPTER FOURTEEN

Pinto arrives at Ningpo in China

Delaying only to help himself to fresh provisions from a village in the vicinity, whose inhabitants had fled in terror, Antonio continued on his way north to Ningpo, still three hundred miles further up the coast. It occurred to him that if the news of the sack of Nouday spread, his appearance at Ningpo would endanger the Portuguese settlement. The Chinese government might refuse to distinguish between the peaceful traders there and the buccaneer visitor, and, labelling all Portuguese as robbers of the sea and their abettors, descend upon the settlement and destroy it, a fate which in fact overtook it five years later. On arrival, therefore, at the anchorage among wooded islands that lay on the outer side of the haven in which it stood, he sent messengers with a letter stating that he would not enter the port unless the Portuguese were willing that he should do so. His messengers were also to relate how he had defeated Koja Achem and was bringing back their merchantman which the pirate had taken.

The Portuguese settlement, which seems to have been some miles from the Chinese city of Ningpo, was a sort of municipality, consisting of a thousand houses, with a council, a justiciary and various administrative officers.[1] The messengers arrived very late, but their relation of how Antonio had saved the Ningpo merchants from the total loss of a very rich ship made such an impres-

[1]Some authorities think that Pinto is exaggerating, and that Ningpo was no more than an anchorage and rendezvous for illicit trade, winked at by the local mandarins, who had been bribed; a place like Lintin, the nineteenth-century opium smugglers' depot.

sion that there and then, though it was the middle of the night, the councillors ordered to be rung the bells of Our Lady of the Conception, as the principal church was called, thereby signifying the holding of a general assembly. The merchants hastened to the hall, and when they heard the news, passed a resolution to send Antonio a reply, thanking him for what he had done and inviting him to enter the port. He need not, they said, worry about Nouday, because the whole country was in such a state of commotion, owing to there being no less than sixteen bandits operating with large forces against the government, that a small matter like the sack of an unimportant coast town would pass unnoticed. They proposed to give him a public reception and asked him to wait where he was anchored until they had had time to make the necessary arrangements.

While he waited, Antonio was visited on board by most of the prominent merchants, who brought him presents of eggs, fruit and fowl. On the morning appointed for his entry, boats full of musicians were sent to escort his ships to the inner haven. The sun had not yet risen and a full moon was setting in a clear sky, when the sound of their flutes and hautboys was heard. There was every variety of boat, each profusely decorated with bunting, their decks spread with splendid Turkish carpets. Soon the anchors were raised and the ships moved in procession slowly towards the port. As they neared the settlement, they found all the craft in the place were drawn up in two lines, leaving an avenue between, and had the appearance of a floating forest or orchard, for the sampans and junks were dressed with greenery, even branches of fruit trees on which hung oranges and lemons.

On coming to anchor near the shore, Antonio was greeted by a salute of cannon. Crowds of Chinese were looking on. Astonished at the lavishness of the reception, they were asking themselves what sort of a great dignitary Antonio might be, and were told, says Pinto, that he was the man who shod the King of Portugal's horses. The Chinese took this for simple truth and were the more amazed at the acclamations. Evidently there are greater Kings in the world, one of them said, than are mentioned in our histories. If even his smith is worthy of such honour, the King of Portugal must be richer than the King of Cochin China. That he is, put in a second, and, were it not blasphemy to say so, might even be compared to the Son of Heaven.[1]

And now an oared boat came alongside Antonio's junk to carry him to the wharf. On it was a chair of state under a canopy, about which was seated a troupe of young Chinese girls, singing a song of welcome and accompanying themselves. Antonio was invited to take his seat in the chair and was rowed toward the wharf, from which came a medley of music, the modes of China, Malaya, Borneo, Siam, for Ningpo was a port where merchants from all the states of Asia congregated to trade under the protection of the Portuguese municipality, as they were later to do at British Hongkong and Shanghai.

Antonio was formally received on the wharf by the heads of the members of the town council and conducted to a sedan-chair which was waiting. Though he made a show of declining to enter it, they insisted, and he was carried into the settlement by eight Portuguese dressed in new clothes, with a guard of halberdiers walking beside and police on white horses to keep back the crowd.

In the centre square a further reception had been arranged. The two senior residents of the settlement, Tristan da Gaa and Hieronimo de Rego, each made a speech, in the course of which Antonio was compared to Alexander the Great on account of the generous way he was giving them back their property, and to Scipio, Hannibal, Pompey and Julius Caesar because of the bravery of his conduct. The speeches ended, they started for a thanksgiving service at the Church of Our Lady of the Conception. After going a little way Antonio saw at a window the arms of the Faria family, not painted but, as it were, played in pantomime by living actors, for the coat represented a famous action

---

[1]This imagined conversation is an excellent example of Pinto's method. In a subtle way he suggests that though the Chinese were ignorant of Europe, some of them had an intuitive feeling that it was a great and extraordinary place, a view which was true and which, had it been held by the Chinese governments of the succeeding centuries, would have enabled China to modernize itself and avoid falling behind the West.

by the founder of his house, who was killed in the wars between Portugal and Castile. An ancient gentleman, clad in crimson silk, came forward and in an address referred in feeling terms to this gallant ancestor of the Farias and, again thanking Antonio for his services to the community, begged him to accept a trifling present for distribution to his soldiers, as an earnest of what it was proposed to offer him on a future occasion. Whereupon five chests containing silver ingots to the value of five thousand pounds were brought. But Antonio, though he thanked the old gentleman profusely, declined to accept the present. Having been compared to Alexander, he felt, perhaps, that some such gesture was indispensable.

A covered litter was waiting, and the gentlemen present wanted to carry him in it to the Church. But he excused himself, saying that the honour was too great, and insisted on walking. A procession was accordingly formed to music, and they paraded down the long street, decorated with triumphal arches and whose air was sweetened by clouds of incense. At the door of the Church eight priests were waiting, who conducted Antonio, while the Te Deum was sung, to a red-velvet chair on a dais near the altar.

After the celebration of the mass, the Vicar of the Church rose to deliver the sermon. He was an elderly person of striking features, but of no education and quite incapable of a sermon in the grand manner. Nevertheless, after the learned and elegant orations which had been delivered that day, he felt it incumbent to show himself a man of letters and had prepared what he thought was a fine piece of rhetoric. It consisted of extravagant compliments to Antonio, decked out with what classical tags he could muster, but so jumbled and off the point, that the Captain blushed and hung his head. On and on went the sermon, and two or three of his friends, seeing how distasteful it was to him, went up to the Vicar and, in an effort to get him to stop, pulled his surplice. But he seemed not to notice, and only after they had tugged several times did they manage to gain his attention. With a start he looked down on them and said: 'Don't interrupt! I will not stop. Why should I, when all I am saying is simple truth and may be sworn to on the Gospels? I myself had a share of thousands in our ship and can't overpraise the man who killed Koja. What a dog that pirate was! Please God he stays for ever in Hell! Let us all say Amen to that!'

This caused such a roar of laughter in the Church, that not a word could be heard, and he had to sit down, says Pinto.

The day's festivities were concluded by a banquet. Pinto describes it in detail, his object being to show what a luxurious life was lived in China. It would be impossible, he says, to get such a dinner anywhere else in the world, certainly not in impecunious Portugal. Not only was the food good beyond imagination, but it was served with wonderful taste and in a setting of enchantment. Pinto is very right in drawing attention to this aspect of Chinese culture. More than any people on earth the Chinese have perfected the art of eating, and for centuries before the Ming had been the world's greatest purveyors of luxury goods. In his description of the banquet, Pinto shows his full comprehension of this cardinal fact, in such contrast to the misery of Chinese prisons and the cruelty of their punishments. He is the first European writer to grasp the paradox and to disclose the strange mixture of softness and hardness that is Chinese civilization.

The banquet was held out of doors in a garden surrounded by chestnut trees and full of roses. Little streams of water were led among the flowers, and fountains threw up jets of water so high that it floated down like dew. Three long tables were laid, and ranged on side tables was the food in finest porcelain. The waitresses were Chinese girls, and as they served each course music was played by other girls no less charming to look at. When it was over, Antonio talked of going back to his ship, but his hosts would not hear of it. Two of the best houses in the place had been placed at his disposal; he could stay there free as long as he liked. This invitation was accepted, and he and his companions moved into the houses, which were side by side and connected by a passage. During the winter months which followed they much enjoyed themselves. There was always something new to do, fishing, hawking, hunting deer and wild boar; and in the evenings comedies, dancing, concerts, farces, not to speak of a round of exquisite dinners. The only cloud was that Panian, the pirate without whose help they could not have defeated Koja Achem, got ill and died suddenly. Antonio was much affected by his loss, and gave him a splendid funeral, 'the last duty which one can render a friend.'

CHAPTER FIFTEEN

The expedition to the royal tombs

———————— ✦ ————————

We have now reached a point in the *Peregrination* where a change comes over the nature of its narrative. Hitherto, as I have tried to indicate in my running commentary, Pinto has shown himself to be intimately acquainted with the places and way of life which he describes. Though it is impossible to be sure that the events occurred in the mould and sequence he imposes upon them, it is certain that he is not inventing, but drawing on personal experiences. Now he wants to take the reader inside China, the rich, ancient and highly civilized country of which the West at the time had very little knowledge. A revelation of some of its secrets would make his book far more entertaining. Indeed, to leave China out of his immense panorama of Asiatic life would upset the balance. His ambition, an enormous ambition in the sixteenth century, was to describe his experiences in every country of the Far East, experiences which were generally connected with historical events of importance in each. We have seen him treating, in his autobiographical mode, of the Turkish and Achinese threats to Portuguese Asia, and of piracy, with its commercial and moral implications; later he will deal with capital events in Japan, Burma and Siam. To omit China from such a scheme was clearly impossible. He must have adventures in China on which to hang an impression of that country.

During the Ming dynasty foreigners were forbidden to penetrate into China, but they traded, legally or illegally, at certain ports. Ningpo was such a port and, as we have seen, no objection had been taken to the Portuguese building a settlement; they traded at Ch'uan-chow and elsewhere, too, they managed to procure stores and provisions. By meeting Chinese in the coastal ports, listening to what they had to say of the interior, studying their institutions in the ports, and observing the products offered for sale, they could form a limited, but not altogether reliable, idea of inner China. These sources were all open to Pinto.

There was, however, one way by which the regions beyond the ports could be visited. That was by being made prisoner by the Chinese and taken there. Some Portuguese are known to have had that experience, though few of them survived to tell the tale. Pinto now relates a story of how he was made prisoner, describes why he was taken to Peking, the most wonderful city in all the East, and which, more than any other, had excited Western curiosity, and how he succeeded afterwards in getting out of the country.

While some scholars allow that he did what he declares, others, led by Schurhammer, point out the insuperable difficulties of accepting the fact. Two of these difficulties are the fancifulness of his place-names and the confusion of his dates. In the cases where he had direct knowledge of a region and had had adventures there, he is able to write an account which is so correct and interwoven with such authentic touches that one cannot tell how far it has been arranged. When he had not that direct knowledge, though he makes vivid use of his hearsay information, he cannot avoid what we now see to have been obvious mistakes and improbabilities. His account of China is convincing in parts, and it is to those parts that I shall draw attention.

The story begins in the following way. Antonio, wondering what to do next, was told by a Chinese corsair about an island called Calempluy on which were the tombs of seventeen Chinese Emperors, and resolved to rob them. Now, there is nothing unlikely in this conception as such. Royal tombs all over the world have attracted bandits from time immemorial. The tombs of the Chinese Emperors have continually been robbed. The most famous of all Chinese imperial tombs, that of the first Emperor of the Ch'in dynasty, was plundered in 206 B.C.; that of Ch'ien Lung

The expedition to the royal tombs

(1736–1795), the last great Emperor of China, in 1926. (In the private collections of this country are objects taken from that tomb.) The project was therefore in the tradition.

But though the idea of plundering an imperial tomb can be reconciled with the Chinese background, there remains a difficulty which precludes us from accepting the story as it stands. No such place as Calempluy is known. That it was supposed to lie in some waters in the region of Nanking, and so at no great distance from Ningpo, follows from the sequel, but Pinto's lengthy description of how he and Antonio got there is impossible to follow and is rendered still more obscure by the statement that the voyage took eighty-three days and that nearly a thousand miles were covered. If to that we add that no imperial tombs exist or are recorded to have existed on an island in those parts, enough has been said to show that he was counting on the ignorance of his readers, which indeed was complete in regard to the topography and history of China.

Pinto provides a minutely detailed description of the tombs and their surroundings, but to anyone even slightly acquainted with China it is evident that his model is a group of Buddhist monasteries. The gilded pagodas, the hermitages, the Buddhas, the monks, are all there along with the usual gardens and fruit-trees. Imperial tombs are a Confucian foundation and are laid out on a totally different plan. So exactly does our author hit off a Buddhist atmosphere that we begin to suspect that at some time or other he was guilty of pillaging some monastic settlement.

When Antonio lands with his soldiers from his two ships and enters one of the monasteries, he pretends that he is a shipwrecked mariner and has come to ask alms. The Abbot does not believe this and Pinto makes him say, in effect, that robbing a religious foundation is a mortal sin. The normal attitude of a sixteenth century Catholic towards Asiatic religions was far other than this. Pinto must have been the only Portuguese of his day who believed that he was endangering the salvation of his soul by plundering a heathen sanctuary. At the time of writing the *Peregrination* he had come to feel, true Catholic though he was, that the

118

The expedition to the royal tombs

East believed in the same God as the West and that an Eastern religion, though it had limitations and abuses, was a holy thing. In his indirect way he repeats this again and again in the course of his narrative. It is as if in his early days out East he had done things which he later saw to be wrong and for which his conscience pricked him. As Antonio (perhaps the character throughout is meant to be himself, though an Antonio de Faria is known to have existed) begins to break open the coffins and steal the silver in them, the Abbot is made to say: 'If you hope to obtain pardon for the sin you are now committing and so save your soul from perishing, you must, before you die, do three things—surrender what you have stolen, do penance, and distribute your goods to the poor.' As will be seen, this is what Pinto did before he left the East.

The journey to Calempluy now begins to take on an inner meaning. Outwardly it is used to lead up to adventures in China, but inwardly it is a kind of allegory of the journey of Pinto's own soul. Indeed, it can be argued that the whole *Peregrination* has the double meaning of an outward and inward journey.

The Abbot continued to admonish Antonio, who made excuses, but admitted that what he was doing was a very great sin. One of his men, a certain Nuno Coelho, here interrupted, declaring that 'the law of God commanded him to act in this way', which may be taken as an expression of current Catholic opinion that the plunder of a non-Christian sanctuary was a meritorious act. To which the Abbot replied: 'I have lived to see what I never expected—evil actions justified by claiming God's sanction.'

While this conversation was going on, the soldiery were behaving in an outrageous manner: smashing the coffins, flinging them out of their places and scattering the bones over the ground.

'Tell them at least not to spit on the altar,' the monk begged Antonio, 'and to gather together the bones of the Saints.' In using this term to describe the dead, Pinto seems to abandon the story that they were Emperors, as if his mind were so full of some real desecration that he forgot his fiction.

Having as much silver as they could carry, the Portuguese with-

The expedition to the royal tombs

drew to their two ships, intending to return the next morning for more. But the alarm was raised. The monk, 'though very old and his legs so swollen with the gout that he was not able to stand, much less go,' managed to crawl to the next monastery and call for help. About midnight the Portuguese saw beacon-fires and feared that the Magistrate of the nearest town would send soldiers. Antonio hastened ashore with a few men to reconnoitre. Bells were ringing and he heard many voices. His guides begged him to go back, but he climbed steps to a terrace, and ran up and down it like a madman. Presently he came upon a monk and constrained him to speak, 'else he would use him in a strange fashion.' The monk admitted that help was on the way. There was nothing for it but to retire, and Antonio, tearing his hair and beard in rage, re-embarked, and ordered his ships to weigh anchor. 'We were so desolate and sad that we scarce spoke a word,' says Pinto, not only, it seems, because they were baulked of their plunder, but because the parting words of the monk rang in their ears: 'Labour to save yourselves as you will, yet shall you not effect it, for be sure that all creation, the earth, the air, the winds, the waters, the beasts, the fishes, the fowls, the very trees, will pursue and torment you.'

When they emerged from the maze of nameless waterways that surrounded Calempluy, into the open sea of the Gulf of Nanking, a typhoon caught them. They did all they could to ride it out, cutting down masts and jettisoning cargo. But at midnight those on Pinto's ship heard the lamentable cry, 'Lord, have mercy upon us,' coming from the other, and they knew that Antonio was cast away. At dawn there was no sign of him and his company, nor were they ever seen again.

So, his despairing cry ringing over the dark waves, Antonio passes from the story. He was a brave man, faithful to his comrades; honest, much liked and respected by his compatriots; a good Catholic who, after his piratical cruise, went to mass and even carried a chaplain with him on his raid of the tombs. Redeeming though these qualities were, Pinto condemns him through the mouths of Asiatics and shows how God took his life away in spite of his wild midnight cry for mercy and forgiveness. But Antonio is a symbolical figure. In condemning him, Pinto intends to condemn all the Portuguese in Asia. His fear is that God, for their sins, may take away from them all that they have won so laboriously by their arms. He is the first European to speak on behalf of suffering Asia, the prey of Western marauders, merchants and intolerant priests. And in his condemnation of his own people, he includes himself, the associate of Antonio, the man who had done the same as Antonio, who in a sense was Antonio.

With these interpretations in mind, one perceives how far is the *Peregrination* from being a romance of adventure. In that mode of writing the adventurer is a hero. But there is no glorification of Pinto in his book. At Calempluy the monk says of the Portuguese that they are 'monsters of the night, all their ambition placed upon money, and so greedy that all the silver in the world could not satiate them.' Pinto does not except himself from that denunciation.

In the chapter which follows, his intention is to show that, though he was spared from drowning, he had to undergo sufferings worse than death as a divine punishment.

CHAPTER SIXTEEN

Pinto wanders begging in China

———❖———

Soon after Antonio went down with all hands in the Gulf of Nanking, the ship on which Pinto was travelling drove ashore. Of those on board, fourteen Portuguese, eighteen Christian servants and seven Chinese mariners escaped with their lives. The place was a desolate and rocky promontory without inhabitants. Making their way as best they could up and down steep hills and through woods and marshes, they eventually reached the camp of some charcoal-burners, whom they begged to direct them to a place where they might find food and shelter. The charcoal-burners said there was a poor-house further on, and one of them added: 'I wish we could help you, but all we can do is to let you share our supper. You can sleep here if you are too tired to go to the poor-house.' Whereupon, some rice was given them, though it was only two mouthfuls apiece, so wretchedly poor were their hosts.

Struggling on as fast as their weakness permitted, they reached the poor-house after nightfall. The four men who were in charge received them charitably. The next morning, on being asked to give a full account of themselves, they declared that they were subjects of the King of Siam and had suffered shipwreck on a voyage to Ningpo. The King of Siam was known to employ foreigners and their explanation was accepted. Moreover, as the King was, at least in name, a tributary sovereign of the Emperor of China, his subjects were not regarded in the same way as those whose rulers paid no tribute. Asked what they planned to do, they replied that they hoped to find at Nanking a ship going to some Siamese port, on which they would engage themselves as rowers, but begged, as they were weak after their shipwreck, to be allowed to stay at the poor-house until they felt better. And they asked for clothes, as many of them were half-naked.

The guardians replied that they would do what they could, but that the poor-house had little funds. As for staying there, the rule was that no one could remain longer than three days, or five at the utmost, except women with child or men too sick to travel. A subscription was got up in the village, a small one of fifty houses inhabited only by labourers; and two ounces of silver, half a sack of rice, a little meal, some haricot beans, onions and a few old rags were collected. In addition, two further ounces of silver were bestowed on them from the funds of the poor-house.

For these humble kindnesses the Portuguese were profusely thankful. When the guardians sent them on their way, they gave them a letter to another poor-house, which was situated in a small town and had more ample resources.

On reaching this town, the Portuguese went straight to the poor-house and presented their letter to the guardians, who happened at the moment to be holding a committee-meeting. The clerk read it to the members, who listened carefully, seated round a table. When he had finished, a room was promptly allotted. It was neatly furnished with a table and chairs. A good dinner was provided, and the Portuguese were left to go to sleep. Next morning they were sent for and their names entered in a register; an accounts formality, it was explained. They told the same story, which was not questioned, and on asking leave to stay, as several of them were ill, were given the permission. A doctor attended them, and they were treated with such goodness and charity, that they broke down and wept when they tried to thank the guardians.

After a stay at this place, they set out again, resolved as before to walk to Nanking, begging as they went for food and shelter. But the city was a great distance off, and to find the way was not easy. Outside a village where the road forked they sat down by a well, wondering which turn to take. Presently two or three people approached to draw water, and seeing strangers with beards sitting at the well, were frightened and ran back to the village. The villagers came out and, standing at a distance, stared without speaking. Then they seemed to debate, and after a while sent an old woman to ask the Portuguese why they sat round the well which the villagers used. They told her the story that they were of Siam and asked whether there was a poor-house. She said there was not, but that she would go and inquire what could be done for them. After some discussion they were invited to the temple, and given food and mats to lie on. Next morning they begged from door to door and collected in that way a little money.

So far they had received nothing but extreme kindness from the poor country people, who did not suspect them of being sea-rovers nor dreamed they had been plundering royal tombs. No police or officials had yet been met with. But their luck was not to hold. Near the next village, when they sat down under a solitary tree to rest, three boys who were tending cattle espied them. Their beards, their strange eyes and their foreign manner so startled the boys that they ran towards the village, screaming 'Thieves! Thieves!' The Portuguese tried to slink away, but the villagers, rushing out with sticks and lances, and seeing, as they supposed, thieves making off, pursued them, shouting and throwing stones. Presently they grew bolder and closed in, seized the Portuguese, tied their arms behind their backs, beat them and dragged them half-dead to the village, where they put them into a cistern of water, which was up to their waists and full of leeches.

'In this miserable place,' says Pinto, 'we remained two days, which seemed two hundred years to us, having neither rest nor anything to eat all the time.' At last a man from the village where they had been lodged in the temple happened to pass, and, hearing that they were in the cistern, said a mistake had been made and that they were not thieves but shipwrecked mariners. He carried his point, and they were taken out of the cistern that evening and allowed to depart, weak and sore from the sucking of the leeches. Not knowing where they went in the rain and the dark, they came to the gate of a cattle-pen and lay down on a dung-heap until the dawn.

Pinto wanders begging in China

Continuing the next morning, they climbed a little hill and saw spread below them a plain full of trees and in the middle of it a large house, standing alone beside a stream. Attracted by its pleasant aspect they went towards it and sat by a fountain outside the gate of its courtyard. Afraid to knock at the gate, they remained for two hours without seeing anyone. At length a youth of sixteen or seventeen, most gentlemanly looking and mounted on a white horse, came from the direction of the wooded country. He had a falcon on his wrist and dogs at his heels, and his servants carried his bag of two hares and five pheasants. The house was his father's, and on seeing the Portuguese at the gate, dirty, ragged and covered with sores, he was sorry for them and stopped his horse. 'What can I do for you?' he asked them.

'We answered as well as we could,' says Pinto, 'and told him the story of our shipwreck.' It was evident from the young man's face that he was touched. 'Wait here,' he said, 'and I will send you something to eat.'

He went into his courtyard and presently an old woman came out, dressed in a long plain garment with a rosary hanging from her neck. She said kindly but severely: 'Our young master has sent me out to you. You can come in, but mind you behave properly, or they will take you for a pack of idle vagabonds.'

They followed her humbly into the outer courtyard, which was surrounded by galleries, like cloisters, on the walls of which were frescoes depicting women on horseback hunting with falcons. Out of this court was a flight of stone steps that led up to the door of a hall. Inside they saw a lady of about fifty years of age. She was seated on a carpet and beside her were two girls, very pretty and charmingly dressed, evidently her daughters. Behind them nine maids, dressed in red-and-white silk gowns, were busily sewing. A little to one side was a couch, on which reclined an elderly person of venerable appearance. He appeared to be unwell. Standing behind his head was the young gentleman they knew.

It was evident that the old man was the master of the house, and the Portuguese knelt down at his couch and asked him for charity, explaining their destitution in tearful voices.

Pinto wanders begging in China

It was the old lady who spoke. 'Come, come,' she said. 'No need to go on crying. We know you want alms, and that is enough.'

An idea now suddenly occurred to the old gentleman. He had heard that the Portuguese were remarkable doctors and, guessing that his visitors were of that nation, asked them whether they could prescribe for a fever.

Before they could answer, one of the daughters put in: 'I think they would rather have something to eat, than be asked what they probably know nothing about.'

Her mother thought this very pert. 'I wonder whether I shall ever get you not to speak until you are spoken to?' she said.

'Of course you will, Mother,' replied the girl, smiling; 'meanwhile let these poor strangers have some food.'

But the old gentleman would not be put off and began asking the strangers a string of questions. They answered to the best of their ability, and told him, too, of their shipwreck and how they hoped, by begging their way, to get to Nanking and find a ship. The old man listened with a thoughtful air and at length, turning to his son, he remarked: 'I hope you have been attending. These men's story ought to make you thank God that He has given you a father able to shield you from the hardships of life. But I am afraid you are too happy-go-lucky for that. All you think of is to go hawking.'

To this the young gentleman made no reply, but looked into his sisters' eyes and smiled.

The master of the house now ordered food to be brought in and had it placed so that he could see the strangers eat. 'Fall to,' he said. 'I like people with a good appetite, having none myself on account of my illness.' Chopsticks were provided—'two little sticks made like a pair of scissors,' explains Pinto, rather inexactly, to his readers, who had never heard of such things. But he and his companions did not attempt to use them and ate with their hands. Their disgusting table manners made the young people giggle, though the old gentleman watched with bland interest. After the meal, the Portuguese said grace, an act which seemed to touch their host. With a pious gesture he declared how moving it was to observe that even strangers from beyond the boundaries of the Empire, men totally ignorant of the truth, thanked Heaven for benefits received, a simple and natural show of gratitude which, in his opinion, might be as pleasing to Heaven as one made with the proper ritual. Whereupon, he gave them some pieces of linen and four ounces of silver, and, as it was late, said they could sleep in the house.

This is a very brilliant description of a Confucian family of the upper class. No contemporary of Pinto's has given so penetrating a glimpse of Ming China nor, indeed, has any subsequent writer bettered it. All the essential characteristics of the Confucian way of life are touched on. The passage proves that Pinto actually met such a family, for the scene could not have been written otherwise. No amount of reading or hearsay would have sufficed. The contention, put forward by some critics, that he only had a seafarer's smattering, picked up in the ports, becomes ridiculous. He understood China in a more balanced way, not only than his contemporaries, but also than the long list of later writers who first overpraised and then underrated her. Since we have to admit that in this part of his Chinese adventures he is marvellously correct, we must believe, in default of any evidence to the contrary, except the general one that all Pinto's narrative is arranged, that in fact he had direct experiences beyond the ports, though what precisely these were we shall never learn, as he had his own ultra-historical reasons for presenting his life story in the way he did.

CHAPTER SEVENTEEN

Pinto suffers in Chinese prisons

So far, in the tale of his Chinese adventures, Pinto has emphasized the benevolence of the Chinese, which tempered the
divine punishment which he had incurred for his sins. But
now he discloses the hard side of their character, the instrument
used by God to inflict penalties more dreadful than shipwreck and
destitution, a sort of purging as terrible as a sojourn in Hell. This
part has been found by his critics to contain so many fanciful
names and improbabilities, that they reject it altogether. But the
journey, as I have suggested, is more a vision than reality itself.
Nevertheless, we can follow it; the core of it makes sense and
could have happened. Indeed, other Portuguese of the period are
known to have suffered in a similar way, as I will mention.

After leaving the delightful old gentleman's house, the Portuguese wandered begging from village to village, while they made
for Nanking, as far as they could gauge, keeping off the main
roads and away from large towns, for fear that they might be
arrested as strangers. By taking this roundabout route, and frequently missing their way, two months were consumed, in which
time they could easily have reached Nanking had they been able
to go straight there. A day came when, still fifty miles from the
city, they were tempted to enter the important town of Taiping,
for a beggar gets more in a town than a village. They were going
as usual from door to door, when they happened to pass a window where no less a person was looking out than an Imperial
Commissioner from Peking on a tour of inspection. Surprised to
see beggars of their sort, he called from the window, and they had

to go into the room where he was sitting. He ordered them roughly to give an account of themselves, demanding: 'Why are you running up and down the world like this?' They replied, as before, that they were Siamese subjects, cast away and obliged to beg their food, until such time as they reached Nanking and found a ship to take them home. The Commissioner seemed satisfied and ready to let them go, when one of his clerks pointed out that under the law he was bound to arrest them; they were idle vagabonds and it was rumoured that they abused the alms given them by behaving in an abominable manner. On hearing this the Commissioner's manner changed. He examined some witnesses, 'who charged us with many foul crimes,' says Pinto, 'of which we had never so much as dreamed.' After this they were taken to prison, with irons on wrists, ankles and neck, where they received a cruel beating. Starving, covered with lice, they remained there twenty-six days. 'Six and twenty thousand years it might have been in regard to the great misery we suffered,' says Pinto, in a comparison of their state with that of the damned spirits of Hell. 'One of my companions died in my arms, eaten up with lice, I being in no way able to help him, and it was almost a miracle that the rest of us escaped alive from those filthy vermin.'

Unexpectedly, on the twenty-seventh morning, they were drawn up out of the dungeon, so weak that they could hardly speak, and after being chained together were marched to the Yang-tse river and put on a boat. It transpired that the Commissioner was submitting their case to the Prefectural Court at Nanking, because he thought it more serious than he had at first supposed, and found his powers insufficient to pass an adequate sentence. Their imprisonment so far, therefore, had been only a remand, and their beating a piece of prison discipline. Their main punishment was still to come.

On arrival at Nanking, they were imprisoned in a vast jail, said to house four thousand criminals. 'One could hardly sit down in any place without being robbed and filled full of lice,' is the way Pinto describes the horrible place. The judge to whom their process had been sent perused it and sentenced them to a whipping and to have their thumbs cut off, as there was evidence that they were thieves in the guise of beggars. Thieves they certainly were, robbers of royal tombs and pirates as well, but luckily for them the Chinese did not know that; the punishment awarded them for crimes of which they were innocent was infinitely less than they would have suffered for those they had committed.

The beating they now received was far worse than on the first occasion, and two died of it three days later, though all of them were treated in the prison hospital, an institution which Pinto cites as another example of the way the Chinese tempered cruelty with mercy. This was further evident a few days later when some prison visitors came to call, men who not only represented a charitable society which looked after the welfare of convicts, but who were allowed to act as prisoner's friend and represent hard cases to the authorities. After distributing some clean clothes and money, they asked the Portuguese who they were in a most sympathetic manner. One of Pinto's companions was that Borralho who has been mentioned as Antonio's business agent. He is stated to have known Chinese, and he now told the visitors the story of the shipwreck and how, having no money for bribes and no one to put their case for them, they had been convicted of disorderly begging and were expecting to have their thumbs cut off. The visitors, persuaded there had been a miscarriage of justice, asked the Registrar to let them see the process. This he did, and after they had read it, they drew up and presented a petition to the Prefectural Court, giving reasons why the rest of the sentence should not be carried out. But the court rejected the petition. Accordingly they petitioned a higher court, which gave leave to appeal to the High Court at Peking. In recording these details, both about the hospital and the appellate system, Pinto is not only commending the Chinese administration, but reflecting on the backwardness of that obtaining in Portugal.

Since the appeal had to be preferred in person at Peking, the prison authorities arranged for the Portuguese to be sent there under guard. The journey was to be by boat up the Grand Canal.

Pinto suffers in Chinese prisons

Before they started, the Prisoners' Welfare Society gave them food, money and clothes, together with a letter recommending them to the head of a similar society at the capital.

Pinto describes their voyage up the Grand Canal. It seems that they helped to row, but he says he could see quite well from the bench and that, moreover, they were taken ashore every evening and allowed to beg, in chains as they were and under the charge of a sergeant, who got half the money they took. At Junquileu,[1] a walled town though not fortified with battlements, Pinto records that he saw a monument on which was written in Chinese: 'Here lies Tuan Nacem Mudaliar, uncle to the King of Malacca, whom death took out of the world before he could be revenged on Captain Alfonzo Albuquerque, the lion of the robberies of the sea.' In 1511 Albuquerque took Malacca from its Malay King, whose uncle, Mudaliar, went to China, says Pinto, and asked the Emperor for help, since Malacca was a vassal state of Siam, which in turn was a vassal of China. When Tomé Pires, the Portuguese Ambassador, after the failure of his embassy, was arrested by the Chinese in Canton in 1521, he was informed that he would be kept in custody until Malacca was returned to its rightful King. But Mudaliar had died long before this of apoplexy after supper, or so a Chinese told Pinto at Junquileu. This is an example of how Pinto weaves into his narrative news of a person in whom the Portuguese of that time were interested. There are three explanations: Pinto really saw the inscription; or he copied it from the Albuquerque *Comentários*, inventing further details about Mudaliar; or he heard of it from another source, if it was a story current on the coast, as it must have been, since otherwise it would not have been in the *Comentários*. One cannot tell, but can admire Pinto's address, for the story, inserted where it is, adds an appearance of naturalness and truth to the account of his journey. It will be noticed as we proceed that Pinto has a knack of being at the right place at the right time. When an event has special news

[1]Not identified for certain. It is called Janquileu on Albuquerque's *Comentários* (published 1557 by his son, Albuquerque having died in 1515), where the inscription is also given, though in slightly different words.

value at his period, he is sure to be a witness of it or a leading actor
in it or have something fresh to say about it. For instance, a much
debated question was what happened in the end to Tomé Pires,
the Ambassador. Did he die in prison after his arrest at Canton, as
did most of his companions, who were put to death, or was he
banished into the interior to die years later? Some said one thing,
some another.[1] Pinto answers the question in the most dramatic
manner by telling a story which must have proved intensely exciting. Even now it has some power to move. It is introduced as
follows. After leaving Junquileu and continuing along the Grand
Canal, the prisoners arrived at a place called Sempitay in the text,
probably the town of P'ei, with which readers of my *The First
Holy One* are familiar, for it was the Eminent Founder of the
Han's home town and where he sang his famous song about the
wind. Pinto and his companions were taken ashore as usual to beg.
As they went up and down the streets, doing rather well, for the
inhabitants were charitable, they were asked for their story and
gave it as before. Presently one of the onlookers, a woman, said
to those about her: 'It is very likely that what these poor strangers
are saying is true, for it is the most ordinary thing that those who
trade by sea find their grave in it. For that reason it is better to
work on land, which is the clay from which God originally made
us.'

Saying so, she gave the Portuguese a small sum of money.
There followed a conversation between them and her. Suddenly
she unbuttoned the left sleeve of her red satin dress and disclosed
a mark tattooed on her arm, as a slave is marked, but the mark
was a cross. 'Do any of you know this sign?' she asked. At once
the Portuguese knelt and replied with tears in their eyes that indeed they knew it well. Then she cried out, raising her hands upwards: 'Our Father, which art in Heaven, hallowed be Thy
Name.' She said these words in Portuguese, the only Portuguese

[1]See the discussion on p. xlix of Armando Cortesão's Introduction to the *Suma
Oriental*, vol. I. Both the writers Castanheda and Correia were out East at the
time. The first is uncertain how Pires died and suggests poison, the second says
he was banished to an unknown town where he lived for a long time.

sentence she knew. 'Tell me at once, are you Christians?' she then demanded earnestly in Chinese.

For answer the Portuguese took her arm and each of them kissed the cross upon it and intoned the rest of the Lord's Prayer. Her tears were falling now and she drew them aside, saying: 'Christians from the ends of the earth, come with me who am your true sister in the Faith, who am perhaps even related to one of you through him who begot me in this miserable exile.' And she made to take them to her house. The sergeant, however, objected, saying that the prisoners had been allowed ashore to beg and that if they stopped begging he would take them back to the ship. Fear of losing his half of the alms made him say this. The lady reassured him: 'I understand your objection,' she said, 'and it is quite reasonable, since I know you have no other source of profit. But I will make it worth your while,' and she took silver from her purse and gave it to him. He was satisfied and let them go.

As soon as they got to her house, they begged her to tell them who she was. 'My name is Inez de Leyria,' she said, 'and I am the daughter of Tomé Pires. My father, after his return from Peking, where the Emperor refused to see him, was arrested at Canton as a spy, because other Portuguese there had caused a commotion. Some of his suite were tortured and beaten to death, but he was banished to this place where now you see me. Here he married a Chinese woman, my mother, and taught her the faith of Jesus, and here he died. Other Chinese were also converted. In that little Christian community I was brought up.'

After telling them this story, which explained the mystery of what had happened to the unfortunate first European Ambassador to the Court of China in modern times, she gave them a very good dinner. 'You shall stay here as long as your boat remains at P'ei,' she said; and to obtain the commander of the escort's permission, she sent him a present. They were with her for five days, for the commander was delayed by his wife falling ill. During this time they met the Chinese Christians of P'ei. Tomé Pires had given them a prayer-book, but it had been stolen, and Borralho wrote out for them in Chinese, says Pinto, the Pater Noster, the Ave Maria, the Credo and the Salve Regina, the Commandments and other prayers. Before they left, a collection was made from the Chinese Christians, who subscribed fifty ounces of silver, which the Portuguese found very useful afterwards for tipping the jailers. Inez de Leyria gave them secretly another fifty ounces out of her own pocket, 'begging us humbly,' says Pinto, 'to remember her in our prayers, since it was easy for us to see how greatly she had need of them.' Much comforted and encouraged by this extraordinary meeting with a Christian and a friend in the midst of the vast extent of China, they returned to their bench on the boat and set off again, not knowing whether their appeal would be successful or whether in the end they would lose their thumbs. But the commander's wife was kinder to them, on account of the present that Inez had sent.

CHAPTER EIGHTEEN

Pinto is released on appeal

───────◆───────

Thefe text of the *Peregrination* is here much drawn out, for
Pinto's intention was twofold: he desired not only to describe the valley of the shadow through which he was
journeying, but also the mystery of the great country of China.
China was part of his enormous canvas of the whole orient and
it was also only part of his pilgrim's progress, for his journeys in
all the countries he visited belong to the same progress. His conception of himself as a wandering soul is the plot which holds his
description of China together, but it is not well held because, in
his desire to make his book also the most complete and elaborate
account of the Far East then in existence, he feels it necessary to
give set descriptions of Chinese manners and customs, cities and
buildings. As his personal experience of the country was limited,
these had to be drawn from hearsay and books. His principal
authority is the work *Tractado em que contam muito por extenso as
cousas da China*, published by the Dominican monk, Gaspar da
Cruz, in 1569, fourteen years before Pinto's death and at a time
when he was writing the *Peregrination*. Borrowing in this way,
without acknowledgment, was the custom of the period. When
Pinto borrows, he writes as if he himself had seen what he describes. Indeed, he embroiders so well upon his original and writes
so much better than Gaspar da Cruz, that his descriptions, until
closely examined, read like originals. To-day, however, we find
them tedious. I shall therefore skip on to the moment when he
and his companions were disembarked at Peking, which is given
as taking place on 19 October 1541, eighteen months after he left
Patani with Antonio.

Pinto is released on appeal

The prisoners had been well treated on the canal journey, but now they were to fall again into the hands of jailers. On their arrival at the prison 'for our welcome we had at the first dash thirty lashes apiece given us,' as our seventeenth-century translation has it. This savage reception put them in great fear. Did it mean that their appeal, instead of a reduction of sentence, would bring an enhancement? And they were haunted by the dread that news of their raid on the tombs might have reached the authorities at Peking. However, on their first appearance before a remand magistrate, they were advised to employ counsel and given five days in which to make arrangements with the Prisoners' Aid Society, a member of which would conduct their defence. In spite of the fairness of this treatment, they were nearly driven mad by the terror of witnessing, while in the precincts of the magistrate's court, the cruel execution of twenty-seven Chinese. On their return to prison, they were loaded with chains, so tightly fixed as to cause great pain. But in a day or so they were visited by representatives of the Society, who promised to engage counsel for their defence.

When the case came before the Court of Appeal their lawyer pointed out that, as the process showed, there was no direct evidence of their having committed robbery or gone armed, and that the lower court had convicted them on suspicion.

Counsel for the government replied. Pinto gives his speech in full, as he does all speeches, letters and other communications, a device which here enables him obliquely to declare again his belief that his sufferings and misfortunes were caused by his own sins. The attorney is made to say that, had the appellants been real merchants, as they alleged, they would not have been prowling about islands and estuaries like pirates. The fact that they were shipwrecked was a just punishment sent by Heaven. Heaven had decreed that they were to be arrested, and was now using the judge as an instrument of its divine retribution.

After the arguments of counsel, the court reserved judgment and remanded the Portuguese to custody, with an order for their reappearance on a fixed day. While they were waiting in jail, miserably anxious about their fate, they received a further visit from members of the Society. 'As we knew that the judge was considering his verdict, we begged the visitors, who had already done so much for us, to do one thing more by going to him and interceding on our behalf,' says Pinto. This request deeply shocked the visitors. They replied: 'We stand for a fair trial and a judgment founded strictly on the evidence given before the court. To go and try to influence the judge now by advancing further arguments, or adducing facts off the record, would be entirely contrary to our principles. And not only this, but were the judge to listen to us, he would be guilty of a dereliction of duty.'

The Portuguese were surprised and much taken aback by this display of integrity and the majesty of the law. 'Please overlook what we said,' they begged, 'and let ignorance be our excuse, in your sight and in God's.'

'We will overlook it,' the visitors replied, 'for barbarians cannot be blamed for not knowing the right. But if justice is administered that way in your country, you ought all to be afraid of the wrath of Heaven.'

This remarkable passage is a veiled criticism of the Portuguese courts. Pinto is describing his conception of an ideal form of judicial procedure and building up a picture of the just judge. That he should put the just judge in China shows that he had grasped the essentials of Confucian morality, an example of his intuition, for he certainly had no academic knowledge of Confucius and his philosophy. But though he is right in making benevolence, justice, incorruptibility and consideration for the feelings of others the cardinal principle of Chinese administration, his account of the trial is fictional and his visitors and judge are no more than ideal types. Indeed, he himself shows that cruelty, injustice and corruption were the general rule.[1] But to keep track of Pinto's flickering thought is not easy, for simultaneously he is writing a story, an autobiography, a history and a criticism.

---

[1] As they notoriously were in the late Ming period; cf. Ricci's account of the same in his *Storia dell' introduzione del Christianesimo in Cina*, lib. 1, cap. IX, section 11. (First published in 1615 in Latin.)

Pinto is released on appeal

On the day fixed for the delivery of judgment, the Portuguese were brought to court tied together on a long chain. An escort of armed police accompanied them. The mob hooted them, for Europeans were always hooted by the lower orders. All this, the chain, the grim guards and the jeering populace, worked so on their nerves that they abandoned hope and walked as if they were going to certain execution. 'How we got to the court,' says Pinto, 'I cannot say, for we were so frantic with terror that we went as in a trance, our only thought to resign ourselves to God's will and to beg Him, if He was resolved to take away our lives, to accept that punishment as satisfaction for our sins'; (if they suffered enough on earth, they would not be punished again hereafter). So they were brought into the court-room and, when it was their turn, knelt down before the judge, their eyes fixed on the ground and their hands raised, as if praying. Judgment was then pronounced, strictly according to the proved facts of the case and the law, and they were acquitted, though before they could go home they must work for a year on repairing the Great Wall.

CHAPTER NINETEEN

Pinto's journey into Tartary

━━━━━━━━━━━◄❋►━━━━━━━━━━━

One can only marvel at the adroitness with which Pinto slips in his phrase about the Great Wall. Having taken the reader as far as Peking, the great frontier capital of the North, he plans to introduce him to a feature in the Asian world view whose omission would hurt the balance of the whole. This radical feature was the steppe. Its inhabitants, called Huns, Tartars, Mongols and many other names since the dawn of Chinese history, were always nomads, mounted on ponies, masters of the bow, partially civilized, who, whenever China was weak, raided her and had conquered her altogether in the thirteenth century. To leave the Tartars out of his *Peregrination* would have been as improper as for a modern writer on world affairs to omit Russia, which is, of course, the steppe again in a modern disguise. Obliged to bring in the steppe, Pinto was confronted with the literary problem of how to effect the transition. As the *Peregrination* was written in the form of an autobiography (and in fact was as far as possible autobiographical), it was desirable that an account of the Tartars should be of personal adventures among them. But by what artifice to fit these on to the Chinese adventures? One perceives how brilliant was his idea of a court sentence involving work on the Great Wall. The fortification had been maintained for seventeen centuries as a bulwark against the steppe. By getting himself sent there (quite a usual Chinese sentence), it would be easy to bring in the Tartars. All that was necessary was to imagine a raid by them. Actually a raid did take place nine years later. Gaspar da Cruz in his *Tractado* of 1569, already mentioned, states that the Tartars made a great incursion in 1550 and that the Portuguese who were in Chinese prisons at the time were delighted because they hoped it would mean their liberation. He records this on the authority of those Portuguese who subsequently returned home. Pinto uses this historical foundation and improves on it; he is freed by the Tartars from his detention on the Wall, and carried by them into Tartary, whence he is allowed to depart and, travelling overland through western China, reaches Tongking and rejoins his compatriots of the China coast. This is one of the parts of his book which is wholly invented. He knew something of China, and his Chinese experiences rest in places on personal observation and happenings. But he had never seen the Tartars or their country and had to draw wholly on hearsay and old books for the background of his plot. The result is that his Tartar experiences lack those authentic touches which vivify episodes founded upon reality. He has nothing contemporary to say, his geography is confused, his place-names are so far from any known that their identification becomes itself a flight of the imagination,[1] and his adventures are either vague or conventional, for, resourceful inventor though he was, he had not enough solid fact to build on.

While it would be neither instructive nor amusing to follow him on these wanderings, which, if they conform to the theme of his soul's progress, are certainly not a journey in the flesh, we should note one episode. Extraordinary to relate, he brings the Dalai Lama on the scene. The Tartars in their withdrawal from China after the failure of their raid take Pinto and his companions westward until, as it appears, they are on the borders of Tibet. In that region, perhaps northern Yunnan or Szechuan (though, indeed, it is impossible to say where he claims to have been), a great ecclesiastical dignitary, whom Pinto expressly calls a Pope, and who is the head of the religion practised by the inhabitants, comes to visit the Tartar King. His temporal and spiritual state, and the

[1] A. S. H. Charignon, in his *A propos des voyages aventureux de Fernand Mendes Pinto* (Peking, 1936), tries to make out a case for Pinto having been captured by the Tartars, but fails to convince. The real test is literary; the adventures do not read like a record founded even remotely on actual experience, either by himself or anyone else.

way he authorizes the local monks to give the people 'bills of exchange for Heaven', are mentioned, as also a sermon which he preached in a nunnery, and which, by its insistence on charity, has a certain Buddhist flavour.

Pinto also pretends that he afterwards went to this Pope's capital, which he calls Lechuna, a town 'such as Rome is among us'. Evidently some rumours of the Dalai Lama had reached him. He even attempts a description of the Lama's palace-monastery and citadel. Far from exact though the description is, he realized that it was a huge monastic settlement, something like a fortified castle; and there is a sentence suggesting that he had some vague and confused notion of the doctrines relating to Boddhisattvas. That Pinto was able to write as much as he did, shows that, long before anything definite was known about the Dalai Lama, he was known to exist.[1] It was not until a century later (1661) that the first Europeans entered Lhassa, the Jesuits Johann Grueber and Albert D'Orville, who travelled there from Peking.[2]

Now, in declaring that there was a sort of Pope in Asia, who had Saint Peter's power to unlock the gate of Heaven and deputed this power to his monks, and who preached a sermon in which there occurred such a sentence as: 'We please God most of all by doing unto those in need, as we would that they should do unto us,' Pinto was running into danger. In sixteenth-century Portugal that was not the way you could safely describe a pagan imposter. As we have seen, throughout the *Peregrination* Pinto makes Asiatic priests, dignitaries and good men speak as if he held that their religious beliefs were in essence the same as a Christian's, an extraordinary view for a man of his day, and he does

[1] There is a section (10. 45) in Friar Odoric's *Travels* (given in full in Yule's *Cathay and the Way Thither*) where the Friar, alleging he was in Tibet about 1328, mentions its 'Pope' and capital, though he gives no description. Pinto no doubt used Odoric and other odd references in early books, together with the unpublished talk of his age, as the basis of his account.

[2] See *China Illustrata* (Amsterdam, 1667) by Athanasius Kircher, where extracts from Grueber's narrative and his drawing of the Potala are given. Lhassa only became the permanent headquarters of the Dalai Lama after 1643. His present monastery, the Potala, was built between 1650 and 1682. But other monastic citadels existed elsewhere from an earlier date.

not always think it necessary to cover himself by some disclaimer. But here he did find it safer to do so, since the case was so extreme. He therefore invents a little comedy. One of his companions, Vicente Morosa, who was listening with the rest of the congregation to the Lama's sermon, amuses himself at the expense of that ecclesiastic by pretending to be deeply moved by his words, so moved that in his devotion he weeps, copies to excess the gestures of the most pious, raising his hands wildly to Heaven, screwing up his face, repeating incessantly a response, like one of theirs but not correct, and generally behaving in a manner so extravagantly devout as to be ridiculous, and which caused the whole congregation, and even the Dalai Lama, to laugh at him. Had they suspected he was laughing at them, adds Pinto, he would have been so beaten that never again would he have been able to laugh.

That the Dalai Lama, on his first appearance in European literature, was made the centre of such a farcical scene, is an extraordinary fact which must be known to very few people.

CHAPTER TWENTY

Pinto's first visit to Japan

———————◆———————

W e now come to one of the most dramatic and disputed
episodes in the *Peregrination*—Pinto's claim to have discovered Japan and taught the Japanese how to use firearms. Before going further into this tangled subject, it should be
said that the word discovery is misleading. The existence and
position of Japan was always known in the East. In the records of
the Han dynasty is an account of a Japanese embassy to the capital, Loyang, in A.D. 57.[1] During the ensuing centuries Japan built
her civilization on the Chinese model and adopted Buddhism. As
was natural, European travellers who came to Asia heard of Japan.
Marco Polo, for instance, has a section about it. Tomé Pires includes it in his *Suma Oriental*. The Portuguese, therefore, knew of
Japan; their merchants at Ningpo must have been fully aware
that Chinese merchants went there to trade. They may even have
seen an occasional Japanese ship, for the Japanese traded, though
in a very small way, in Chinese ports, and Japanese freebooters
sailed the coast. Despite all this—and here is the point—the Portuguese had not made the voyage to Japan at the date (1541) when
Pinto was in Ningpo with Antonio. Reasons can be given for
this: the Japanese trade was not supposed to be valuable; there
were no charts of Japan; the Chinese merchants who went there
did not want competition and gave no information about ports,
facilities, prices and the like. In sum, the Portuguese had not been
to Japan because they had not made the necessary effort to get
there. Pinto's claim that he discovered Japan would, therefore, be
better expressed by saying that he claimed to be the first European

[1]Quoted in *Japan* by C. B. Sansom, p. 18.

to have reached the country. As for firearms, the Japanese by the sixteenth century must have come across gunpowder and cannon in China, though neither seems to have been used in the armies of the great feudatories who ruled and fought in Japan in the fifteenth and early sixteenth centuries. The arquebus they had never seen or heard of. It was the great military invention of the early sixteenth century in Europe, and transformed the old infantry into a firing-line of modern type. The latest models in 1530 were effective up to 500 yards. Pinto's claim is that he, and the two Portuguese who accompanied him, were the first to show an arquebus to a Japanese, explain how to use it and make its powder. That he should advance this claim is characteristic; his method of writing was to record as personal experiences all the important events which happened in Asia during his stay there. But while much that has so far been related from the *Peregrination* cannot be checked against other contemporary writings, his visits to Japan (for he made several) can be, and this has been done at length by a number of scholars. Unfortunately, their conclusions do not agree. What I shall now do is to give his account and draw attention to the criticisms which have been directed against it.

The transition from the Tartar journey to the Japanese journey is effected by a rambling story that, having marched through western China from north to south, Pinto came to Tongking and thence made his way to Macao in search of a Portuguese ship sailing to Malacca. Finding none, he and two of his companions, Christóvão Borralho and Diogo Zeimoto, took passages on a junk belonging to a Chinese merchant-freebooter, who was sailing north towards Ningpo. After passing through the Formosa Strait, they ran into very bad weather, which blew them far out of their course. They sighted the Lu-chu Islands, but could not make land because of the continuing gale, and, driving northward into unknown seas for several days, at last in better weather saw land on the horizon. As they approached, looking for a harbour, they noticed the smoke of a great fire and steered towards it. On getting close, they anchored inshore, but at first could see no houses or men. Presently two rowing-boats came out from the shore and when they were alongside their crews inquired where the ship hailed from. The Captain said he was from China and asked the name of the land. He was informed that it was the island of Tanegashima, off the coast of Kiu-shiu, the southern-most island of Japan.

This, then, was the way that Pinto says he arrived in Japan—a passenger in a Chinese ship which had been driven out of its course by a gale, and whose Captain, one supposes, had not been in those waters before, though he or some of his crew seem to have been able to speak Japanese, unless one of the boatmen could speak Chinese.

The Captain asked for the nearest port, saying he wished to trade his cargo. The Japanese informed him that he was quite close to the principal town, where the Lord of Tanegashima lived. This Lord we know was named Tokitaka.[1]

They had not been anchored two hours in the port before the Lord Tokitaka came aboard with his suite. While he was inquiring what they had for sale, he noticed the three Portuguese. 'Who are those men?' he asked. 'From their beards and features I perceive they are not Chinese.'

The Captain explained: Malacca was their headquarters in Asia, but their country of origin was Portugal, which was at the further end of the world.

Lord Tokitaka was much intrigued by this reply. Turning to his gentlemen, he exclaimed half seriously that the strangers must be the Chenchicogims[2] of the old prophecy, of whom it was said that they would come flying over the water and conquer Japan and the rest of the world; and he added, in his jocular way, that it would be just as well to be on good terms with such people.

[1]Pinto gets his Japanese names recognizably correct. In the case of Tokitaka he gives a rendering of his title, Higobunojo. See Le Gentil's *Fernão Mendes Pinto*, p. 157.

[2]This is Pinto's spelling of the Japanese word Tenjiku-jiu, the fabled land of the West from which these people were to come. But Tokitaka's identification was premature. It was not for another four hundred years that Far Western strangers were to come flying over the sea to conquer his country. Prophecies of the coming of white conquerors were common in many Eastern countries.

Pinto's first visit to Japan

After he had looked round the ship, Tokitaka sat down on a chair on deck and began questioning the Portuguese through a Lu-chu Island woman[1] who knew Chinese. Pinto remarks that he seemed intensely interested in all the strange things that they spoke of, showing a curiosity which, allied, as we know, with a capacity to copy novelties from overseas, has always characterized the Japanese. Before going, he said: 'Come and see me at my house to-morrow and go on telling me about the great world beyond, for I would rather buy that information from you than any commodity you could offer me.'

But the Portuguese had a commodity which he had not yet seen, and which, when he did, he desired more than anything.

Next morning, after an early exchange of presents (fruits from Tokitaka and objets d'art from the Chinese), the Captain went ashore with some samples, taking with him Pinto and his two companions, Christóvão Borralho and Diogo Zeimoto. Tokitaka entertained them to a meal in his house and, after looking at the samples, put the Chinese in touch with the local merchants. Business done, he began asking the Portuguese more questions. He had already heard of their nation, he now declared, from the Chinese and the Lu-chu islanders. Was it a fact that Portugal was bigger than China? The Portuguese assured him that it was. And in the same vein they replied to his other questions. So delightful did he find their conversation, that he insisted that they should sleep ashore that night and had them put up in a merchant's house.

On the following day the Captain landed his cargo and stored it in a warehouse allotted to him. The market was very good, for it seems that Chinese ships did not often call at Tanegashima, and there was a great demand for his silks and rarities. During the next few days he sold everything he had and at his own price, making the enormous profit of twelve hundred per cent.

While this business was going on, the three Portuguese amused

[1]The Lu-chu Islands, the chain which includes Okinawa, from which the Americans flew to drop the atomic bombs, did not belong to Japan at that date. Their King was a vassal of China.

themselves as best they could. In consequence of their misadventures in China, they had, of course, nothing to sell, a matter of regret when they heard of the prices that were ruling. So they went sightseeing and visited temples, whose priests were happy to show them round. And hearing of good shooting in the neighbourhood, Diogo Zeimoto took out his arquebus one morning and went with two Chinese to a marsh, where wild duck were to be had in plenty. As he shot over it, the Japanese, hearing the reports, crowded to the place and watched with amazement as he bagged twelve and a half brace. Lord Tokitaka was riding in the vicinity and also heard the strange noises. On inquiry, he was told that one of the strangers was killing ducks with a weapon of a sort which had never been seen. 'I would like him to show it to me,' he told his attendants. Presently Zeimoto, who had been sent for, came up, his arquebus on his shoulder and the two Chinese carrying the game. When Tokitaka examined the arquebus, he could not understand how it worked, as he had no conception of gunpowder. It must be magic, he concluded. Let me see how you do it, he demanded of Zeimoto, who, pleased at the sensation, fired a few shots and brought down a kite and two turtle-doves.

Tokitaka was a man of ebullient character, and the spectacle excited him to such a degree that he did not think it compromised his dignity to give Zeimoto a seat on his horse's crupper and invite him to ride back to the palace. So they set off, accompanied by the crowd of onlookers, and with four of Tokitaka's footmen walking in front. When they entered the town, he told the footman to shout out that Zeimoto was a visitor worthy of honour and that all should treat him with respect. On reaching the palace he took him by the hand and led him into his courtyard. Pinto and Borralho, who seem to have joined the procession, were also invited in. Zeimoto was given a seat beside Tokitaka, who treated him in the most effusive manner, for instinctively he recognized it as a great moment in the history of his country, as, indeed, was so, for it was the first step in the long course that led to Japan becoming a first-class military power.

Zeimoto, anxious to make some return for the honours he had

received, thought that he could not do better than give Tokitaka the arquebus. This he did a day or so later, going to call with some pigeons he had shot and presenting the arquebus along with them. 'You could not have given me anything I should have valued more, not if you had offered me all the treasures of China,' cried Tokitaka, and immediately in return gave the Portuguese a thousand ounces of silver. 'But you must show me how to make the gunpowder,' he said, 'for this wonderful thing, without the powder, is only a bit of iron.' Zeimoto accordingly told him the ingredients and how to mix them.

Pinto here makes an observation of interest, for it falls in so well with the character of the Japanese as subsequent events have revealed it. Tokitaka's smiths immediately set about copying the arquebus. Hundreds were made, says Pinto, thousands, even hundreds of thousands; for the Daimyos, or feudal Dukes, introduced them into their armies. A civil war was about to break out, and in the great battles that were coming the arquebus had its important part. Of this immediate and rapid copying of the new arm, Pinto remarks: 'It showed how much the Japanese are naturally addicted to war, in which they take more delight than any nation that we know.' [1]

After they had been in Tanegashima three weeks, a messenger arrived from the Daimyo who was Duke of Bungo, a territory half-way up the east coast of Kiu-shiu, the southernmost of the main Japanese islands. The Daimyo's name was Otomo Yoshinori, and Pinto says that he was the suzerain of the Lord of Tanegashima, though in the Japanese records Tanegashima is shown

[1] In Japanese history the sixteenth century is called the Sengoku Jidai, the age of the country at war. The barons were fighting it out. The winning side, with its three brilliant soldiers, Nobunaga (1534–1582), Hideyoshi and Ieyasu, set up a stable central government which lasted until 1868. This government, after 1603, was called the Tokugawa Shogunate. The Shoguns ruled Japan, but maintained the Emperor as an institution. There had been Shoguns of different families from 1192. The difference between the earlier and later Shoguns was that while the first were head of a feudal system, the second created a bureaucracy and were much stronger. Pinto saw feudal Japan just before the Tokugawas tamed the Daimyos. To Pinto the Daimyo of Bungo looked like a king and he called him so.

as under Satsuma, a daimyo-ship opposite it across the strait.[1] The messenger carried a letter addressed to Tokitaka. This stated that the writer had heard of the Portuguese arrival at Tanegashima, and wanted one of them to come to Bungo, as he was most anxious to talk to him about the outer world.

Tokitaka sent for the three Portuguese and explained what he had been asked to arrange. 'I cannot spare Diogo Zeimoto,' he said, 'because he is teaching me to shoot. Which of you two others would like to go?'

Pinto and Borralho replied that they would leave the choice to His Highness; it was a great honour and whichever of the two he selected would be proud to go. Looking at Pinto, Tokitaka then said: 'I shall send him because he is an amusing man. The Duke of Bungo is not in good health and requires to be cheered up. The other is too solemn.' But he added politely: 'A very good quality in matters of more weight.'

That settled, he gave Pinto a liberal sum for his travelling expenses and told the messenger from Bungo that he would be held responsible for his safety. Pinto had been slightly apprehensive about travelling alone into the heart of Japan, without a knowledge of the language or the punctilios, but was now confident that he would be treated as a gentleman; with his arquebus he was less a merchant in appearance than a soldier, a profession which entitled him to privileged treatment.

The next day he and the messenger set out by boat, crossed the strait to the main island of Kiu-shiu and, calling at some ports en route, reached Funai, the capital of Bungo. It was about noon when they arrived, not an hour when the Daimyo received visitors. Though he was known to be looking forward to Pinto's visit, it seemed best not to call until after dinner. Accordingly the messenger took Pinto to his house, and later in the afternoon, after putting on his best clothes, rode with him to the palace. The Daimyo was no sooner informed of their coming than he sent his

[1]See Hans Hass, *Geschichte des Christentums in Japan*, 2 vols., Tokyo, 1904. In Pinto's text the Duke of Bungo is made father-in-law of Tokitaka. This also is incorrect, as it is known that Tokitaka's wife belonged to a different family.

younger son to receive them. The boy, who was only nine years old, made a pretty little speech of welcome, in the form of a set phrase of verse. The messenger prostrated himself and, protesting that only a denizen of Heaven could inspire him with words adequate to express his thanks for such politeness, tried to kiss the boy's sword, but he would not allow it.

Pinto was now told to wait, while the messenger was taken into the presence and handed over Tokitaka's letter. When Pinto was ushered in, the Daimyo received him with great cordiality. He was in bed, as he was suffering from gout. 'Your coming,' he said to Pinto, using also a formal phrase of verse, 'is no less pleasing than rain that falls after the rice is planted.'

Pinto informs us that he was rather confused by the novelty of his reception and the elegant terms in which it was framed, and did not know how to reply. Said the Daimyo to his suite: 'The stranger seems abashed. No doubt he is not accustomed to seeing so many gentlemen. Perhaps it will be better to dismiss him now and call him again when he is more used to our Court.'

This put Pinto on his mettle, and to prove that he was well able to make a courtly reply, he said through the interpreter that, though he was indeed abashed, it was not the presence of the gentlemen that caused him to be so, but the distinguished appearance of the Duke.

The answer was applauded by the Court. 'What a neat reply!' they exclaimed. 'Clearly he is not a merchant, but an ecclesiastic or a captain that scours the seas.'

'I agree,' said the Daimyo. 'But now, no more chattering, for I want to talk to him. And let's hope it will give me an appetite. The pain in my foot is much better already.'

At which, the Duchess and his daughters, who were seated by his bed, devoutly uttered: 'Thank God for that.'

What the Daimyo wanted to find out was revealed in the first question he put to Pinto. 'You have been about a great deal,' he said, 'and in making your way here from the other end of the world must have picked up a lot of things. Have you by any chance heard of a cure for the gout?'

Pinto's first visit to Japan

'I am not a professional doctor,' replied Pinto, 'nor indeed have I made any study of medicine, but on the ship that brought me here from China, they had a bark which, infused with water, was wonderfully successful with most diseases. If Your Highness were to try it, I think it would help you.'

The Daimyo was delighted, and, full of hope, sent to Tanegashima for the bark, a course of which, in fact, did cure him. But that happened after Pinto had left. He was only there three weeks, and every day the Daimyo would ask him about the Western world. They also showed him round, and he saw some of the temple rituals, attended military parades, and went hawking and fishing. They were, of course, most interested in his arquebus, and from the first he was asked to demonstrate his ability to shoot birds with it. The Daimyo had an elder son, who was eighteen. Japanese sources give his name as Yoshinaga. One day he begged Pinto to teach him how to shoot. But Pinto did not want to take the responsibility and put him off, saying that to learn how to handle an arquebus took time. The young man was disappointed and applied to his father. 'Let him have a couple of shots,' the Duke suggested. 'He shall have as many as ever Your Highness commands,' replied Pinto with a flourish.

Yoshinaga could not manage it that morning because he was lunching with his father and had to stay in the palace. In the afternoon his mother unexpectedly asked him to accompany her to a village fête. So it was not until the following morning early that he called at Pinto's house with a couple of friends. Pinto was still in bed. Yoshinaga peeped in and, seeing him asleep on his mat and the arquebus hanging on a hook, thought it would be fun to try it by himself. He had seen Pinto charge it and knew how to do that, or so he thought, as he rammed home the powder. In fact, he filled it right up to the muzzle, leaving only just room for the bullet. He took aim at an orange tree near-by, and one of the friends applied the match. There was a violent explosion; the arquebus burst. One fragment wounded Yoshinaga on the head and another badly damaged his thumb. He was stunned and fell to the ground as if dead. His two friends rushed to tell the Duke, and as

they raced along the street, shouted that the stranger's arquebus
had killed their young lord. A crowd collected and advanced on
the house, waving weapons and uttering imprecations. Meanwhile Pinto had woken up and beheld Yoshinaga lying on the
floor, streaming with blood, the burst arquebus beside him. He
ran to him, held him up in his arms, striving to know if he were
mortally injured. That was the scene when the townspeople burst
in.

In a very few minutes the Daimyo arrived, carried in a chair on
four men's shoulders, so pale and distraught that he looked very
ill. Behind him on foot had hastened the Duchess, supported by
her ladies and her daughters, who were in such a state that several
were weeping. When the parents saw their dear son on the floor,
gashed and his blood on Pinto's clothes, they concluded that the
foreigner must have killed him. Evidently the two friends had
given a totally incoherent account of the affair. A couple of samurai who were present now drew their swords and made at
Pinto as if to cut him down. But the Daimyo shouted: 'Stop!
stop! Let us find out the facts first. There is more in this than
meets the eye. He must have been bribed by someone to do it.
Probably the relations of those traitors that were executed the
other day.' And he turned to the young gentlemen who had accompanied his son and began to examine them severely. Perhaps
to cover themselves, they said that the bursting was an enchantment. On hearing that their lord's son had been killed by an
enchantment, the two samurai were horrified. 'What need,' they
cried, 'to take more evidence? Surely we know all there is to be
known? Let him be put to a cruel death.'

But the Daimyo insisted on sending for the man who had been
appointed to act as Pinto's interpreter. He should have been on
the premises, but had fled in terror after the catastrophe. They
found him and dragged him bound into the room and swore to
kill him if he did not interpret correctly.

The interrogation was entrusted to a monk. Pinto, with his
hands bound, was made to kneel and the monk stood over him,
the sleeves of his gown rolled back and holding a dagger dipped

in the blood. 'Confess!' he cried, 'I conjure you to confess, loudly so that all present may hear, why you killed this young innocent with your sorceries.'

Pinto declares that fright had numbed him into semi-consciousness, and that he was incapable of uttering a word of explanation.

The monk glared at him, incensed beyond measure by his silence. 'Cannot you understand,' he cried, 'that if you do not answer you are a dead man?' And he gave Pinto a violent kick to rouse him, shouting: 'Speak! Confess who have bribed you! What sum did they give you? How are they called? Where are they to be found?'

The kick had the effect of clearing Pinto's head, and he replied firmly that he was innocent and called Heaven as witness of the same.

But the monk did not believe him and was beginning to menace him with torture, when suddenly Yoshinaga opened his eyes and looked about the room. He seemed at once to realize the situation, and with the most charming frankness explained what had happened, said it was all his fault and begged them to untie Pinto's hands.

The Daimyo was the first to recover from his surprise. He ordered Pinto to be unbound and turned his attention to his son's wounds. Four doctors were summoned, but when they saw the condition of Yoshinaga's thumb, all they could do was to stand round and click their tongues in dismay. This irritated the young man, who was in great pain. 'Tell these devils to get out,' he cried. 'I want a doctor who can do something.'

Other doctors were called, all monks of one sort or another, but none of them had the courage to dress the wounded thumb. One of the suite now reminded the Daimyo that there was a wonderful old monk at Osaka, the holiest man living, who by a mere touch could heal the worst wounds. What!' broke in the patient. 'Why, Osaka is hundreds of miles away! My wounds should have been dressed by now and yet you expect me to wait for this old rotten man, who cannot be here for a month. Besides, he is ninety-two and can see no further than his nose.' And he went on: 'The doctor I want is this poor stranger whom you still seem to think wants to kill me. Stop frightening him and clear all these people out of the room.'

The Daimyo had already shown his confidence in Pinto's medical knowledge. But it was rather delicate to beg the man who had been wrongfully suspected and threatened to come to one's assistance. However, he swallowed his pride and said: 'Try to help my son. If you save him, anything you ask is yours.'

Pinto knew that he was still in great danger. The Japanese would kill him if what treatment he was able to give failed to save the young man's life. But there was no alternative; he had to take the risk. So after the room was cleared, he examined Yoshinaga's wounds. 'I believe I can save him,' he told the Daimyo, and asked for a needle and thread, some tow, whites of egg and bandages. When these were brought, he stitched the thumb and head-wound and, soaking the tow in the white of egg, bound it on with the bandages. This was the method he had often seen the Portuguese surgeons use with wounded men after a sea-fight.

The treatment worked; there were no complications and in a day or so it was clear that healing had begun. In five days Pinto was able to take out the stitches. It seemed a miraculous cure, for the thumb, on account of the profuse bleeding, had looked much worse than it actually was. The Daimyo's gratitude was profound (his gout too was better, for the bark had arrived and he was taking it). Presents were showered on Pinto; he was given silks, swords and fans, together with a very handsome fee in silver.

A letter now arrived from the Chinese Captain to say that he was leaving shortly. Pinto asked permission to return to his ship. This was promptly accorded, and the Daimyo sent him back to Tanegashima in one of his own vessels.

So much for Pinto's story. It reads well, is vivid, discloses a close knowledge of Japan, is full of names that can be identified, is, in short, clearly the work of a writer who was in Japan at or about the time when it was first visited by the Portuguese. The main facts are historical: Japan was reached at this date (round about 1542) by the Portuguese; firearms were first introduced by them, and the introduction was at Tanegashima; the son of the Daimyo of Bungo was wounded in the hand by the explosion of an arquebus. But did Pinto play the leading part which he pretends? The specialists who have sought to answer this question have minutely examined what other contemporary writers, European and Japanese, have had to say on the subject. Not one of these writers mentions Pinto. Antonio Galvão, who was in the East at this time and wrote a book on the Portuguese discoveries up to 1550,[1] states that in 1542 three Portuguese, named Antonio da Mota, Francisco Zeimoto and Antonio Peixoto,[2] while on a Chinese junk going from Siam to Ningpo, were blown out of their course 'and after some days saw to the eastward an island in 32° which is called Japan'. Diogo do Couto, who spent most of his life in India after 1556, and who wrote before his death in 1616 part of the work known as *Decadas*, gives the same names as does Galvão for the first Portuguese in Japan. The Jesuit Father P. Rodrigues Tçuzzu, who was a missionary in Japan from 1577 to 1614, accepts Galvão and Couto's version;[3] he had read the *Peregrination* and declares that Pinto invented his story. The Japanese contemporary sources have been examined in detail by Hans Haas in his *Geschichte des Christentums in Japan* (Tokyo, 1904). In two Japanese texts the name of Korishita ta Mota is mentioned as that belonging to one of the first Portuguese to land. Ta Mota and da Mota are clearly the same, and Korishita might be an attempt at Christóvão, Borralho's name, or at the word Christian. One cannot, therefore, say more than that the Japanese texts give a name, part of which is in Galvão's list and part of which may be in Pinto's.

Precision is here lacking, and other contemporary testimony confuses the subject further. For instance, Father Fróis, S.J., writing from Japan in 1578, says that a son (not Yoshinaga) of the

[1] *Tratado dos descrobrimentos antigos e modernos, feitos até a era de 1550*, etc. (not published until 1781).
[2] Diogo Zeimoto is in the *Peregrination* list. The surname Zeimoto is therefore common to both lists.
[3] See his *Historia da Igreja do Japão*, and note 2 on p. 298.

Daimyo of Bungo told him that the Portuguese who cured his brother Yoshinaga of wounds caused by an arquebus was called Diogo Vaz. Nothing more is known of this person or what ship he came on or whether he was connected with either Galvão's or Pinto's list of first arrivals.

Extracts from all the contemporary Portuguese and Japanese sources are given in Schurhammer's *Fernão Mendez Pinto und seine Peregrinaçam*, pp. 66–70, including Fróis's letter above. They are tantalizingly illusive. The German historian Hans Haas in the work already quoted as published in 1904, and the British historian James Murdoch in his *A History of Japan during the century of early foreign intercourse* (Kobe, 1903), after weighing the evidence in the original sources, have both concluded that, though Pinto was one of the early visitors to Japan, he was not among the first, and that his account of his discovery and his introduction of firearms cannot be accepted. Schurhammer concurs in this view, and adds weight to it by adducing additional facts.

On the contrary the Portuguese historians Christóvão Ayres,[1] Jordão de Freitas,[2] and Armando Cortesão,[3] while admitting that Pinto's story is arranged, and contains inaccuracies and contradictory dating, declare it to be an authentic piece of autobiography. The Japanese historian H. Nagoaka is of the same opinion.[4] Professor Le Gentil of the Sorbonne tries to sum up and adjudicate between the contending experts, and on the whole sides with Schurhammer.[5] Professor Boxer of the University of London also sides with Schurhammer.

If the reader wishes to know what is my opinion on this question, I can only repeat that throughout the *Peregrination* Pinto's method of describing the Asia through which he travelled is to combine everything he saw, experienced, heard and read into an autobiographical statement; and he is using the same method

[1]*Fernão Mendes Pinto e o Japão, Pontos Controversos* (Lisbon, 1906).
[2]*Peregrinação, nova edição conforme à de 1614* (Lisbon, 1930).
[3]C.f. his introduction to Tomé Pires' *Suma Oriental* (Hakluyt, 1944).
[4]*Histoire des relations du Japon avec l'Europe aux XVIᵉ et VIIIᵉ siècles* (Paris, 1905).
[5]*Fernão Mendes Pinto* (Paris, 1947).

here. We shall never know what proportion of the material was heard rather than experienced, or was transposed from the third person into the first. Pinto's whole book is a creation whose full significance cannot be assessed by dissecting it according to the rules of historical scholarship. It is a unique picture of six-teenth-century Asia, which provides historical information in the same sort of way as do the immense canvases and frescoes which were painted in Italy during the same epoch. Its subject is the first onslaught of the West upon the East, launched with the objects both of making money and spreading Catholicism. But it does not glorify either of these objects, as do the works of the other Lusitanian historians and epic poets, but rather raises the question whether the Portuguese had not endangered the salvation of their souls by seizing what did not belong to them. They are shown suffering rather than triumphant, losing rather than gaining, as if God's face was turned away from them. Such a theme—and it seems to be the essence of Pinto's book—would have led to its suppression by ecclesiastical authority had it been directly expressed. Driven to invent an indirect method, he adopted that of the traveller to whom statements are made and things happen, both arranged to be relevant, not only to the theme of sin and punishment, but to an Asian panoramic view.

It may be objected, however, that his theme was rather to dis-play himself as a man who had been everywhere, seen everyone, and participated as a protagonist in every important event; that such, for instance, was his reason for claiming to have been one of the first three Portuguese to visit Japan. But this argument is not easy to sustain, because in the whole of his *Peregrination* there is not a word of self-praise or self-righteousness; he does not depict himself as playing an heroic or brilliant part, as directing policy or advising kings, as being treated with honour or as clever or successful. He tends to keep himself in the background and to throw the chief light on some person other than himself. The form is autobiographical, but he is rather an onlooker and ob-server, though smirched with the general evil and suffering for it.

CHAPTER TWENTY-ONE

Pinto is wrecked on the Lu-chu Islands

———————◆———————

Pinto and his two companions sailed directly from Tanega-shima to Ningpo. When the Portuguese of that settlement heard that he had been to Japan and learnt of the wonderful market that existed for Chinese commodities, their excitement was great. The profits to be made by shipping silks and porcelain to Malacca were, though large, only a fraction of what he reported was there to be made. The revelation seemed such a proof of divine favour that they decided to have a thanksgiving service. A procession was organized, and they walked with banners from the Church of Our Lady of the Conception to that of St. James, where a mass was sung and a sermon preached.

This sacred duty performed, they got to business. It was resolved to fit out a fleet of ships at once for Japan. There were nine vessels in the harbour. As not enough goods to fill them were in the warehouses, they began buying hastily from the Chinese. This was done with so little discretion that prices soared, and for a quantity of silk normally sold at forty ounces the Chinese asked and got a hundred and sixty. In this way, regardless of expense, the nine vessels were loaded, and within a fortnight of Pinto's return were ready to set sail. He himself was carried away by the gambling fever and was as eager to go as anyone else. All was haphazard. Some of the ships were out of repair; there were not enough navigators to go round; it was too late in the season and the wind was unfavourable. Nevertheless, in their frantic desire to get rich quickly they would not wait and, tumbling aboard in confusion, weighed anchor, and set out. Luck turned against them at once. After leaving the shelter of the islands covering the approaches to Ningpo, they ran into heavy weather, a gale accompanied by a horrible rain, and seven of the nine vessels were driven on to a shoal.

Undeterred by this catastrophe, even meanly glad because the competition would be less, the Captains of the remaining two ships, on one of which Pinto was a passenger, held on westwards, their intention being to sight the Lu-chu Islands and follow the chain northwards to Japan. They safely made the Grand Lu-chu, now called Okinawa, where a second gale caught them. The two ships lost touch and Pinto's was driven towards a lee shore. Having abandoned all hope of saving their bodies, the Portuguese knelt to an image of the Virgin, praying that she would intercede on behalf of their souls. Soon afterwards the ship was flung on rocks that lined the coast. It rapidly went to pieces and only thirty survivors, among them a few women, reached the shore.

Such was the manner of Pinto's arrival on Okinawa. I have heard Americans speak of the charm of its inhabitants. They are given the same character in the *Voyage of His Majesty's Ship Alceste to the Island of Lewchew*, written by her surgeon, John McLeod (1816). Indeed, all accounts speak of their sweet nature, and this real goodness provides the plot of the story that follows. Some commentators doubt whether Pinto was ever on Okinawa, but he seems to have divined its chief characteristic. The drama he develops has an atmosphere of its own. We are neither in China nor Japan, but in a place between, with a particular aroma, which he could hardly have seized had he not at least seen something of the Lu-chu. The object of the story in the general plan of the *Peregrination* is to drive home from another angle his criticism of his own countrymen's behaviour in the East, and to continue the demonstration of how suffering brought him to a realization of his own demerits.

The part of the coast on which the survivors of the shipwreck found themselves was remote from habitation, a desolate shore. On getting to the beach, they had been cruelly scraped against the rocks; bleeding, in tatters, and without food, they set out to find help and shelter.

Pinto is wrecked on the Lu-chu Islands

They had gone a long way and were much exhausted, particularly the women, two of whom died, when a boy who was tending a herd of cattle saw them and ran uphill to give his village the news. Presently the villagers came out in a body, some of them on ponies, and headed down to where the Portuguese awaited them on their knees, a most pitiable group of suppliants, the two dead women lying in front of them. Six of the mounted men reached them ahead of the rest and, perceiving their utter destitution, were so touched with compassion that they galloped back and stopped the villagers, telling them not to do the strangers any harm.

The villagers now seemed to consult together, as if debating who the strangers might be, and whether they were dangerous or truly unfortunates. But since there was a law that any unknown persons seen wandering about had to be taken into custody, the mounted men approached again, accompanied this time by six constables on foot. 'We must arrest you,' they said gently, giving orders to the constables to tie the Portuguese together in groups of three, 'but there is no need for you to be frightened, for the King of Lu-chu is a man who is good to poor people.' And they swore on oath to do them no harm, though the Portuguese found it hard to believe them.

The mounted men now gave the order to march, and they set off, surrounded by the constables. But the women—there were three besides the two who had died—fainted after going a short distance. The constables were obliged to carry them, in spite of which two more died before sunset, when the party reached its destination, a town, in whose temple the Portuguese were locked up for the night.

Next morning as soon as it was light, the ladies of the town paid them a visit. Pinto often depicts oriental women as kind; in his story of Lu-chu the island women are made to act with a charity and compassion which could not have been greater, he observes, had they been Christians, though he is careful to make the observation oblique. The ladies had with them dishes of fish and rice ready cooked and, as they distributed them, spoke words of comfort, straight from the heart, for there were tears in their eyes. And seeing the extreme need which the strangers had of clothes, six of them went round the town collecting garments, saying to the people: 'You who profess to follow the law of the Lord, who is so generous to us, come out of your houses and look at the flesh of our flesh, which the Lord has chastised, and give alms lest his compassion be turned away from you, as it has been from them.' The people gave liberally in response.

Having made his point about the goodness of the Lu-chu islanders and their belief in a heavenly Lord identical to a Christian's, Pinto introduces the minions of the law, who even in so humane a setting have a sinister air, since to Pinto justice is always harsh and seldom fair. At three o'clock in the afternoon, he says, a messenger arrived from the capital with orders from the Minister of Justice to bring the Portuguese before him.

The Governor of the town communicated this order publicly to the people, who, knowing what it meant in pain and misery, even if the Portuguese were acquitted, declared that they would not obey it. The messenger was told to go back to the Minister and explain the innocence and destitution of the strangers and say that the townspeople desired to treat them with kindness and charity. The next day, however, officials from the Minister's office arrived with a mounted escort and, after binding the Portuguese, marched them to the capital, where they were paraded through the streets on the way to the law courts. 'The crowd,' says Pinto, 'seemed touched by our wretchedness, seeing us half-throttled by the chains about our necks.'

They were charged with being robbers of the sea, the standing accusation directed by Asia against Europe. They replied, as Europe has always replied, that they were merchants; violence and robbery were no part of their policy; all they wanted was to trade. But, said the prosecutor, you took Malacca by force and killed many of the inhabitants. That was war, they objected, not robbery.

The retort to this excuse, which the prosecutor is now reported

161

as making, is really Pinto's own opinion that the Portuguese dominion in Asia rested on an impiety (and he would have held the same about the subsequent Asiatic empires of Britain and Holland). The prosecutor cries: 'War, not robbery, you say! But can you deny that he who wages war robs? He who attacks, does he not kill? Who conquers, does he not commit wrong? And his motive of gain, is that not a thief's?' And he goes on: 'Your nation is guilty of all these crimes, the reason that God has permitted the waves to engulf you.'

In spite of this grand denunciation of the Portuguese empire, the court is represented as inclined to mercy, as if Pinto's intention were to ascribe to it an almost saintly forbearance. A message is sent to the King advising him to show clemency, and he is about to do so when a Chinese buccaneer puts into port, who had once been worsted by the Portuguese in a sea-fight. Hearing of the situation in which his enemies were, he saw an opportunity to avenge his losses. In an audience with the King he alleged that the appearance of the Portuguese in Lu-chu was part of a dark plot, since it was the custom of that nation to come to a country pretending to be traders, when in fact they were spies, and after having discovered its weaknesses and won over its inhabitants, to start a rebellion and seize the kingdom.

Pinto here puts into the mouth of the Chinese buccaneer the suspicion which then and afterwards haunted all orientals; Europeans who came ostensibly to trade and preach Christianity, to neither of which objection could be taken, were a disrupting influence and as such highly dangerous, for having caused disaffection inside a country, they took advantage of it to increase their power, until finally the country fell into their hands. It was fear of this insidious growth of power which led the Chinese a few years later to destroy the Portuguese settlement at Ningpo. Half a century later this very accusation was made against the Jesuits in Japan and so alarmed the Shoguns that the Jesuits were expelled and Christianity proscribed. Later again, the Chinese, after observing how the British managed in the name of trade to get possession of India, became afraid that the same would happen in

Pinto is wrecked on the Lu-chu Islands

China if the British secured a foothold there, and refused them a settlement or entry of any kind, until in 1842 they were obliged by force of arms to cede them Hongkong. Pinto shows his profound understanding of the East's appreciation of the Western danger by causing the buccaneer to whisper this same suspicion in the ear of the Lu-chu King. It had immediate effect. The King gave up his idea of clemency and ordered all the Portuguese to be quartered.

The sequel is one of the most moving episodes in the *Peregrination*, and gives Pinto scope to show without reserve how women could be good without being Catholics.

The King, who held his Court at some distance, sent a messenger with the death-warrants. On reaching the town, the man went first to his sister's house and confided to her the purport of his visit. She was much shocked and immediately hurried to her niece, who was the Minister of Justice's wife. This lady had given shelter in her house to the surviving Portuguese woman, who happened to be the wife of one of the prisoners, and, when her aunt told her the dreadful news, she called the woman and broke it gently to her that her husband had been condemned to death. The woman fainted and, on coming to, had hysterics and tore her face with her nails. This disfigurement, which was a custom strange to that part of the world, created a sensation when it became generally known, as it shortly did, on account of the loud cries the woman uttered. Many of the principal ladies called on the Minister's wife, and when they saw the Portuguese woman's grief and bleeding cheeks, were very distressed. Something must be done, they felt, and after a discussion decided to send a letter to the Queen Mother, begging her to intercede with the King on behalf of all the prisoners. 'There has been a miscarriage of justice,' they wrote, and described the wild despair of the Portuguese woman. 'God will listen to her cries,' they continued, 'because He helps those whom the world abandons, and, if the sentence is carried out, will visit us with fire and hunger.' They asked her to act 'as a saint would act,' and go urgently to the King, her son, and persuade him to pardon the prisoners. The letter was signed by a hundred of the principal ladies of the town, and to deliver it went the daughter of a high official.

The girl arrived at the palace at two o'clock in the morning. She had very little time, for the execution was fixed for the day after. She went straight to her aunt, who was a lady-in-waiting. This excellent lady promised to inform the Queen Mother, and before dawn entered her room by a private door and sat down at the foot of the bed. When the Queen Mother woke and saw her there, she exclaimed: 'What is it? You haven't been sleeping here all night? Or is it special news?'

'I have news,' said the lady, 'and am sure Your Majesty will find it as extraordinary as it seemed to me when my niece suddenly arrived in the middle of the night.'

Whereupon the Queen Mother desired that her niece should be called in. The girl entered at once and prostrated herself, and after the usual submissions and compliments presented her letter.

'Read it to me,' the Queen Mother directed, which she began to do, but had not gone far before the Queen, with tears in her eyes, exclaimed: 'Enough. No need to hear more now. God grant that the poor wretches do not lose their lives. They have suffered amply. Leave it to me.'

Not till the next morning, however, was it possible to see the King. It seems that he was not altogether happy over the execution and had had an alarming dream about it. So he was in a mood to be persuaded, and when he heard the letter read and his mother's earnest support of the petitioners, he reprieved the Portuguese, ordering at the same time that a ship be provided to take them back to Ningpo. These commands were received at the capital just in time. The people were delighted and made much of the prisoners on their release. They were given dinners in the best houses and such generous presents that when they sailed on a Chinese junk, the Captain of which had undertaken to land them safely at Ningpo, they all had substantial sums of money in their pockets. As a final touch Pinto makes the Minister of Justice admonish them to return thanks to God for their deliverance.

Besides the interpretations which I have already suggested, the

Pinto is wrecked on the Lu-chu Islands

little drama of Lu-chu stands for the idyllic aspect of the orient. The East has many faces, and Pinto describes them in turn, giving to each kingdom its most characteristic features. From the Lu-chu he will take us to Burma. There the face that we shall see is not a woman's but a tyrant's.

CHAPTER TWENTY-TWO

Pinto is sent to Martaban in Burma

————————◆————————

Pinto states that he reached Ningpo safely and, after a short stay there, embarked for Malacca on a ship belonging to a Portuguese merchant called Tristan da Gaa. Fortune had been adverse in the China seas, but he believed that he could count on the friendship of Pero de Faria, still Captain of Malacca,[1] to give him opportunities in another direction. On arrival he went immediately to see him. The story he had to tell was a long one, but he says nothing of the conversation except that de Faria, anxious to help before his term of office at Malacca expired, found him a new job, not unlike his missions to Batak and Aru, but more important.

The mission was to Burma; Pinto was to take ship up the west coast of the Malay peninsula to Martaban, on the mouth of the Salween river, a town of the greatest importance, for it was an entrepôt on the trade route from China to the West, via Siam. Ships from China often discharged their cargo at Ayuthia, the Siamese capital. From there the goods were carried west by two roads, one via Tenasserim to Mergui, whence they were shipped to India and beyond; the other to Martaban over the Three Pagoda Pass, and so to Bengal. Martaban was a larger and richer town than Tenasserim and had been a great trade centre for centuries. On Pinto's arrival at Martaban he was to go to the Viceroy and make a trade agreement with him, whereby certain goods

[1]It is known that Pero de Faria left Malacca for Goa in 1543 (see Schurhammer, op cit., pp. 27, 28, 29). The Burmese scenes which Pinto is about to describe are generally dated 1541 onwards in the Burmese chronicles, though the Siamese chronicles give a slightly later date. Nevertheless, the discrepancies are not great. We are somewhere about the year 1542.

which were in demand at Malacca would be sent down the coast regularly. Who the Viceroy was, and the relation in which he stood to the Burmese Government, will be described further on.

In addition to this, Pinto was to find and give a message to a free-lance Portuguese called Lançarote Pereira, who was operating as a buccaneer on the Tenasserim coast with a hundred men and four small galleys, or foists, and persuade him to return to Malacca and reinforce de Faria against a rumoured attack by Achin, the aggressive Mohammedan power in Sumatra. Lançarote Pereira was the same sort of sea-rover as Antonio had been, but he was operating nearer home and, the text suggests, contrary to Pero de Faria's wishes, though the latter had no power to stop him. He was also, as will appear, one of those mercenaries who sold their services, as arquebusier or gunner, to any Eastern ruler who would employ them. There were many such in Burma, and Pinto will give us a vivid picture of them as part of his whole panorama of the Portuguese in Further Asia.

The junk on which Pinto embarked had as its commander a Mohammedan resident of Malacca called Mahmud. It was a large vessel and towed a long-boat, well fitted up and armed. Setting sail, they steered north along the coast of Malaya. On reaching the Sembilan isles at the mouth of the Perak river, Pinto transferred himself into the long-boat, so as to be able to hug the coast and inquire in the river-mouths whether any prahus of Achin had been seen, and gather news of the whereabouts of Pereira. In this way he worked up past Kedah, where he had had his alarming experience with the Sultan, and, passing Junkseylon, entered the archipelago that continues past Kra to Mergui of Tenasserim. These islands are all similar in appearance, as I know well from having visited many of them in 1932, and must look to-day as they did in Pinto's time. They are thickly wooded, often surrounded by a white beach of coral and shells, some of them large and mountainous, with waterfalls and glades, full of game and occasionally inhabited. Whether large or small they are of surpassing beauty: a shimmering green at midday in the blue expanse; at nightfall a dark bulk lapped by the phosphorescent swell.

Pinto is sent to Martaban in Burma

At one of them they dropped anchor on the twenty-third day of the voyage. Pinto calls it Pisandurea, but since his time the British Admiralty has renamed most of the islands and one cannot identify it. That it was on the Tenasserim coast and not far from Mergui is clear from the text, and it may have been what is now called Domel Island. Men were landed to fetch wood and water, and the women went ashore to wash the clothes. In the afternoon Captain Mahmud's son asked Pinto to go shooting. He agreed and got his arquebus. Walking through the forest they came to an open place and saw a herd of wild pig rooting near a marsh. Delighted at their luck, for wild pig are seldom seen so conveniently in the open, they discharged their firearms and knocked over two of the beasts. Then with a shout they ran towards them. But on getting closer, they saw with horror that what the creatures had been digging for were corpses, numbers of which were lying about, some half-eaten. The stench was unbearable. Puzzled and agitated, they hurried back to inform Captain Mahmud.

Mahmud was a man of great experience. On hearing the news it struck him that there might be a pirate in the vicinity, who had buried the bodies of men he had slain. If so, there was grave risk of being surprised at a disadvantage. Accordingly he re-embarked the women, though the washing was only half done, and, collecting his men together, sent a party round a neighbouring headland to see if a pirate ship might be hidden there, and himself with forty armed men went to view the dead bodies. All had gold bracelets on their arms and jewelled daggers at their waists. That these valuables were still on the bodies proved that the idea of a pirate was wrong. 'I see now what it is,' said Captain Mahmud to Pinto. 'These men were Achinese of rank, officers in their army. One can tell that from the style of the bracelets and daggers; moreover, the custom in Achin is for officers to be buried with their arms and ornaments. They must have been killed in a battle.' And he went on to argue that an Achinese force must have gone up the river to Tenasserim and there been heavily defeated. The dead had been carried back and buried on this island.

Pinto is sent to Martaban in Burma

A search was then made for further bodies and altogether thirty-seven were exhumed. Such heavy casualties in officers suggested that a large force had been annihilated. Captain Mahmud took the daggers and bracelets and ordered the corpses to be buried again, so disgusting a piece of work that several of his men fell sick afterwards. On return to the junk, he told Pinto to send back the long-boat with a message to Pero de Faria, reporting that the Achinese had suffered a defeat in this region, a piece of news which would relieve his anxiety.

This done, they continued the journey up the coast, looking for Mergui and the entrance to the Tenasserim river, where more might be learnt of the Achinese defeat and Pereira's whereabouts perhaps ascertained. As they tacked through the many channels between the islands that screen Mergui harbour, they came to an islet, from which a boat put out. Six men were in her, dark-complexioned fellows, Malays by appearance, who were wearing, however, the red caps which Portuguese seamen generally wore. The one who seemed in most authority, though he was so ragged that patches of his skin showed through his clothes, inquired if any Portuguese were aboard. Pinto was lying down in his cabin, as he was unwell, and the Captain asked him to come on deck. The sight of him seemed to rouse the men in the boat to great joy; they clapped their hands and gave a cheer. Coming close alongside, their leader said: 'Sir, before I presume to speak to you, will you kindly read this letter,' and unwrapping it from a filthy piece of rag, he handed it up. It was a Portuguese testimonial declaring the bearer to be a Christian, newly converted by Pereira, who had given him his own name of Lançarote. He was King of the island, and the Portuguese were indebted to him for valuable intelligence which had helped them to win a sea-fight. The signatories of the testimonial, who were Pereira himself and his three Captains, earnestly begged any Portuguese who might read it to preserve him from wrong and right him if necessary.

When Pinto had finished reading, he cordially invited Dom Lançarote aboard (for he had taken the noble prefix in virtue of

169

his office). 'My power was so small,' he writes, 'that it could not reach further than to give him a bad dinner and the red cap I had on, which, worn though it was, was better than his own.'

When Pinto asked him what he wanted, Dom Lançarote explained that he was in a predicament. Because he had befriended the Portuguese and turned Christian, one of his Mohammedan slaves had risen against him and seized the island, reducing him to the poor state in which they saw him. 'Since I perceive you are alone on this junk,' he said to Pinto, 'I realize you cannot help me. Therefore, take me with you as your slave.' So he declared, and broke down, weeping.

Captain Mahmud, who was a very good-natured man, was so affected by his grief that he gave him some rice and a suit of clothes. 'Where is your enemy?' he asked kindly, 'the man who took away your island?'

'In the village,' replied Dom Lançarote, 'not a mile from here.'

Captain Mahmud looked at Pinto: 'Supposing you were captain, what would you do for this poor fellow, whom I see you are sorry for?'

Pinto, though he knew well what he would like to do, had not the face to say it. But the Captain's son, a high-spirited young man, who had been brought up among the Portuguese at Malacca and understood that Pinto was bound in honour to help a Christian in distress, asked his father to lend him twenty mariners and he would set up the King again.

The Captain, who had guessed that this was what Pinto had in mind and who wanted to oblige him, readily consented. Pinto's gratitude was in accordance with the custom of the time, when a European, without demeaning himself, could humbly acknowledge his indebtedness to an Asiatic. He threw himself at the Captain's feet and, embracing his ankles, declared that for such a favour he would ever be his slave.

The junk was brought close to the shore and a force of sixty men, natives of Java and Borneo, armed with thirty arquebuses, bows and arrows, lances and grenades, landed and set out for the village. The Captain's son went in front and Captain Mahmud himself came behind with a flag on which was painted a cross, given him by de Faria as a means of showing that he was a Malaccan subject in case of his meeting with Portuguese ships. Dom Lançarote guided them to the village, where they found some forty men waiting for them, but armed only with lances and one arquebus. The first volley put them to flight; and they were pursued and cut down. In the village were women and children. Captain Mahmud's rough mariners were for slaughtering them and sacking their houses, but they cried out that they were Christians, and at Pinto's instance the sack was called off. Thus was Dom Lançarote restored to his realm, an island three miles in circuit, whose inhabitants lived entirely by fishing, but who carried themselves as proudly, says Pinto, as if they were the nobles of a real capital, a vanity highly characteristic of the Malays.

Before Pinto left the island, he dedicated a church, to be used by Dom Lançarote and his Christian subjects. So ends this very curious account of the Mergui archipelago in the sixteenth century. Pinto is the first European writer to describe it at any length[1]. His story of a Christian King and a Christian islet may sound, in spite of its circumstantiality, like an invention, but I must admit that I myself in 1933 came upon an island in this same archipelago, whose inhabitants met me on the beach with a hymn and led me afterwards to their Christian church; they were Karens, whose presence there could be plainly accounted for, but the sound of whose singing in that lonely isle was to me as unexpected and unlikely as was to Pinto Dom Lançarote's letter.

[1]The Venetian traveller Nicolo di Conti (who travelled overland to India a century earlier) mentions it.

CHAPTER TWENTY-THREE

The surrender of Martaban to the Burmese King

———————◆———————

A week or so later the junk entered the estuary of the
Salween and anchored some distance below Martaban.
Though he seems to have made inquiries at Mergui and
Tavoy, Pinto had failed to get in touch with Pereira. Nor was he
better informed about the latest developments in Burma. What
was happening at Martaban was very different from what he
expected.

The history of Burma is a record of how the Burmese made
themselves the ruling race in that region. Besides numerous tribes,
there were four principal peoples in Burma: the Burmese, the
Shans, the Talaings and the Arakanese. The Burmese became the
dominant race by establishing the Pagān dynasty (1044-1287). Its
Kings ruled a united Burma. The dynasty fell after a Tartar invasion in 1287, at the time when Kublai Khan was Emperor of China.
The Tartars afterwards withdrew and left the inhabitants to govern
themselves. During the three centuries that followed the Burmese failed to re-establish their hegemony. The country was
divided into four independent states: the Shans in the north and
east, the Arakanese on the west littoral, the Talaings in the south
and the Burmese in the centre. The Viceroy of Martaban, whose
name was Saw Binnya,[1] held his position under the Talaing King.
But in 1531 a remarkable personality became Burmese King under
the title of Tabin Shwé-ti.[2] His ambition was to bring the whole
country again under Burmese rule as at the time of the Pagān

———

[1] This is, in fact, a title meaning the Lord of Wisdom. Pinto writes it as Chau-
bainha, quite a close approximation for him.
[2] The title means 'The Topmost Golden Parasol'.

The surrender of Martaban to the Burmese King

dynasty. He was associated from an early date with an even more striking person, who is generally called by his later title, Bayin Naung,[1] and was, perhaps, the greatest man of action in Burmese history. In 1535 these two set out on their adventure to reunite Burma. The first step was to overthrow the Talaing kingdom, by far the wealthiest and most civilized of the four. The Talaing capital was Pegu, fifty miles north of Rangoon. Tabin Shwé-ti and Bayin Naung entered it as conquerors in 1539. The Talaings, however, did not give in; their two other principal towns, Prome on the Irrawaddy, one hundred and eighty miles from Rangoon, and the enormously rich Martaban, held out under their governors. After a failure before Prome, the Burmese King marched against Martaban, and his army was besieging that city when Pinto entered the mouth of the Salween. A trade envoy, he had stepped into a war. The situation was further complicated by the fact that there were Portuguese mercenaries on both sides. A certain Paulo da Seixas commanded a contingent for the Viceroy of Martaban; on the Burmese side the contingent was under João Caeiro; and Lançarote Pereira, whom they had been searching for all up the coast, was with him.

Of all this Pinto and Captain Mahmud knew nothing (or only vague rumours) when they dropped anchor after midnight some way into the Salween estuary. At first it was quiet, but presently they heard an occasional cannon-shot. At dawn Captain Mahmud called a council to decide what to do. Was it safe to proceed? After a debate they resolved to go on and find out exactly what was happening. The anchor was raised and on the flood-tide they sailed up the estuary. On rounding a point before midday the city came into view. It was clear that a siege was in progress. The blockading army could be seen outside the walls. They went forward cautiously and anchored at a safe distance from the many boats which invested the city on the river side. As a sign that the ship was a neutral merchantman, they fired the salute usually fired by such vessels on entering a port.

Their flags announced that they were Portuguese subjects, and

[1]Meaning 'The King's Brother'.

173

soon afterwards a boat put out from shore containing six Portuguese. Pinto was much relieved to see them. They came on board and explained the situation: the Burmese King had a huge army and was pressing the assault; it would be most imprudent to try to enter the town and communicate with the Viceroy; it would also be useless, since Martaban was likely soon to fall; the best course would be to land and get in touch with João Caeiro, with whom they would find Lançarote Pereira. Caeiro, they said, was a very nice man, a close friend of Pero de Faria's, for whom he had a great admiration, both as a nobleman and because of his character.

This advice meant joining the Burmese side and throwing over the Talaing Viceroy, an old ally of Malacca and to whom their letters were addressed. But there seemed no alternative, and Pinto went ashore and was taken directly to see João Caeiro, the commander of a force of seven hundred Portuguese, well-armed men who drew a large pay.

When Pinto showed his letters and explained his mission, the chief part of which was to persuade Lançarote Pereira, and, for that matter, any other Portuguese fighting men, to return to Malacca and defend it against Achin, João Caeiro pointed out that, as Captain Mahmud had supposed after finding the corpses, the Achinese had, in fact, suffered a defeat in Tenasserim of so severe a kind, that it would be a long time before they would again be a threat to Malacca. In the circumstances, though he professed the most devoted loyalty to the King of Portugal, there seemed no point in going to Malacca. Pinto agreed, and asked him to put it in writing.

Since the season was unsuitable for sailing back at once to Malacca, Captain Mahmud stayed on and traded as he could with the Burmese. Pinto went to stay with João Caeiro and was a witness of the concluding phase of the siege of Martaban. The pages of the *Peregrination*, wherein he records what he saw, are among the most powerful in the book. The high moral standpoint from which he has viewed the behaviour of his compatriots in Asia is maintained, and in a scene of great intensity he declares himself ashamed of them. His judgment of the King of the Burmese, soon afterward to be crowned King of Burma, is no less severe; he denounces him as an inhuman tyrant.

When the Viceroy, Saw Binnya, found his resources in men and material running out, he tried to come to terms with King Tabin Shwé-ti. If he would raise the siege, he offered him a sum down of thirty thousand viss of silver, a viss being seven and a half pounds' weight, and an annual payment, as his tributary, of sixty thousand ducats a year. Tabin Shwé-ti replied that he must surrender unconditionally. Saw Binnya sent a second message, asking that he might be allowed to leave Martaban in two ships, the one containing his wife and children and the other the contents of his treasury; the Burmese King could have the city and all its accumulated riches. Tabin Shwé-ti replied as before that he must surrender unconditionally. A third envoy was sent with instructions to offer everything, provided the Viceroy and his family were allowed to escape and take their own private money and jewellery. That he must surrender unconditionally was again the answer.

Saw Binnya then tried another move. The Portuguese on the Burmese side were under obligations to him; it seems that João Caeiro and also Lançarote Pereira had originally been in his pay and that, though he had treated them very liberally, they had, before the siege began, gone over to Tabin Shwé-ti, who had won them with larger pay and more certain prospects. Saw Binnya now hoped to win them back again by an offer so lavish that no man could refuse it. He sent his own Portuguese Captain of mercenaries, Paulo da Seixas, to João Caeiro's tent, disguised in Burmese clothes, with a letter to this effect: 'I wish to become the King of Portugal's vassal. Come, therefore, with ships to the wharf called the Temple wharf, where I shall be waiting with all my treasure in gold and precious stones. If you take me off, I will pay half my treasure to the King of Portugal. The other half I will divide so liberally among you and your men that you will all be wholly satisfied.'

On reading this letter, João Caeiro summoned a council and

declared that he must accept the offer, because he could not refuse what would be a fortune for His Majesty of Portugal. The council wanted to know whether the Viceroy's treasure was really as great as it was reputed to be. Paulo da Seixas was put on oath and stated that he could not say for certain what was its value, but that he had seen with his own eyes a fairly large building full to the roof with bars of gold, enough to load two ships; that he had also seen twenty-six chests, which Saw Binnya himself had told him was the treasure of the Talaing King, and which Tabin Shwé-ti had failed to seize when he took Pegu, the capital. Nor was that the whole of the treasure, da Seixas declared. There were reserves of gold in the chief pagoda that would fill four ships. And he had been shown, too, a solid gold image of Buddha, which belonged to the Shwe Dagon pagoda at Rangoon, and was studded with rubies and emeralds, in his opinion the most valuable image in the world.

The council found it difficult to believe this statement and, after sending Paulo da Seixas out of the room, the members began a debate that became acrimonious. There was a party which violently disliked João Caeiro, and they could not bear the thought of his triumphant return with all this money to Portugal, when the King, after receiving so splendid a gift, would certainly make him an earl or a marquess, or, at least, send him back as Viceroy of the Indies. There were others, too, who thought it was too risky; Tabin Shwé-ti might well find out and they would all lose their lives. This timid section supported those who were blindly jealous of Caeiro, and swayed the council to vote against him. And they threatened to denounce him to the Burmese if he disregarded their wishes. Paula da Seixas had to be sent back with a refusal.

When the Viceroy Saw Binnya got this message, he fainted, for he saw it meant his ruin, if not his death. On coming to, he said: 'All I wanted was to save the lives of my wife and children.' And he bewailed the ingratitude of the Portuguese, on whose old friendship he had relied. But Paulo da Seixas had been faithful to him to the last and now, all hope being gone, he told him to escape. 'Take your young Talaing wife and two sons with you,' he said, 'and this pair of bracelets, take them as a parting present. Yet, when you think of me, let it not be on account of them, but because I have always truly loved you.' And he charged him to tell Caeiro and his Captains that he would arraign them before God for their base ingratitude.

Pinto says that the following night Paulo da Seixas crossed over to the Portuguese camp in the Burmese lines with his sons and wife, a beautiful woman, whom he took with him afterwards to Goa and married properly with Catholic rites. There he showed the bracelets to two lapidaries, who bought them from him for sixty thousand pounds and sold them afterwards for double that amount to an Indian Rajah.

A few days later Saw Binnya hung out a flag of surrender. The Burmese King's marshal of the camp, a Talaing who had joined him, called Smim Payu, sent a horseman to the wall. The Viceroy asked him to obtain a safe-conduct for an emissary. When this had been procured, the Arch-abbot, an old and saintly man, was sent with a letter to King Tabin Shwé-ti. In it the Viceroy said: 'I, Saw Binnya, am resolved this night to render myself, my family and all my possessions to Your Majesty, to do with as you think fit. But if you are merciful, you will acquire the merit of a merciful man. My only request is that I be allowed to enter a monastery. My emissary, whose saintly character is his guarantee, will make, if required, a more ample statement.'

In this way Saw Binnya surrendered, his only condition that his life and his family's be spared. The Burmese King accepted the condition. By the former terms offered, Saw Binnya personally would have escaped him; now he would get his enemy into his clutches. The Abbot was sent back with a reassuring message.

CHAPTER TWENTY-FOUR

The Burmese King's terrible vengeance on Martaban

Next morning the Burmese army paraded to witness the surrender of the Viceroy, who was to come in procession from the city to the camp. Pinto had never seen such a display of Asiatic might. Round the King's tents were grouped his elephants, two thousand five hundred and eighty of them, the castles on their backs gay with banners, and each one wielding a mighty sword in his trunk. Round them in a square was the Burmese cavalry, twelve thousand five hundred strong, the horses richly caparisoned, the riders in corselets, carrying lances, swords and shields. Beyond the cavalry was the Burmese foot, amounting to twenty thousand, like a field of rich colours. There was a tumultuous sound of voices and music. Officers galloped about, dressing the lines and shouting orders. The foreign mercenaries, thirty-six thousand in number, were stationed in two files, forming a lane from the King's tents to the city gate, a distance of two miles. The real strength of the Burmese army lay in these mercenaries, who, besides Portuguese, included Greeks, Venetians, Turks, Jews, Armenians, Moguls, Indians and men from Java and the islands. All had been ordered to put on their best uniforms.

About one o'clock in the afternoon a cannon was fired, the signal for the opening of the gate. First there issued the troops which the King had sent to conduct the Viceroy to the camp. Towering in the chasm of the gate were seen the rolling mass of three hundred war-elephants, their castles full of armed men. After these were come out, there followed other elephants, plated with gold-leaf and with ruby collars, on which rode divers great Burmese lords. Then appeared in the gate he whom all were assembled to see, the Viceroy Saw Binnya, mounted on a small elephant, in token, as it seemed to Pinto, that he had put away the vanities of the world. He was habited in a robe of black velvet and his hair was shaven off, as were his eyebrows and moustache; and to render himself to his conqueror in all humbleness, he had a rope halter round his neck. He seemed about sixty years old, his features grave and generous, though his mien at the moment was sad and afflicted. Beside him on the elephant was the Arch-abbot, who had taken on himself to act as his advocate. Outside the gate was watching a crowd of women, children and old men. When these poor folk saw their lord come out, with the cord on his neck and so fallen from his former glory, they uttered seven times a dreadful cry and struck their faces with stones until the blood poured down. Saw Binnya passed through the mournful throng, and it was seen that behind him was a litter on which was carried his wife, a royal Princess, for she was the daughter of the Talaing King, who had died after the fall of Pegu, his capital. With her were four children, her two boys and two girls, the eldest not seven years old; and about the litter her ladies walked, thirty or forty, of wonderful beauty, their looks cast down as they leant on their waiting-women. When the Princess saw the populace weeping, wounding themselves and crying aloud, the horror of the moment overwhelmed her and she fainted.

The litter was lowered so that her women could attend her. On perceiving this, the Viceroy protested that he must stop and go to her; whereon his guards let him dismount. He knelt beside the litter and prayed to heaven that, as his wife and children were innocent, the divine wrath, which had cast him down, might pass them by. The intensity of his pleading was so great that when he had spoken he fell forward on his face. Even the Burmese of the guard, though little inclined to compassion, showed by their faces that they were touched. As for the crowd of common people, they uttered another piercing cry of horror. At last Saw Binnya raised himself and, taking water from the attendants, filled his mouth and spurted his wife. She sat up and he put his arms round her, and, trying to comfort her, used consolations, says Pinto, which might have come from the lips of a Christian.

But now the guards, afraid to delay longer, obliged him to re-mount his elephant and proceed. When he had ridden on a short distance, he came to the lane-way which had been formed by the foreign mercenaries, placed first among whom were the Portu-guese under João Caeiro. The seven hundred of them were in buff coats, great feathers in their caps and carrying their arque-buses on their shoulders. Caeiro himself, with a gilt halberd in his hand, which he used for keeping off the crowd, was wearing a suit of red satin. Saw Binnya no sooner perceived him than he seemed to sink on the neck of his elephant, and said to his guards: 'I swear that to look at these wicked and ungrateful men is more painful for me than all the pain of this surrender. Send them away, for otherwise I refuse to go on, and you can kill me here.'

Having said this, he turned away his face in grave disdain. 'And, indeed, all things well considered,' writes Pinto, 'there was every excuse for him to condemn us as he did.'

The Captain of the Burmese guards was very irritated at the procession being held up a second time. He thought the Viceroy had reason for his plaint and, since he himself also disliked the Portuguese, he turned his elephant abruptly towards Caeiro and gave him a very nasty[1] look. 'Get out of this, and that instantly!' he shouted. 'Men like you blight any ground. May God forgive the fool who put it into His Majesty's head that you could be of any use to him.' And he went on insultingly: 'Shave those beards off and stop pretending to be gallant men. Without them you will look like women and we can make use of you in a way that will be worth the money.' At which the guardsmen forced the Portuguese out of the line and drove them away with contumely. 'Not to lie,' comments Pinto, 'I never felt so sensible of my countrymen's dishonour than on this occa-sion.'

After this, Saw Binnya went on until he came to where Tabin

[1]Our Commonwealth translator has: 'a scurvy look.' A French seventeenth-century translation has: 'le regardant d'un œil de travers.'

The Burmese King's terrible vengeance on Martaban

Shwé-ti waited in front of his tent, attended by the principal lords of the kingdom. There he alighted from his elephant and threw himself down at his conqueror's feet, lying a good while, as if in a swoon, without uttering a single word.

Presently the Arch-abbot, who was by his side, addressed the King on his behalf: 'Here is a spectacle for pity. Your Majesty will do well to imitate the clemency of God, never so much moved as by a voluntary submission such as this.'

The King renewed the assurances which he had given before the surrender, and committed the Viceroy into the keeping of a high officer. He was anxious to lay hands at once on the enormous treasure, fearing that during the night his soldiers, particularly the mercenaries, might get into the town and obtain possession of it. For the next forty-eight hours he was engaged in removing it. The town was then delivered to the soldiery. A cannon was fired, the signal that they were free to begin the sack. So frantic was the rush to the gates that three hundred men were stifled in them. 'There was an infinite company of men of war of different nations,' writes Pinto, 'the most of them mercenaries without king, without law, or the fear of God. They went to the spoil with closed eyes and were so cruel minded that they would kill a hundred men for a crown.' The sack lasted for three and a half days. The warehouses were full of merchandise from every country in the East, including pepper, incense, lacquer, aloes, camphor, silk and porcelain. In the houses of the rich were found quantities of gold, silver and precious stones. Sixty thousand persons were killed during the sack. When there was nothing left, Tabin Shwé-ti ordered fire to be set to the palaces, monasteries and houses of the lords, many of them splendidly carved and gilt. The flames spreading, all Martaban was consumed, even the towers and walls being utterly destroyed.

But Tabin Shwé-ti's vengeance on the Talaings, who had dared to resist him after the fall of their King and capital, was not yet complete. The day after the end of the sack, Pinto noticed that twenty-one gallows had been erected on a hill, where the King had moved his tents, and with five companions he went to find

181

out the reason. As they drew nearer, they saw horsemen lining the way, as if a procession were about to pass up the hill. Such, indeed, was the case, for presently they caught sight of a group of women, bound four and four together, and behind them, conducted by mace-bearers, the Princess, Saw Binnya's wife, attended by her ladies. Her children were also there, each held by a horseman before him. The women were the wives and daughters of the Viceroy's principal commanders. Walking by them were monks, who strove to comfort them as they went upwards to where the gallows stood. Most of the women were between the ages of seventeen and twenty-five, 'very white and fair, with bright auburn hair,'[1] and so slender and delicate that they had not the strength to endure such a march, and now one, now another, would sink to the ground. More pitiable still was the crowd of their little children who came behind, three or four hundred of them, naked and holding white wax lights, and each with a cord about his neck. The rear of the procession was brought up by a hundred elephants.

In the King's camp on the hill a vast concourse of soldiers and others was waiting to witness the executions. After the procession had reached the foot of the gallows, a proclamation was made by a crier, in which it was stated that the women, numbering one hundred and forty, were to be put to death because they had in-cited their husbands and fathers to resist the Burmese King, with the result that twelve thousand of his soldiers had been killed before the city. When the crier was done, a bell sounded, signify-ing that the executions would begin. The hangmen made ready, and the women, after embracing each other, turned to the Prin-cess to bid her farewell. She was lying, only half-conscious, in the lap of an old lady. Speaking for the rest, one of them said: 'Your most humble servants, who are about to die, beseech Your Lady-ship to place yourself so that we shall be comforted by the sight of you while we are dying.'

But the Princess, out of her wits with anguish at the thought

[1]That Talaing women should have seemed so to Pinto is strange. Their natural complexions were probably blanched with white powder and they may have been wearing yellowish turbans or head-scarves.

of what was about to happen to her children, could only murmur in a voice that was scarcely to be heard: 'Do not go away so soon, my sisters, but help me to sustain these little ones.' And she buried her face in the old lady's bosom, unable to utter another word.

The hangman now seized the women and hung them from the gibbets by the feet, a lingering death that kept them a full hour in dreadful agony. While they hung there, strangely groaning, the Princess and her four children were taken to a separate gallows. The Arch-abbot was with her and strove by encouraging words to give her strength. She held her four children tightly, and having kissed them many times, for they were terribly frightened, she said weeping: 'Oh! my children, my children, how happy would I think myself, if I could redeem your lives with the loss of my own a thousand times, were it possible!'

One of the hangmen approached and began to bind her two boys. 'My friend,' she implored him, 'do not be so void of pity as to make me see my children die. If you do that, you commit a great sin. For God's sake put me first to death.'

But he would not desist, though he allowed her to take her children once more in her arms, and she kissed them over and over in a last farewell. When he again laid hands on them, suddenly her heart stopped and the old lady who held her saw that she was dead. The hangman, however, was not to be baulked. He seized her, dead as she was, and hung her up by the feet, and hung her four children, two on each side.

The sight of this inhuman cruelty drove frantic the Talaing conscripts in the Burmese army, says Pinto, and, uttering a great and hideous cry that seemed to make the very earth quiver, they broke into a mutiny, which was suppressed with difficulty. That night the Viceroy Saw Binnya was thrown into the river, a great stone tied to his neck; and many of his officers suffered the same fate.

If the reader asks how far this tremendous scene of high tragedy is historical, the answer may be put in the following way. It is certain that Pinto resided in Burma for some time and may, as he declares, have been at the siege of Martaban. The Burmese chronicles, after recording the fall of the city, do not mention the execution of Saw Binnya and his wife, but such executions were normal in Burmese history and it is likely that this one took place. Pinto was in a position to ascertain what happened, and having gathered the main facts, perhaps partly by his own observation and partly from witnesses, he had the literary ability, twenty-five years or more later, to throw them into the form of a tragedy. We can compare him here to a historian in the grand manner, not to a chronicler and certainly not to the modern specialist working methodically from written sources. The scene he describes may be conceived of as his effort, on the basis of his information, whatever precisely that may have been, to imagine the surrender and death of the leading Talaing personalities after the fall of Martaban as viewed by the victims themselves. He was evidently profoundly moved by the event, and his description is meant to be a condemnation, not of the people, but of the tyrant, of Burma. The implication of the Portuguese in the cruel deed is an additional reason why he was ashamed of them. That he was able to compose in the fifteen-sixties such a piece of writing proves that he had literary genius. The historical novel had not been invented, nor the descriptive article for the newspaper. Neither the medieval romances nor the Italian *novelli* would have been of the slightest use to him as models. The picaresque novel was still in the future and when it did come was never tragic. The great Cervantes did not publish until 1604. Except for passages in the Greek and Roman historians (and there is no sign that he had ever read them), he had nothing to guide him. He managed, however, to give his contemporaries in Europe a most realistic peep into Burma.

CHAPTER TWENTY-FIVE

Pinto becomes a slave in Burma

———————◆———————

Nine days after these executions, the Tyrant of Bramaa, as Pinto terms King Tabin Shwé-ti, left Martaban and returned to Pegu, the former Talaing capital and now his own. He took with him João Caeiro and his Portuguese regiment. Not more than three or four Portuguese remained in the ruined town. One of these was Gonçalo Falcão, a man of good family, to whom the King had given a title at the time when he came over to him from the Viceroy's side. Pero de Faria, knowing that Falcão was an old resident of Burma and could be of service to Pinto, had addressed a letter to him in that sense. Pinto had called on him with this letter shortly after his arrival, and frankly told him of the treaty which he had been sent to negotiate with the Viceroy. It now occurred to Falcão that he might insinuate himself still further into the King's good graces if he denounced Pinto as an emissary whose reason for coming to Martaban had been to offer the Viceroy Portuguese reinforcements. Accordingly, he went with this tale to the newly appointed Burmese Governor of Martaban and, declaring that Pinto should have been arrested long ago, urged him to apprehend him now. The Governor, on learning that Pinto had come on a ship with a rich cargo, saw that there was money in Falcão's suggestion, and ordered not only Pinto's arrest, but the seizure of the vessel and everyone belonging to her. They were thrown into prison, and the vessel with its cargo was confiscated. After a month, during which they were abominably treated in the prison, Pinto was summoned to stand his trial for treason and the rest were put into a boat without oars or sails and sent drifting down the estuary on the tide. After terrible hardships, two of them reached Malacca and told Pero de Faria that in all probability Pinto had already been executed.

In fact, he had a very narrow escape. There was no evidence against him except his own papers, and these only showed that he had been instructed to renew an old trade agreement with the Viceroy. To get him to admit that he had secret instructions to offer men and arms, he was tortured. They beat him, and molten lac, which is like sealing-wax, was dropped on him and burnt holes in his flesh. In his agony, however, he happened to say that if they put him to death, Captain João Caeiro would hear of it and complain to the King. This frightened the Governor's advisers, for Caeiro had influence. Moreover, if the King learnt of the matter in that roundabout way, he would suspect them of trying to defraud him (as, indeed, they intended to do), and would send a man down from Pegu to assess the cargo. As he would be sure to over-value it, not only would they make nothing, but would be heavily out of pocket. A light sentence on Pinto would cause no stir, and as no one would question the accounts, they could value the cargo at a moderate figure and keep the balance without risk.

The Governor found this to be prudent advice and, instead of the death penalty, ordered Pinto to be detained as the King's slave with the loss of all property.

As soon as Pinto was sufficiently recovered from the torture to be fit to travel, he was sent in chains to Pegu, where he was made over to the King's Treasurer. There he found eight other Portuguese, slaves like himself. They had been shipwrecked on the coast and the Burmese had refused to let them go. They all became, it seems, attached to the Treasurer as military orderlies and had to accompany him wherever he went.

Important events were impending. Tabin Shwé-ti, having taken Pegu and Martaban from the Talaings, had still to take their third city, Prome, before he could call himself master of their kingdom. To make himself King of all Burma, a further campaign was necessary; he must take Ava, the capital of the Shan dominion in the north. The attack on Prome began six months or so after the fall of Martaban. Pinto describes how the King em-

barked his army in twelve thousand boats, descended the Pegu
river to Rangoon, turned north into the creeks of the delta,
passed Henzada and Danubyu, entered the main stream of the
Irrawaddy and so arrived before the walls of Prome. The Talaing
lord of Prome was only thirteen years of age, but had been married to his aunt, who was the daughter of the Shan King. She was
a courageous woman of thirty-six, and on her fell the task of
saving the town. As soon as Tabin Shwé-ti appeared with his
army, she offered to pay homage. But he was angry with Prome
for holding out against his authority for so long. He declined her
homage and ordered her to surrender, though he promised that
if she did he would recompense her for the loss of her estates. Re-
membering what had happened at Martaban when Saw Binnya
surrendered, the Princess refused to obey and sent an urgent message to her father, the King of Ava, for help. Before help could
arrive, the Burmese King, assisted by a traitor, took the city.
Pinto says he was an eye-witness of the terrible massacre which
followed. 'Even now when I think of it, I am horrified,' he writes.
'The inhumanities committed were beyond imagination. The
King ordered all the dead children that lay up and down the
streets to be brought and, causing them to be hacked very small, he
gave the bits mixed with bran, rice and herbs to his war-elephants
to eat.[1] This done, the Princess was brought before him, the wife
of the poor little lord, a very white and beautiful woman, and he
caused her to be stripped naked and publicly torn and mangled
with whipping. Afterwards he had her led up and down the city
and exposed to other torments till she gave up the ghost. Her dead
body was tied to the little lord, and they were thrown into the
river, a heavy stone about their necks, a kind of cruelty that

[1]Our knowledge of tamed elephants in this country is confined to the poor
clownish creatures of the circus, or the broken-hearted beasts at the zoo to
whom an infant may safely offer a bun. Even those of us who have worked
them in the forests and timber-yards of Burma know them only as beasts of
burden. What a war-elephant was like is impossible to imagine, an animal
trained to be obediently ferocious, in battle to wield a mighty sword and, as
an executioner, to kill men by tossing, trampling and rending them. Such
monsters relished a bran mash flavoured with babies. It was usual to give them
a drink of spirits before a battle.

seemed very dreadful to those who were watching. For a conclusion of his barbarous punishments, the King caused all the gentlemen of the town that were taken alive to be impaled and, so spitted like roasted pigs, to be thrown into the river; whereby may be seen how past all imagination were the injustices inflicted by the tyrant on these miserable wretches.'[1]

The King of Ava's help arrived a fortnight too late. The Shans came hastening down the river in four hundred canoes under the command of the late Princess's brother. But they were defeated at Myédé after a battle in which the Shans, who were much outnumbered, fought tenaciously. Thereafter, Tabin Shwé-ti made a reconnaissance in force up the river as far as Ava itself. Pinto, taken along in the train of the Treasurer, saw this town and remarked on the strength of its fortifications, which may be seen to this day, standing at the point of junction of the Mu river with the Irrawaddy, whose swift stream is here a mile wide, though four hundred miles from the sea.

There now comes in the *Peregrination* an episode which is generally considered to be an invention, perhaps the only complete invention in the book, for even in such passages as the journey to Tartary Pinto is describing a real place with the help of information derived from others. But Calaminham, the kingdom to which he declares that he travelled with his master, the Treasurer, who was sent as ambassador, cannot be located and is a fiction. The alleged reason of the embassy sounds convincing enough. Tabin Shwé-ti, before attacking the Shans, may well be supposed to have wanted an ally who would invade them from the east while he besieged Ava on the west. Calaminham was supposed to be a large Buddhist kingdom east of the Shans, north of Siam and south-west of Tongking. But no kingdom answering to Pinto's splendid description ever existed in that area. More-

[1]The Burmese chronicle, the *Hmannan Yazawin*, says the lord of Prome was executed later and that his wife became a concubine of Bayin Naung, the colleague of Tabin Shwé-ti and his successor. But the cruelties described by Pinto were characteristic of Burmese kings and we cannot easily reject the testimony of a man so generally inclined to take a flattering view of orientals and, as we shall see, who held the Church of Burma in great esteem.

over, his claim that he reached it by navigating rivers eastwards from Ava is impossible, because except for a few small rivers that are not navigable for any distance, the main waterways here, the Irrawaddy, the Salween, the Menam and the Mekong, flow from north to south in distinct watersheds divided by mountain ranges.

What can have been Pinto's object in inserting at this point a long and detailed account of a kingdom which was not anywhere? The answer appears to be that it was a literary contrivance that enabled him to throw together into a connected narrative a quantity of varied information which he had gathered about religious practices pertaining to India, Burma and Tibet. He did not properly understand Hinduism nor appreciate the distinction between the two forms of Buddhism, the Mahayana and the Hinayana, and, despairing of disentangling them, he treats them as existing all three in one place. In point of fact, he was not entirely wrong. While it has been the practice of modern writers to demarcate the geographical boundaries of these three forms of oriental religion, they are not in actual practice so insulated. Even in Burma, which has always prided itself on the purity of its Hinayana faith, there have always co-existed important elements of Hindu and Mahayanist worship, though the orthodox monks have not countenanced them; for instance, to-day the Burmese still invoke, under a local name, the old Hindu god of the sky, Indra, to visit the country before the rains. Pinto was particularly interested in the phantasmagoria of oriental beliefs, because he conceived that not only behind them all was the conception of a supreme God like the Christians', but also that definite Christian doctrines had always been current in Asia since the time of the Apostle St. Thomas. By positing such a place as Calaminham he was able to jumble all these elements together.

It were tedious to follow him here in any detail, but we may dip into his narrative, which will be found to illuminate his own outlook and give startling glimpses of practices which certainly did exist in the East and which he was the first European to write of at length.

When the embassy entered Calaminham they went to a famous

pagoda called Tinagoogoo before continuing to the capital. This pagoda stood on a hill and had something of the lay-out of the Shwe Dagon at Rangoon. They happened to arrive at the time of a festival, which, as Pinto describes it, was like the festival of Juggernaut.[1] The famous car festival of Juggernaut had been heard of at his time; Friar Odoric (1330) had mentioned it and stated that pilgrims threw themselves under the cars; Nicolo Conti (1420) refers to it, as does Couto, Pinto's contemporary. A later traveller, Sonnerat, in his *Voyage aux Indes* (1782), says the suicides had decreased; a hundred years later again they were a rare exception. But in the sixteenth century the car procession was reputed to be an occasion of nightmare, the most dreadful scene of religious frenzy in Asia. Some Indian must have told Pinto about it. He was both horrified and impressed, horrified by its bloody nature, impressed by its devotees' wild longing for salvation, and he composed his account, pretending that he had seen everything he describes on the road leading to the pagoda of Tinagoogoo. His reconstruction of the scene is by far the most horrid that has ever been penned.[2]

The procession of the cars, he says, was three miles in length, and as it came in sight, appeared to be led by a concourse of priests, most on foot but some in palanquins, who were robed in green satin with stoles of carnation. Carried also were shrines of deities, the porters wearing yellow robes. Then came the cars, in all a hundred and twenty-six, four or five stories high with as many wheels on both sides. In each rode at least a hundred priests, and on the highest part was a silver image, wearing a crown shaped like a mitre and a necklace of precious stones. Boys holding silver maces conducted the cars, and acolytes censed the idol with burning perfumes to the rhythm of music, uttering thrice in

[1]Our corruption of the Sanscrit word Jagannātha, Lord of the World, the title under which Vishnu is worshipped at Puri in Orissa.

[2]Brother Sebastião Manrique, whose adventures I have written of in my *The Land of the Great Image*, extracts Pinto's description of the cars and uses it as the basis of his account of a similar festival at Mrauk-u, the capital of Arakan, a dishonest attempt to discredit Burmese Buddhism, for it can never have occurred in that region.

a voice of lament: 'Lord assuage the pains of the dead that they may praise thee peacefully.'

The cars were dragged by long ropes on which as many as a thousand persons were pulling, for to pull was to win a measure of salvation. Such a multitude sought for a place at the rope, that there was not room, but merit could also be gained by placing the hands on those who pulled or even on those who so placed their hands, so that each car advanced with as many as six or seven lines of men to each rope. The crowds of onlookers were very dense and mounted pikemen cleared a passage, striking hard anybody in the way, though no one, not even those grievously hurt, protested.

The drumming became more tumultuous, as suddenly a band of men, smeared with sweet odours, wrapped in silk, and wearing gold bracelets on their wrists, issued from a building. A lane-way was instantly made for them by the crowd. They rushed towards the cars and, after making a profound salutation to the god, laid themselves flat in the path of a car. The wheels passed over them and, such was the car's weight, cut them in pieces. Those who saw their death cried out: 'Would that my soul were now with theirs!' as if the devotees were already safe in paradise. Priests then descended from the car. They had platters in their hands and heaped them with the severed members of the dead. Climbing again to the top of the car, they held these aloft, so that all could see that the sacrifice was accomplished. 'May you too prove worthy to become saints!' they cried to the vast crowd looking up at them.

After hundreds had sacrificed themselves so, there came on the scene other martyrs, a band of frantic devotees, dancing before the cars and slashing themselves with razors. They seemed to be in a state which rendered them wholly insensible to pain. Not content with gashing their flesh, they cut off lumps of it and, fixing them on the points of arrows, shot them into the sky, vociferating, as they did so, that it was on behalf of the souls of their dear ones that they made this gift of their living flesh to God, the most precious gift they had to give. The arrows streamed over the crowd and fell. Such was the rush to pick up the gobbet of flesh, as if they were a potent relic, that many were stifled. As the self-mutilation proceeded, the scene became more desperately macabre. The wretches stood, dripping with blood, without ears, without noses, still slicing their flesh and shooting arrows, until at last they drooped down and lay dead. The priests sitting on the top of the cars, watching like vultures, again descended and, cutting off the fanatics' heads, held them up to the people, who prostrated themselves.[1]

Pinto makes a comment on these scenes of suicide which reveals his point of view. To the average man of the period they would have seemed no more than demonism; but he says what struck him was how much harder the devotees strove to win salvation than did Christians. As we shall eventually see, Pinto himself was to renounce the world, and so had in some sort an affinity with the devotees. Nevertheless, that he was able to catch a glimpse of the real state of mind of the fanatics who threw themselves under the cars proves him to have been a man of rare perception. Not until three hundred and fifty years later do we find a thinker with the acumen to state their case. Renan writes in his *Avenir de la science* (1894):[2] 'The English thought that they were acting in accordance with moral decency by forbidding processions bloodied by self-immolation and the suicide of the wife on the husband's pyre. How mistaken was your contempt, you tame

[1] Religious suicide, not unknown in Europe, was always a feature of oriental life, where the climate predisposes to greater hysteria. In my *The Land of the Great Image* (pp. 77–85) I cite the case of the tree of death at Prayāga in Bengal, from which devotees threw themselves, as it is described by Hsüan Tsang, the Chinese pilgrim of the seventh century. In the same place is given Fra Manrique's account of the devotees who swung on hooks until they died, as also the more extraordinary suicide of those who offered themselves to sharks on the island of Saugar. In 1667, Daniello Bartoli published his *Dell'historia della compagnia di Giesu*, in which the curious will find on p. 133 some observations on religious suicide in Japan at that time, suicide by drowning, and by jumping off a cliff. The latter resembles the jump from the tree of death, for in both the god of the place calls to the devotees to jump and be carried to paradise. But, indeed, on this topic it would be possible to collect an immense documentation, which would include *sati*, the suicide of the wife on the husband's pyre. We may regard Pinto's account of the mass suicides at Tinagoogoo as a résumé of all that he had been able to learn about a subject which evidently fascinated him.

[2] Quoted by Professor Le Gentil in his *Fernão Mendes Pinto*, p. 62.

business men! Do you not realize that the fanatic who joyfully places his head under the wheels of the car of Juggernaut is a happier and more admirable man than you? Don't you see that he does more honour to human nature by testifying, irrationally, no doubt, but with great force, that there are aspirations in man that rise superior to finite desires and ordinary self-love? True, if one held these acts to be no more than a sacrifice to a chimerical deity, they would be absurd. Rather, one should see in them the fascination which the infinite can exercise over mankind. But you English, with your petty morality and narrow common sense, would circumscribe the superb overflow of humanity's deepest instincts. There is an audacity, a spontaneity, in these great and picturesque excesses of the spirit, which reason can never reach and which will always be preferred by the artist and the poet.'

This view accords exactly with Pinto's, that the devotees of his Tinagoogoo were prepared to go further than any Christian to wring from the infinite a promise of safety.

A couple of days after the procession of the cars, Pinto was taken by the ambassador inside the precincts of the pagoda, where a number of hermits lived. Their penances were harsher than any practised by Catholic cenobites. In the first grotto were men dressed like the monks of Japan. Pinto was told that they ate only herbs, haricot-beans and wild fruit, a rule more restricted than that followed by the Franciscans or the poorest begging friars. At another grotto the hermits were in deep holes in the rock and their food was insects and sorrel juice. They meditated day and night with their hands closed, one within the other. Further on they saw hermits, of so sick a look and of such bad colour that they were horrifying, whose sole nourishment was various kinds of filth. After that they came to those 'who spend their whole life in crying day and night on those mountains, Godomen, Godomen,[1] and desist not until they fell down stark dead on the ground for want of breath'. And lastly, they saw the sect of hermits who shut themselves in narrow closed cells, in which they lighted bonfires and smothered themselves in the smoke.

[1]Gautama, one of the names of Buddha.

Pinto becomes a slave in Burma

Such kinds of hermits, yogis, recluses and anchorites were to be found at that date, and continue till the present day, in India, Tibet, China and also, to a less degree, in Burma and Siam, though never all of them in one place. The austerities mentioned by Pinto are facts and he might have added others of an even grimmer sort, such as the holding aloft of an arm until it stiffens and withers, the keeping tight closed of a hand until the nails burrow through and come out at the back, and the burial in a grave, from which a bamboo tube to breathe through comes up to the surface.

Besides the reason hinted at above why there was some affinity between Pinto and these men who renounced the world so as to make sure of heaven, another reason can be put why he was interested in them. The Popes had laid the duty on the Portuguese of converting Asia to Catholicism, and missionaries were sent out to achieve that object. For them to succeed they had to set a high example of sanctity. But since Asia had its saints, who sought by such extreme austerities to reach an apprehension of the divine, the missionaries' task was very difficult. How could they compete with the devotees? Even the penances of the greatest of their missionaries, Saint Francis Xavier, were much less severe. To Eastern eyes, they were bound to seem less utterly devoted to God, than the saints whom they sought to displace. Throughout the *Peregrination* Pinto is continually citing instances of the deeply religious feeling of orientals, as if he realized, what has since turned out to be a fact, that Asia could not be converted to Christianity. The fiction of Calaminham, with its picture of a humanity prepared to go any lengths in order to make sure of paradise, may have been invented to convey that opinion indirectly.

CHAPTER TWENTY-SIX

The Arch-abbot's funeral

The Burmese ambassador's reception at Timplan, the capital of Calaminham, is related in detail and at wearisome length. But one chapter is curious enough, that devoted to a conversation in which an abbot is made to show a knowledge of the fall of man as related in the Old Testament, but to be ignorant of his redemption as related in the New. He had, however, heard a report that a missionary from overseas had in former days been put to death at Rangoon for saying that God once made himself into a man and had been crucified. On Pinto's explaining the significance of the crucifixion as a promise of redemption, the abbot was much moved and offered a prayer to God that the time might soon come when everyone would know of this promise.

The abbot gives the name of the missionary as Tomé Modeliar, and calls him the servant of God. It is thought that here Pinto is referring to St. Thomas the Apostle, who was believed to have been martyred in the East. While the martyrdom was generally supposed to have taken place at Mylapur, a suburb of Madras, where a shrine commemorating it still stands on a hill called Mount St. Thomas and where there is a cross with an inscription in Pahlavi dating from the seventh century, rumour persisted that he had died elsewhere. Indeed, the exact place was a favourite subject of speculation at that period. Pinto, whose custom, as we have seen, is to claim that he had first-hand information about every interesting topic of the day, is writing in characteristic vein when he makes the Calaminham abbot disclose the secret that Rangoon was, in fact, the place.

The Arch-abbot's funeral

But how are we to reconcile the prayer put into the abbot's mouth with Pinto's views, as they have been so far revealed? Did he think that when the peoples of Asia heard of the Christian way to salvation they would follow it, as the abbot suggests might be the case? But we have seen how the sight of the devotees and hermits made him doubt this. In addition, there was the notorious reputation of the Portuguese, which was no advertisement for Christianity. So Pinto returns in his indirect way to the point he has been continually making throughout his book: his countrymen, though Christians, are despoilers and pirates, and therefore must be ineffectual missionaries. That is the deadliest of their sins; though Asia knows of God and is crying out for His revelation, they have failed to impart it. As we shall see, this argument has particular relevance to his own case.

The journey back from Calaminham is given in the same sort of unintelligible detail as the journey thereto. The nomenclature does not convey anything until suddenly we find that the party is in Martaban, whence they travelled on to Pegu.

Shortly afterwards the Arch-abbot[1] died, the head of the Church, who had preached mercy to the King at Martaban. In a lengthy dissertation on his funeral and the appointment of his successor, Pinto not only develops further some of the views which have just been discussed, but declares that while tyranny was the characteristic of the Burmese Kings, the Burmese Church stood for charity and compassion. That he should insist on this point shows his grasp of essentials, for the great achievement of the Burmese was that they had adopted as their religion the Hinayana form of Buddhism and, in spite of bad kings, wars, invasions, and anarchy, had carefully fostered its high morality through the centuries. He is correct in laying stress on the immense respect in which the monks were held and on how kings, tyrants though they might be, listened contritely to their reproofs.

[1]Pinto calls this personage the Roolim of Mounay. Mounay was presumably the name of his monastery, or some Burmese name like it. It was not in the town of Pegu, but at a considerable distance into the country. Roolim is a corruption of the Burmese word Yahan or Rahan, the highest monastic grade.

The Arch-abbot's funeral

As soon as the news of the Arch-abbot's death reached Pegu, the King went to Mounay to attend the funeral. Nowadays, when an important abbot dies, he is embalmed and the funeral does not take place for six months at least, but in the sixteenth century it may have followed at once. The ceremony itself remains in essentials as Pinto describes it; the body, in a coffin, was placed on a high ornate catafalque and burnt. But an event, which he says took place immediately before the burning, belongs (if it happened) to a time that is past: six monks committed suicide by taking poison at the foot of the catafalque. From what he has already stated about religious suicide, we can understand how relevant that event was to his conception of the orient.

The ceremonies were concluded by a sermon preached beside the ashes by an abbot of royal blood. In the course of it, after praising the deceased for his virtues, he turned to King Tabin Shwé-ti and said: 'If the Kings who now govern, or rather tyrannize, over countries were to consider the little span of their life and the punishment that awaits them hereafter, they would realize that the cattle feeding on the grass were more fortunate. God made them Kings to rule with mercy, to be easy of access, and to punish justly. But the real object of their laws is to squeeze money, and a man is put to death so that his property can be confiscated.'

It is related that when Tabin Shwé-ti heard this, he was deeply affected and promised to reform, as his royal predecessors are often said by the Burmese chroniclers to have done, when admonished by their Arch-abbots or Royal Chaplains. But in bringing into his sketch of Burma such a scene, Pinto is not only using it to record an essential characteristic of that country, but is also thinking of Kings in general, particularly the Kings of Portugal. His insinuation is that the autocrat of Portugal would do well to follow the example of the tyrant of Burma and meekly receive a similar reproof.

In connection with the funeral ceremonies one or two points should be noted as showing how well Pinto knew Burma. For instance, the King and Court made lavish gifts of cloth to the monks of the Order, who had attended in thousands. That the Portuguese merchants, who happened to have in stock a quantity of material imported from Bengal, were able to sell it for that purpose at a large profit is a true touch. Again, the ashes of the Arch-abbot's body were collected, placed in an urn and carried by the King himself to a funerary shrine. In this procession of the ashes the King walked with the urn on his head, the most honourable of all positions, for in the opinion of the inhabitants of Further India the head had (and still has) an extraordinary symbolical importance; to touch another's head is a disrespect which may be resented by anyone. So when Tabin Shwé-ti placed the Arch-Abbot's ashes on the top of his head, he signified that the Throne took second place to the Church. Pinto also notes, though without fully appreciating its meaning, the King's release of hundreds of caged birds and little fishes in jars, an act of compassion that would be counted against his cruelties in the final balancing of his merits and demerits. These little condescensions, though ritualistic in character, allow us to see the King in a pleasanter light.

During the election and installation of the Arch-abbot's successor, Tabin Shwé-ti continued to demonstrate his respect for the Church. Bayin Naung, the King's foster-brother and successor on the throne, was sent to fetch the new prelate. Tabin Shwé-ti met him at the head of his Court and prostrated himself at his feet. The new Arch-abbot bade him rise and sit beside him, and touched him thrice on the head, a capital crime for any other person in the realm, but which the King took for a great honour. They embarked together on the royal barge, the Arch-abbot sitting up on a throne like a statue of the Buddha and the King kneeling at his feet. The barge was rowed by grandees with gilded oars; on prow and stern was an orchestra, and singers chanted sacred hymns. On reaching Mounay, where the installation was to take place, the King carried the Arch-abbot on his shoulders from the barge on to the shore, and thence princes and grandees bore him in turn to the pagoda.

When all the many ceremonies, which Pinto describes in detail,

were ended, the Court moved back to Pegu. The reduction of
Ava, prepared for by the alliance with Calaminham, would
normally have been Tabin Shwé-ti's next campaign, but he preferred first to send Bayin Naung against a town called Savady
in the text, and which may have been Tharrawaddy in the deltaic
creeks, and in that case was the fourth Talaing stronghold, Pegu,
Martaban and Prome being the other three. In the course of the
operation, the Treasurer, who had the rank of Colonel, was
ordered to attack a village in the jungle, from which the besieged
were being provisioned. Pinto and the other Portuguese in his
bodyguard accompanied him. On the way they ran into a strong
force of Talaings and were disastrously routed, most of the Burmese being killed. Pinto, however, was lucky, and with his compatriots escaped from the field unhurt. They were soon lost in the
jungle and, straying at random among the countless streams and
wide creeks of that region, eventually came upon a hermitage.
The hermit gave them shelter, and it seems that there the idea
came that they might be able to get out of Burma, if they could
reach Bassein, a port on the western side of the delta, which was
frequented by Portuguese ships. As slaves of the King, they could
never hope for leave to go home. Indeed, it was not easy even for
a foreign mercenary, who had made a free contract of his services,
to get a passport out of the country. Now was their chance, for
they were supposed killed, and they would not be pursued as
runaways. Their master, moreover, had been among the slain.
But to find the way to Bassein was not easy; and to reach it without a boat impossible, as the delta is a vast swamp in a maze of
tidal creeks.

After leaving the hermit, they were lucky enough to find a
canoe moored on the mud. Setting their shoulders to the gun-
wale, they pushed it into the water and escaped without being
detected. Next day they arrived at a nunnery, where they were
given provisions, and after great difficulties and misadventures, at
last reached Bassein. By a piece of luck a Portuguese ship was in
the river, on the point of weighing anchor for Bengal. Her
master consented to take them on board and they sailed with him

to Dianga in Chittagong, the frontier town between Arakan and India, where was a Portuguese settlement of pirates and slavers, countenanced by the King of Arakan because they guarded the frontier for him and provided him with a regular supply of Indian slaves.[1] There Pinto found a foist about to leave for Goa and, getting a passage on her, arrived safely and in good health at the capital of the Indies. On landing, he learnt that his old patron and good friend, Pero de Faria, was living in the city, for his appointment as Captain of Malacca had ended in 1543. De Faria, it will be recalled, had been told by the survivors of Captain Mahmud's ship that Pinto had been executed by the Burmese, and will certainly have been very surprised to see him, looking strong and well, though, as on previous occasions, without a penny. 'To him I rendered an account of all that had passed,' writes Pinto. 'He was sorry for me and made me a present of some money and goods, obliged thereto, not only by his habitual generosity, but because I had lost some merchandise of my own while on his service to Martaban. A little later, that I might not miss the season for sailing east, I embarked on a ship belonging to him which was bound for Malacca and the Straits of Sunda, resolving once more to try my fortunes in the kingdoms of China and Japan, and see if in those countries, where I had so many times lost my coat, I could not find a better one than I had on.'

[1]Cf. the full description of Dianga in my *The Land of the Great Image*.

CHAPTER TWENTY-SEVEN

Pinto joins the King of Java in his attack on Pasuruan

Pinto says that he landed at Malacca the day that de Faria's successor in the Captaincy, Ruy Vaz Pereira, died. That fixes the year as 1544, for the date of Pereira's death is on record. In general the dates scattered about the *Peregrination* are confused for reasons impossible to elucidate. But in this case there is support; by Burmese chronology, Pinto was in Martaban in 1541/42, and he says that he was detained in Burma about two and a half years. We may therefore adopt with some show of reason the date 1544 as representing the point of time which the narrative has reached. As he arrived in India from Portugal in 1538, his travels so far will have occupied six years.

After a short stay at Malacca, his ship took him on to Java to load a cargo of pepper for sale in China, a new line of business which the Portuguese had begun to develop two years previously. Bantam was the port they traded at, and the ship put in there. It was the capital of the feudal kingdom of Sunda, which was situated in the west corner of the great island. At this period Java, unlike Sumatra, which was split up among independent small royalties, had a supreme ruler to whom the other kings owed allegiance. This personage was called the Pangeran or Emperor of Demak, his dynasty having been founded in 1517 on the overthrow of the Hindu-Buddhist Madjapait dynasty. Java had been the seat of a great Hindu and Buddhist civilization for hundreds of years,[1] and some of the inhabitants still adhered to

[1]The magnificent stupa of Borobudur is in the centre of the island, perhaps the most famous of all Buddhist shrines.

those religions, as now does Bali, off its eastern tip, an island we know so well from photographs, and which, as it has retained its original culture largely unspoilt, provides us with a picture of what Java itself was like in Pinto's time. But the Demak dynasty was Mohammedan, and the Emperor's ambition was to spread that religion over the whole of Java. If diplomacy failed, he tried war, and when Pinto landed at Bantam, a war against the Hindu-Buddhist King of Pasuruan, whose territory faced Bali over the strait, was on the point of beginning. An envoy arrived at Bantam from the Emperor calling on the King of Sunda to bring his contingent of soldiers, as he was bound to do as a vassal. After her departure, for she was a woman, women being used by the Javanese in diplomacy, the King of Sunda collected his forces and invited forty Portuguese, who were among those in the town, to accompany him at an attractive rate of pay. Pinto declares that he made one of the party and so was an eye-witness of the campaign against Pasuruan. The Dutch historian P. A. Tiele (writing in 1880) opines that he did not go in person, but wrote his account from information received, a possibility always present throughout the *Peregrination*, as we know. 'For all that,' Tiele adds, 'Pinto provides us with a document which cannot be disregarded, for little is known of Javanese history at this period.' It is, however, known that the Emperor of Demak did engage in such campaigns, with the ultimate object, after uniting all Java under the Prophet, of overwhelming Malacca, the same ambition as that harboured by the King of Achin.[1] One may, therefore, safely conclude that the campaign, of which a glimpse will here be given, is historical, though its presentation is literary, as is all else in the *Peregrination*.

The King of Sunda's contingent numbered seven thousand men and was embarked in forty sailing vessels. The fleet followed the north coast of Java until it reached Japara, about half-way along, and there joined the Emperor's main forces, which were large and had for their transport a thousand junks, as well as rowing vessels.

[1]For this important fact and for Tiele's views, see Schurhammer, op cit., pp. 83 and 84.

Pinto joins the King of Java in his attack on Pasuruan

Pinto presents what follows as a drama, full of colour and movement, and having an unexpected climax. The Emperor sailed from Japara and, rounding the eastern end of Java, arrived at the mouth of the river leading up to Pasuruan. Since his junks had too deep a draught to cross the bar, he sent his rowing vessels in, which destroyed the shipping in the river. The army followed, either in small boats or by marching along the banks, and occupied a position outside the town walls. The Emperor had plenty of cannon and calculated that he could easily batter his way in. Some of his guns came from Achin, where they had been made under the supervision of a Portuguese renegade. 'As for his name,' says Pinto severely, 'I am content to pass it over in silence out of respect for his family, which was a noble one.' But Pinto himself was now fighting for a Mohammedan King and helping to mount this same ordnance so that it would rake the town. We must see in this a veiled confession: among his many sins he had helped the great enemies of Christendom, if not against Christians, at least against Hindu-Buddhists. But the Buddhist King of Pasuruan was as good as a Christian could ever hope to be, admits Pinto. 'He was young, had many excellent qualities, was much beloved, no manner of tyrant, very affable to the poor, and good to widows.'

This model King now called upon his troops for a sally against the invader. A supreme effort must be made, even if it meant certain death, to storm the platform on which the cannon were mounted. So well did he know how to inspire his men, that volunteers for this dangerous exploit immediately came forward. They were paraded in an open space outside the palace. When they were ready, the King harangued them, declaring his utmost confidence in their devotion. And to encourage them better, he took a cup of gold and drank to them all, causing their captains to pledge him and asking pardon of the rest, for that the time did not permit them also to pledge him. This done, the volunteers annointed themselves by rubbing their chests and limbs with a perfumed oil, a sign that they dedicated themselves to death.

Pinto is here describing a desperate sort of loyalty, that has been noticed by all writers on the Malay world. The devotee (for he is almost in the state of mind of the fanatic who sacrifices himself to a god) rushes into the enemy ranks, slashing and killing, and is so difficult to stop that even when wounded with a lance, he will press against the point till run right through, in his efforts to come at his adversary.[1] The Malay word *amoq*, which has become our amuck, in the phrase to run amuck, was used to describe the devotee, but later came to refer only to the nervous crisis of a man who, after brooding over his wrongs, kills everyone within reach. Pinto knew the term well and calls the King of Pasuruan's devotees *amacos*.

The gates of the town were opened and the *amacos* sallied out and, going stealthily at first, insinuated themselves into the Emperor's lines, when suddenly, as if possessed, they made their frenzied onslaught. In spite of their fewness compared with the huge forces of the Emperor, they made a terrible slaughter. Pinto says that he and the other Portuguese, who were acting as the King of Sunda's bodyguard, could not save him from being thrice wounded by a lance, and that several of them were killed in their efforts to get him into safety. Such was the confusion that the *amacos* penetrated to where the Emperor was, and he had to jump into the river with a dart sticking in him.

This reverse, and others that followed, did not discourage the Emperor of Demak. His troops and cannon were so much more numerous that he felt sure he could wear down the besieged. He was preparing a mass assault on the walls, when without warning a catastrophe overtook him. One must admire the art with which Pinto presents the climax. No European reader could possibly guess it, though, as we shall see, he has been prepared to understand it.

Two days before the assault was timed to begin, the Emperor was sitting in council with his officers. A heated discussion had arisen over the tactics to be employed, so much so that he had been obliged to ask the leaders to put their opinions in writing. His mouth being dry with much speaking, he called rather testily

[1]See the account of the Macasser rising against the King of Siam in my *Siamese White*, p. 128. Like the Javanese they also were of Malay race.

to his page, a boy of thirteen, son of the Paté or Lord of Surabaya, to bring him a chew of betel, the little parcel of betel-leaf, areca nut and lime, which acts as a mild stimulant and stomachic. The page was inattentive and did not hear, so he called a second time. Again the page did not hear, and it was not until a lord had pulled his sleeve that he hastened to bring what was wanted. After the Emperor had helped himself, he said to the page, who was kneeling below him with the tray of golden boxes: 'Are you deaf, that you couldn't hear me?' And giving him a light smack on the head, hardly more than a pat, he continued the discussion with his councillors. The boy, however, was mortally offended. His head had been touched; he had been humiliated before all the lords of the council; though the son of a nobleman, he had been treated with contempt. This, of course, was morbid nonsense. It was the Emperor who had touched his head, nor had anyone paid attention. Nevertheless, so hypersensitive and neurotic was he, that he went aside sobbing and, after brooding by himself awhile, became frantic for revenge. So returning to his place, which was close beside the royal chair, he suddenly drew his little ornamental dagger and plunged it into the Emperor's breast. The wound chanced to be mortal, and the Emperor fell, uttering the words 'I am a dead man'.

There was utter consternation. The sudden murder of their Pangeran stupefied the proud Javanese Patés. He lay there the victim of an extravagant punctilio, pushed till it became a lunatic excess. Recovering their wits, they crowded round him, striving to see what remedy to apply. But he was stone dead with a punctured heart. The page was seized and put to the torture. Had he been set to do the deed by conspirators unknown or perhaps by an offer of money from Pasuruan? But in his torments he cried again and again: 'I did it of my own free will, to be avenged of the blow that the Emperor contemptuously gave me on the head, as if he were striking some dog that barks in the streets at night, unmindful that my father is Paté of Surabaya.' For punishment he was impaled, the stake coming out at the nape of his neck, and along with him were impaled his father, three of his brothers and seventy-two of his relations, so cruel an execution, says Pinto, that it caused insurrections throughout Java and the attendant isles.

The murder of the Emperor ended the campaign. The King of Sunda, as the senior feudal lord, re-embarked the army, though the King of Pasuruan made another sally and badly mauled it. When they got back to the capital, Kartasura, which was close to Borobudur, the Emperor was buried, but violent disturbances marked the election of his successor. Pinto and his companions, alarmed at the unrest in the country, asked the King of Sunda's permission to leave. This he gave, and a present besides. They found their ship at Bantam ready loaded with its pepper, and sailed for China according to the original plan.

This little Javanese drama of the sixteenth century which Pinto has arranged for us is composed of the essentials for a comprehension of the island's history at that date—the eastward drive of Islam, which, in fact, never got any further; the warlike aristocracy and the feudal army that was both military and naval, but had no elephantry; the fanatical devotee as a type of soldier; and the morbid streak that might drive a man amuck or out of demented pride cause him to murder his lord. The picture is exotic, and Pinto, as its creator, should be regarded as the first in a long line of European writers who saw the orient in this light.

CHAPTER TWENTY-EIGHT

Pinto in Siam and again in Burma

O ne of the company that sailed with Pinto was a Portuguese called João Rodriguez. He had been captured by the Demak forces in front of Pasuruan, dressed as a Javanese and speaking the language. I mention him in this connection with the exotic because he was an early case (I know no record of any earlier) of the European who becomes a Buddhist monk. He was attached to a pagoda and had taken a monastic name. Later on, the Jesuits sometimes used to dresss in a religious garb of the orient and closely identify themselves with its ecclesiastical etiquette,[1] but this was in order to insinuate their own Catholicism in such a way as to make it less strange and offensive. The Christian who became a real Buddhist monk was rare, though it has happened many times since; I myself have met English Buddhist monks in Burma. This João Rodriguez told Pinto that he had been in Java twenty-three years. 'I was shipwrecked on the coast,' he said, 'and would to God I had died, instead of sinning as I did. The inhabitants used to try to persuade me to their way of thinking. At first I held off, but the flesh is weak. I was poor and far from my native country. By giving in, I obtained the favour of the present King's father.'

Pinto, for all his sympathy for Asiatics and his appreciation of their point of view, was a convinced Catholic in the sixteenth-century sense of the word, and could only agree that Rodriguez had committed a grave sin, though not nearly as bad as turning Mohammedan and fighting against Christians. His comment is: 'The man's story astonished me very much, for it was so new and

[1]Cf. de Nobili and Ricci.

strange. I tried to console him as best I could, using such words as I judged necessary in the circumstances of the time and place. And I invited him to return with us to Bantam, and go thence to Malacca.' In fact, Rodriguez accompanied him to China, where he found a ship for Malacca. There he confessed, and for penance had to act as a servant in the Hospital for Incurables. He died there afterwards, says Pinto, 'showing every sign of being a true Christian. Our Lord was merciful in allowing him to return and die in His service after so many years as an unbeliever.'

The pepper ship on which Pinto was travelling put into Chincheo (Ch'uan-chow), the port on the China coast in the Formosa Strait, where the second Portuguese settlement lay. But trade had been disrupted by Japanese privateers, who, as I mentioned, when considering in its proper perspective the 'discovery' of Japan, had operated in those seas for a long time. As business was not good at Chincheo, Pinto tried a port further down called Chang-pu. There his ship, along with several others, was set upon by Japanese rovers, but managed to escape into the open sea. It is not clear what course was set, though the direction was southerly. Somewhere in the South China Sea between Cambodia and Borneo they ran into bad weather. The ship was much battered and one night was blown on a reef. The mariners were Chinese and constructed a raft, while the Portuguese prayed. At dawn, when the Portuguese saw them launching it, a very ugly scene took place. The Captain, Martin Estevez, begged the Chinese to take him on to the raft, addressing himself particularly to his own servants. They said it was impossible, and a savage fight began. 'We were in imminent danger,' writes Pinto. 'It was a moment when even a father does not care for his son, or a son for his father. Every man for himself was the word.' Forty Chinese were on the raft and the Portuguese, who numbered twenty-eight, drew their swords and attacked them. The Chinese were armed with hatchets. No quarter was given in the horrible affray. All the Chinese were killed, but not before they had killed or mortally wounded twenty of the Portuguese. It was an affair, says Pinto, passing belief in its brutality, and showed what a beastly miserable thing life was, when people who had been living together and on the best of terms for weeks were carried by their sins to such an extremity that, balanced on a few planks tied with rope, they fought each other to the death, as if they had been mortal enemies or worse.

The survivors set out on the raft, having some children with them and servants. They rigged up a bit of cloth for a sail, but having no compass, did not know where they were going. On rafts the same sort of things have a way of happening. After four days one of the Negro servants died and, as they were starving, they ate his corpse. A week passed, by which time only seven Portuguese and four servants were still alive. On the twelfth day they reached a coast which at first appeared to be uninhabited, but where they came upon some islanders from Papua in a small vessel loaded with timber. By promising these men a reward, they overcame their reluctance to have anything to do with them, and were allowed on board. The Papuans brought them to a village, where a merchant from the Celebes purchased them for six pounds. On his ship they remained until it called at Batavia, then the seat of the King of Calapa, another of the Javanese Emperor's vassals, who paid ten pounds for them and, with extraordinary generosity, sent them free to Bantam, the port from which they had set sail.

Pinto was none the worse in health for his experiences in the pepper trade, but he had lost the money which Pero de Faria had given him in Goa. Stranded in Bantam, without a penny, he was dependent on the charity of the Portuguese there. He was lucky in being able to make friends with two merchants who were taking a ship to Siam and who invited him to accompany them, even lending him some money 'to try fortune once again,' as he says, 'and see whether by force of importuning her, she would not treat me better than heretofore.'

This seems to have been the turning-point in his career as a merchant. It is curious how very little he speaks of business, though during the whole vast length of the *Peregrination* his voyages and land journeys are made with that object. Nowhere, however, is there mention of how he transacted his affairs, nor details of the profits he made nor in what way he secured his money. We must assume that when at last he did begin to prosper, he was able to arrange bills of exchange on Goa and build up a balance there. His voyage to Siam would appear to have laid the foundations of a fortune, which, as we shall see, was very considerable. But it is not about the making of it that we shall now read, but rather a description of Siam at this period. He knew the country well, as well as he knew Burma, better than he knew China or Japan, and his account of it was the first by a European. He arrived at a moment when a struggle with Burma was about to commence which, beginning in 1547, was to lead to three invasions and three famous sieges of the capital, Ayuthia, by Tabin Shwé-ti and Bayin Naung. How long he stayed in Siam is not clear. It was some time in 1545 when he got there, but he collects into one section all that he has to say about the country and covers the years up to 1548. Then he winds up the story of Burma's unification under Bayin Naung before returning to recount his own later adventures. This part of his book contains several memorable scenes and descriptions. My intention now is to touch on these, thereby conforming to the plan of the *Peregrination*, one of the principal aims of which, as I have stated, is to give a complete picture of sixteenth-century Asia.

Pinto says it took his ship twenty-six days to sail from Bantam to Ayuthia, which is forty miles up the Menam from Bangkok, the present capital. The great river splits up at this point of its course into several wide streams which, after a detour, come together again. On one of the flat islands so formed the city of Ayuthia stood. But not only was it completely surrounded by the waters of the Menam, but canals were dug across it in such numbers and leading in so many directions that it was possible to reach many of the houses by boat. It resembled the modern Bangkok, which is also a city of canals. The best account of what Pinto saw there is not in the *Peregrination*, but in a long letter which he wrote in 1554 at Malacca to the Jesuits in Portugal, about which I shall have more to say further on. In this letter, after mentioning the canals that gave Ayuthia a look of Venice, he refers to the royal palace, a forbidden enclosure of shining gilt, from which the King seldom emerged, though when he did, he went on an elephant, surrounded by his bodyguard, and accompanied by his lords, a vast procession of splendid elephants, with dancers and clowns at the head of it. The King himself would throw down silver from a bag that he carried. 'I also saw him,' says Pinto, 'go for an airing on the river. His barge was bigger than a galley and had wings after the fashion of a fabulous bird, oars with gold designs, and the deck richly decorated. Behind his barge were twelve others with empty thrones, to which prostration had to be made, as if he were sitting on them.'

Next comes mention of the White Elephant, always a distinctive feature of the Court of Siam, and at that date of particular importance since it was a principal cause of the Burmese invasion of 1547/48. Tabin Shwé-ti, as the greatest King of Burma for centuries, wanted the White Elephant because to have it would make him the senior monarch of the Hinayana Buddhist Church. Its possession, also, would, he knew, help him in his efforts to unify the country; the people of the Talaing and Shan parts would have to look up to him, for a White Elephant was like a divine mandate. Pinto had sight of the sacred animal. He says: 'Once I saw the White Elephant being taken to bathe in the river. He was shaded from the sun by twenty-four servants carrying white parasols. His guard numbered three thousand men. It was like a procession on a day of festival. Before and behind went about thirty lords on elephants. He had a chain of beaten gold on his back and thick silver chains girding him like belts. Round his neck were more silver chains. They told me that on feast days he wore gold chains, but silver chains when he was going to his bath. In his trunk he carried a golden globe, of about twice the size of a man's head, that seemed to be a cosmographical sphere. They had a stage for him to stand on at the water's edge. I did not see the ceremonies with which they washed him, but I am told they were very many. The streets through which he passed were beflagged and decorated like in Portugal for the big bull-fights or royal feasts.'

This particular elephant died soon afterwards, but another was found to take its place. Tabin Shwé-ti failed before Ayuthia in 1548 and went home without a White Elephant. But in 1564, his successor, King Bayin Naung, sacked the city and carried away its White Elephant, and three others of the same kind which were also there. These elephants were kept in Pegu, and Ralph Fitch, the first Englishman to visit Burma, saw them in 1584/5 and describes them in his *Travels* in much the same way as Pinto, though he was present at a bathing ceremony and noted that a gentleman washed the White Elephant's feet in a silver basin. One of these four animals was captured by the King of Arakan in 1600 when he sacked Pegu, and was taken to the Arakanese capital, Mrauk-u, where it was seen in 1640 by Father Manrique, the Portuguese Augustinian Friar, as I have related in my *The Land of the Great Image*.[1] In short, the sacred animal which Pinto writes of, and its successors, were closely connected with two invasions of Siam and one invasion of Burma, another example of Pinto's instinct for picking out the essentials of the Eastern scene. In all the wide expanses of lands and lordships between Mrauk-u and Ayuthia, the White Elephant was the most precious object. And, more than the common religion of the Hinayana, it was a unifying link, for the King who held it could claim dominion over all the others.

Pinto lived in the Portuguese quarter of Ayuthia and began to lay out his borrowed capital on commodities to sell afterwards in China and Japan. The city was the great mart of exchange between the Middle and Far East, and was full of traders from all parts, each nationality having its own quarter. After he had been there a month or so, news came of a rising in the north. The vassal King of Chieng Mai, whose state lay on the Salween immediately south of the Shan states, had revolted against his suzerain, the King of Siam, and in alliance with other northern lords had marched south into the royal domain. The King of Siam, says Pinto, was so appalled by this insurrection that without a moment's delay he left the capital and set up a camp beyond the

[1]See p. 156 of the same.

river. There he summoned all his vassals to join him within twelve days; and he sent a special message to the Portuguese in their quarter, inviting them to accompany him north as his body-guard, with a promise of 'pensions, graces, benefits, favours and honours', including permission to build a Christian church. A hundred and twenty of them agreed to go, Pinto among them, as he says. By this time he had had a wide experience of fighting; there were his many sea-fights in the China seas and his service in the bodyguard of the Treasurer of Burma and the King of Sunda. But this was to be his first sight of an elephant battle.

The King's lords came flocking in and at the expiry of the twelve days he departed up-river, his army in rowing boats, and his elephants, of which he had four thousand, marching overland. Twelve days took him to where lay the army of Chieng Mai. It was largely a cavalry force. After a preliminary skirmish in which the Chieng Mai horse routed his foot, he attacked with his elephants, supported on the wings by artillery and foreign arquebusiers, both Portuguese and Turkish. Chieng Mai could not sustain the shock; the elephants charged with impetuosity and screaming; it was all over in half an hour. Chieng Mai fled up the river with the loss of thousands of men. The King did not follow him at once, but at his leisure advanced northwards, punished rebels, destroyed towns that had helped them, received oaths of alle-giance, posted garrisons and, after some months, returned to Ayuthia.

Here he immediately became the victim of a palace plot. The Chief Queen, whose title, according to a Siamese chronicle,[1] was Si-Chuda-Chan, had a lover, one of the lords of the Court. The King had been away six months and now she was four months gone with child. She was, however, one of those relentless women, who seem to have been more numerous in Asia than in Europe, and had already decided on her course. After giving the victorious King a splendid welcome, she put a slow poison in his drink, which killed him in a week without his suspecting her. His son

[1] Translated by Pallegoix in his *Description du royaume de Thai*, etc. (1854), p. 78, vol. II.

by her was made King, but as he was only nine years of age she was appointed Regent. As soon, however, as her son by the lord was born, she resolved to marry her lover, with whom she was infatuated, and raise him to the throne after she had put her lawful son out of the way.

Intrigues of this kind have been common in the East, several such being recounted in the annals of the Court of China and one, almost identical, I found in the Arakanese chronicles and inserted in my *The Land of the Great Image*.[1] The present case, whose authenticity is fully supported by the Siamese chronicle already mentioned, is worth tracing in detail from the *Peregrination*, for it shows precisely how an oriental Queen brings off such a coup.

As Regent the Queen had the support of a powerful clique, and she began to take measures to increase its authority. Her first step was to get the royal minor into her power. He had his own apartments, his staff and his guards. By representing to the Council that she was not satisfied with the sufficiency of the guards and feared for his safety, she was able to reinforce them with so strong a contingent of her own foreign mercenaries that, in fact, he became her prisoner, though nothing of the kind was apparent on the outside. Her next move was to bring charges of treason against two leading noblemen whom she knew were opposed to her. She was able to persuade the tribunal that they were guilty. They were executed and their estates transferred to lords belonging to her party. There was some murmuring at this, for the innocence of the two lords was widely known. The Queen, as if bending to criticism, and declaring, moreover, that her health was not good, asked leave to resign from the Regency and suggested that her lover should take her place, at least for the time being. The Council concurred and he was appointed. Under the Queen's secret direction, he continued her policy of strengthening their party by appointing supporters to central charges in the administration, either by transferring those in them to distant posts or by bringing accusations that led to their downfall. This was done so cleverly that the Queen's party was greatly aug-

[1] See p. 239 *seq.*

mented. When she and her lover felt themselves to be sufficiently strong, they openly arrested the remaining lords who stood out against them and had them put to death. The moment had now come for the final *coup d'état*. The mercenaries who guarded the young King made away with him, and the Queen had little difficulty in obliging the Council, which consisted largely of her nominees, to elect her lover, whom she had recently married, to be King of Siam. This happened in November 1545, says Pinto. The popular conscience was shocked, and in January 1546 the murderous pair were killed at a banquet by two lords who, if they had acquiesced so far through fear, were now heartened by the change in public feeling to act as they did.

Having introduced his readers to Siam by means of an elephant battle and a Clytemnestra drama (surely a very brilliant literary stroke for a man who in the ordinary way might have been expected to jot down laboriously some methodical notes like Tomé Pires), Pinto launches into his narrative of the invasion of Siam by Tabin Shwé-ti, the Topmost Golden Parasol. There were Portuguese mercenaries on both sides in this great affair, so that if Pinto was not in Ayuthia at the moment, as he would lead us to suppose that he was, he had the first-hand evidence of his compatriots to draw on. He rightly assesses the event as one of first importance in the Asia of that day, since Ayuthia was the largest and richest city between India and China.

Before the invasion the Siamese lords had chosen a new King, the brother of him who had been poisoned by the late Queen. He was taken from his monastery, of which he had been abbot for thirty years, and crowned with the title of Maha Chakra Padhi at the beginning of 1547.

When the Tyrant of Bramaa, for so Pinto continues to term Tabin Shwé-ti, learnt of the usurpation, the death of so many eminent lords, and now of the accession of a monk, without experience of war and alleged to be timid, he felt the moment had come for a stroke at Ayuthia. His council was of the same opinion. The ministers pointed out that victory would entitle him to take the style of Lord of the White Elephant, and that in consequence every King in the whole Hinayana Buddhist world would have to acknowledge his overlordship. And they went on, much more fancifully, anticipating the flattering submissions of nineteenth-century Burmese ministers, who promised London to their Kings, that after possessing himself of Siam 'he might, through the same territories, and with the succour of the princes his allies, pass into *China*, where was the great city of *Pequin*, the incomparable pearl of all the world,' as Cogan, our Cromwellian translator, phrases it.

Tabin Shwé-ti, who was a man of war of immense ambition, got ready his army for the invasion, by far the most ambitious of all his campaigns. The territory between Martaban and Ayuthia is two hundred and twenty miles broad, but is so tangled a piece of forest and mountain that in the twentieth century our military advisers did not believe the Japanese could march through it. There are various passes, and Tabin Shwé-ti's main body took that leading over the Three Pagoda Pass behind Tavoy, which debouches at Kanburi, eighty miles from Ayuthia. Besides his very numerous infantry, he had five thousand war-elephants, an artillery train and his Portuguese bodyguard under the command of Diogo Suarez de Mello, perhaps not more than five hundred men, but very well armed, all arquebusiers and gunners, and of proved courage. De Mello was the King's great favourite, who had estates worth two hundred thousand pounds a year, and was Governor of Pegu and now Marshal of the camp. He had left Portugal the year after Pinto. So rapidly was it possible for a Portuguese adventurer to rise to unimaginable fortune.

The Burmese army was preceded by a large force of pioneers who cut a road through the jungle. The King did not wait to reduce Kanburi, which was a fortified town, nor any other fortified places, but pressed on directly to Ayuthia without opposition from the Siamese King, who awaited him, shut up behind his walls. Thus the siege of the city began.

Of the many assaults that were made on the walls the strangest was that in which the war-elephants were engaged. These were divided into twenty troops. The soldiers on their backs were

Pinto in Siam and again in Burma

Talaings and Shans, arquebusiers who drew double pay. Small cannon were also mounted in the howdahs. When the elephants were under the wall, their riders were close to the top and able to fire point-blank at the defenders. Moreover, the elephants themselves dragged down with their trunks a bamboo stockade which served as battlements, so that the Siamese had no cover and were forced to retire. Some Turkish mercenaries now raised ladders, got a footing on the wall and slid down into the city, but were cut to pieces by a rush of Javanese mercenaries, who attacked with the mad fury of *amacos*. The elephants were withdrawn, but the King of Burma ordered a second and more violent assault. 'Whereupon,' says Pinto, 'the conflict grew much hotter than before, and continued half an hour and better. I do not know what passed, and can only say that we saw streams of blood running everywhere and the air lit with fire. The noise was such that the earth seemed to totter. It was a dreadful thing to hear the discordant din of the bells, drums and trumpets, mingled with the boom of the great cannon and the dreadful yelling of five thousand elephants.' But the Burmese failed to break in, and when many of the elephants had been wounded a retreat was sounded.

Such, we may be sure, was one episode in this exotic siege, so different on account of the elephants from anything that Pinto's contemporaries had seen or heard of. Indeed, he says a little further on, when describing an artillery duel which took place during a storm of thunder and lightning: 'It was, to say the truth, a thing which was never seen, read of or imagined and such as put everyone beside himself, for some fell flat on the ground, some crept behind walls, and others got into walls.'

In spite of his elephants, his Portuguese mercenaries, of a Greek who invented a variety of combustibles, and engineers who made him high towers on wheels, from which to shoot down into the streets, Tabin Shwé-ti failed to take Ayuthia. When the rumour of his ill success reached Burma, the Talaings began to hope again, and a lord, Smim Htaw, who was related to the late Talaing King, plotted a rebellion. News of this, more than any other reason, says Pinto, caused Tabin Shwé-ti to raise the siege. He marched home in October 1548.

The *Peregrination* now proceeds to describe what happened in Burma on Tabin Shwé-ti's return, and covers the years 1548 to 1554. The chief events were that Smim Htaw broke out into open rebellion; that Tabin Shwé-ti was assassinated in 1550; that the Talaings re-entered their capital, Pegu, and restored the Talaing dynasty by crowning the Lord of Sittaung under the title of Smim Saw Htut; and that Bayin Naung, Tabin Shwé-ti's successor, was occupied until 1554 in putting down this rebellion and re-taking Pegu.

Pinto describes these events, but in fact during most of the time they were taking place he was moving about the Far East on business. As we have seen, he was in Ayuthia in 1545. Having bought goods there, he departed, as he had previously planned, to China and Japan, returning at the end of the same year. The Ayuthia siege was in 1548, and he may or may not have been present. After that, in pursuance of his business, which at last was prospering, he made several other journeys, including what was his third trip to Japan. In 1552 he visited Burma again, and so was in that country when the Talaing pretender, Smim Htaw, who succeeded Smim Saw Htut, was worsted by Bayin Naung and that great King brought all Burma firmly under his rule. After 1552 there occurs a sudden change in Pinto's life, the dramatic climax of his adventures.

Bearing these dates in mind, we will follow the text of the *Peregrination* and first refer to two or three striking episodes connected with the Talaing rebellion and the final triumph of Bayin Naung. Then we shall return to 1546 and discuss Pinto's second visit to Japan. From this point there develops a continuous narrative leading straight up to the climax aforesaid.

The first episode is the fall of Diogo Saurez de Mello, the Captain-General of Tabin Shwé-ti's Portuguese mercenaries, and one of the richest and most powerful men in the kingdom. Pinto, as has frequently been shown, was a severe critic of his countrymen's behaviour in the East. In recounting what he calls the

abominable case of de Mello he is citing the most notorious of
their misdemeanours.

After the assassination of Tabin Shwé-ti in 1550 and the re-
storation of the Talaing dynasty under Smim Saw Htut, Saurez
de Mello and his men, to save their lives, were obliged to transfer
their services to the Talaing side. Now, four years previously,
de Mello, then at the height of his favour with Tabin Shwé-ti,
had been guilty of a disgraceful abuse of power. One afternoon,
when he was on his way to the palace at Pegu, accompanied by
a great train of horse and foot, he happened to pass a house where
a wealthy merchant, a Hindu it appears, was celebrating the
marriage of his daughter. Attracted by the sounds of music and
air of festivity, de Mello stopped his elephant and asked what was
going on. When told it was a wedding, he sent in a message of
congratulation to the merchant, wishing long life to the married
couple and even offering to be of service to them. The merchant
was quite overwhelmed. That the first grandee in the kingdom
should call and be so exceedingly polite was an unheard-of
honour. He hurried out to prostrate himself and, to show how
much he appreciated the compliment, called out to his daughter
to pay her respects. When she came, he led her by the hand to de
Mello at the door and told her to give him in acknowledgment
of his vast courtesy a ring that she had on her finger. She obeyed
gracefully, kneeling before him. She was exceptionally pretty,
and de Mello, who was accustomed to take any young woman
he fancied, put out his hand and pulled her towards him, saying:
'God forbid that so pretty a girl should fall into other hands than
mine!' So spoilt was he by the most abject compliance with his
whims, that it did not occur to him that he might be refused,
even though the girl was in the act of being married. He was surprised when begged to let go his hold, and did not deign to answer as the father continued to supplicate him, offering money,
all he had, even his own person as a slave. In despair the poor old
man made as if to pull his daughter back. This enraged de Mello,
and turning to the captain of his guard, a Turk, he shouted:
'Kill that dog!' The Turk drew his scimitar, and the merchant,

terrified, took to his heels, leaving his daughter, her hair all tousled, in de Mello's grasp. The bridegroom now rushed forward to rescue his bride, but was immediately cut down with the kinsmen who were with him. All the women in the house started to scream. In this tumult, and before she could be dragged away, the girl took a string that she had round her waist and managed to strangle herself. On seeing her dead, de Mello expressed no regret at what he had done, but only displeasure that he had been prevented from enjoying her. 'Such was this black and abominable action,' says Pinto, 'and I desire to be excused from entering into further particulars out of regard for the honour of the Portuguese nation.' But he continues: 'From the day of this abhorred act till four years later the good old man, her father, was never seen to go out of his house. But at length the better to demonstrate his grief and his deep sense of having been wronged, he covered himself with an old tattered mat and went about begging, or he would lie naked on the ground, his face in the dust.' But as long as Tabin Shwé-ti was King, he knew it was useless to complain against the favourite. After the King's assassination, however, and the seizure of Pegu by the Talaings, he decided to appeal to Smim Saw Htut. To be sure of obtaining audience, he adopted the following procedure. Going to a temple, he took an idol from the altar and, holding it in his arms, went to a square in the city. There, his white beard reaching almost to his waist and with a cord round his neck, he shouted loudly three times to attract attention. When enough people had collected, he harangued them, declaring in the name of the god in his arms that he was about to demand justice from the King against 'the accursed stranger who had wronged him, the most wicked man that was ever born in the world.' And he called on those present to accompany him.

His words whipped the crowd into a state of wild excitement, which increased as its size increased, until the square was full of a shouting multitude. Screaming for vengeance against de Mello they surged through the streets and came to the outer court of the palace. There they shouted, demanding to see the King.

Pinto in Siam and again in Burma

Alarmed by the noise and what seemed like an insurrection, Smim Saw Htut showed himself at a window, and called out to know what was the matter. He was answered with yells of 'Justice! justice!' On inquiring further he was informed that it was against de Mello that they were clamouring. 'Deliver him to us!' was the cry.

The King hesitated. 'What am I to do in so extraordinary a case?' he asked his gentlemen. They advised him to satisfy the crowd and hand over de Mello. Accordingly, he sent a sergeant of police to arrest and deliver him to the people.

When the sergeant came to de Mello's house and told him that he was wanted by the King, the shock was so great that it bereft him of speech. But collecting himself, he told the sergeant that he had a bad headache and offered him a great weight of gold if he would give him a little time. The sergeant refused and forced him to set out, holding him fast in the middle of the guard. When passing through the bazaar, they met de Mello's son, who dismounted in alarm and ran to his father. 'What has happened?' he cried. 'How is it that you are being led along like this?'

'Ask it of my sins, and they will tell you better than I can,' replied de Mello, 'for in the strait in which I stand all seems to me like a dream.' The two embraced, but the sergeant ordered the young de Mello to go. When he delayed, the guard beat him, and he fell to the ground, his head bleeding. At sight of this, his father fainted. On coming to, he asked for water, and having drunk, began to pray: 'Si iniquitates observaberis, Domine, Domine quis sustinebit?'

Presently the procession reached the square before the palace, where the vast crowd was howling for de Mello's blood. He was dreadfully afraid and knelt down, praying God that what he might suffer at their hands should be held to indemnify him against punishment in hell. 'This said, he ascended the stairs that led to the square,' says Pinto, 'and a Portuguese that assisted him told me afterwards how at every step he kissed the ground and called upon the name of Jesus.'

When the half-crazed old man, who still held the idol in his arms, beheld de Mello at last within his power, he began to shriek and to demand of the crowd that it stone him. Immediately stones were flying everywhere. Many persons were hurt by mistake, but enough hit de Mello to kill him. His corpse was torn to pieces and, in a frenzy of hatred, fragments of it were paraded in the streets. 'Such was the end of the great Diogo Saurez,' concludes Pinto, 'a King's favourite, which of all is the most absolute title.'

While Bayin Naung was gathering his forces to suppress the Talaing rebellion, the Talaings quarrelled and fought among themselves, with the result that Smim Htaw, who had started the revolt against the Burmese, got the better of Smim Saw Htut, and was crowned in his place. Pinto's sympathies were with Smim Htaw, whom he regarded as a patriot struggling against the Burmese tyranny, and as a man of much higher character than Smim Saw Htut. But Bayin Naung was a far more able general; by 1552 he was ready to strike, and utterly defeated Smim Htaw in a pitched battle north of the capital. Smim Htaw fled with a few followers, leaving open the road to Pegu. Next day Bayin Naung marched on the city.

Pinto was living in Pegu at the time, engaged apparently on some profitable trading venture. He thus found himself in an alarming situation. His sympathies had been pro-Talaing; his fighting compatriots under de Mello had gone over, as we have seen, to the Talaing side. How would Bayin Naung treat the Portuguese he found in Pegu? If his life was safe, what about his merchandise? Bayin Naung had some ferocious hill tribes in his pay along with other foreign mercenaries, men who counted on a sack. It turned out, however, that the Burmese King was averse to sacking Pegu, as he proposed to live there. He decided to pay off his mercenaries, making them a very liberal present in compensation. It was a delicate business, which the Portuguese inside the city, at his request, helped him to compose by acting as arbitrators, an interesting fact which shows their standing in Burma. This done, he made a triumphal entry into the capital, 'seated on a very mighty elephant, harnessed with gold, and followed by three thousand war-elephants with castles of divers inventions, besides a world of other people, as well as horse and foot.' This was a leading event in Burmese history, since the dynasty of Toungoo, thus established, lasted for two hundred years; another example of Pinto's remarkable knack of weaving into his narrative the most significant events.

The last scene of this Burmese drama was the execution of Smim Htaw. In reading the passage in the *Peregrination* one has to know that the Talaings were more civilized than the Burmese; that they had begun to rule in Pegu from A.D. 825 over the lower part of Burma; and that, though subject to the Burmese of the Pagān dynasty (1057-1287), they had continued after its fall to rule independently. Smim Htaw was therefore the last of a long line of sovereigns, whose Court had for seven hundred years been ahead of any other in Burma except the Pagān Court; though Pagān drew much from Talaing culture at the start. Indeed, it may be asserted that, though the Burmese conquered the Talaings, Talaing culture conquered the Burmese. Such is the background of Smim Htaw's execution, and it will be seen that in composing his elaborate picture of it, Pinto understood very well its essentials. He has given it, however, the twist which he gives to all his reconstructions, making it illustrate some of his *idées fixes*, such as the approximation of oriental to Western religious thought, the ignoble behaviour of his compatriots in Asia, and particularly his conception of the tyrant King.

Smim Htaw, after fleeing from the battle, hid himself on the Arakanese frontier. His identity leaked out and, to get a reward, a villager informed against him, and he was sent to Pegu with an iron collar about his neck. In the audience that ensued, Bayin Naung addressed him with cruel raillery: 'Welcome back to Pegu, my King! I have an honour to confer on you, greater than ever you could guess and that will prove my friendship. See this ground where I have set my foot. I give you my permission to kiss it.'

Smim Htaw, who crouched prostrate before the King, his face to the floor, made no answer nor any motion. His conqueror continued in a jeering voice: 'What is the matter with you? Has the sight of me and the honour I have done you been so overwhelming that you have nothing to say?'

Like an actor in high tragedy, the fallen lord replied: 'For me to speak would be useless. Only the elements, using storm and thunder for words, could express the horror of my predicament.' There was so much to say, so little chance of moving the tyrant's heart.

Bayin Naung now called in Smim Htaw's daughter, who was his prisoner, to look at her father in his humiliation. 'You may give him a cup of water,' he said with false pity. She was a favourite daughter and had been betrothed to one of the Shan princes, but her future had ended with the Talaing defeat. Life now held nothing for her. Embracing her father, she cried: 'We have loved each other. Take me with you. In your sad passage you will need a daughter to comfort and look after you.'

Smim Htaw was oppressed with anguish at the thought of the misfortune in which he had involved her; he tried to speak, but could not utter a word. His pain was so great that he seemed to lose consciousness. At the sight of him crouching inertly there, some Talaing lords who were present wept.

It is always a dangerous thing to show sympathy for a tyrant's victim, for nothing irritates him more than tears. Pinto describes Bayin Naung as falling into a homicidal rage, and handing over the lords and the Princess to his executioners. 'Then no longer enduring the sight of the Xemindoo,[1] he commanded him to be taken to a close prison, where he passed the night following under heavy guard.'

Though Pinto is building up the picture of an oriental despot, he evidently thought Bayin Naung was less of a monster than Tabin Shwé-ti. He explains that the King had grounds of policy for his resolve to put Smim Htaw to death. As long as the rebel was alive, he would be a rallying-point for the Talaings, who had been defeated with such difficulty. His execution was inevitable.

The morning after his audience with Bayin Naung the ex-

[1]This is Pinto's rendering of Smim Htaw.

King was taken in procession from the prison. The citizens of Pegu had been ordered by proclamation to assemble and were there in great numbers. It was a long cortège, with tapestried elephants and arquebusiers marching with their matches lighted. Heralds proclaimed the crimes of Smim Htaw; he was a rebel and must die. 'Yes, let him die without pity,' was chanted in response by another group of criers. There followed a guard of horse and foot 'and in the midst of these came the poor patient, mounted on a lean ill-favoured jade, and the executioner on the crupper behind him, holding him up under both the arms.' He was in rags, his skin showing through the rents, and wore a crown of straw,[1] decorated with mussel-shells fastened together with blue thread; onions were tied to his iron collar. But though he was reduced to so deplorable a state and his face through suffering was hardly human, nevertheless, says Pinto, 'he had something of I know not what in his eyes, which manifested the condition of a king. There was beside observed in him a majestical sweetness, which drew tears from all that beheld him.'

For a king to be dragged in such guise through his own capital city was the height of disaster, yet the contrast to his former glory was made even more evident when the procession reached the main thoroughfare from which so recently he had marched out at the head of his war-elephants against Bayin Naung, an occasion of splendid pride, 'one of the most marvellous sights that has ever been seen in the world,' says Pinto, 'in the opinion of those that saw it, of which number I was one.'

In this street the Portuguese merchants were assembled in a body under their leader, Captain Pacheco. One of them, a man of low birth and of lower mind, says Pinto, having a grudge against Smim Htaw because he had once refused him audience, now called out: 'You refused me justice when I appealed, and now justice is being done to you. To-night I will have supper on a bit of your flesh and will invite my two dogs to share it.'

[1]Pinto says the crown was like the wicker case used for carrying a chamber-pot at that date in Portugal. If so, the resemblance cannot have been intentional, for the implication would have had no meaning for a Burmese crowd.

Pinto in Siam and again in Burma

This abominable pleasantry made some of the Portuguese laugh, but it shocked Captain Pacheco, who told the man to shut up.

Smim Htaw was visibly pleased by this consideration and, since he could not reward Captain Pacheco, having not the smallest token to give him, said what the Captain appreciated more than any gift: 'Would to God I had an hour longer of life to profess the excellency of the faith wherein you Portuguese live; for, as I have heard said, your God alone is true.'

It may be thought that this remark lacks verisimilitude, and is not only an invention but a clumsy one. Yet one cannot be sure. It could have been uttered as an exquisite politeness. It could even have been true, for the Christian faith had admirers throughout the orient. At the moment of execution a man is moved to cling to any hope. To pay the Christian God a compliment could do no harm, and was in the nature of an insurance. Nevertheless, it would be rash to accept the statement, and it may amount only to Pinto's indirect way of saying that a good man of another religion was very close to being a Christian. What follows supports this. On hearing Smim Htaw's remark, the executioner hit him in the face and made his nose bleed. But the fallen King, as if he were a Christian saint, remonstrated gently with the executioner and called him brother.

Pinto does not dwell on Smim Htaw's death. He writes: 'So passing on in the same order as before, he finally arrived at the place where he was to be executed, with so little life that he scarcely thought of anything.' He mounted the scaffold, a judicial officer read out his sentence, and with one blow the executioner struck off his head. But a curious sequel is described at length. Three hours after the execution a bell was sounded and a number of robed figures, some of them monks, appeared on the scaffold, where the body still lay, covered with a yellow cloth. Silence was imposed on the crowd, and Bayin Naung's uncle, a very old man, addressed the spirit of the dead King, asking pardon on behalf of his nephew for what had been done. His Majesty, he said, returns to you the kingdom of Pegu and agrees to hold it for you as your lieutenant; he will pay you homage and obey your commands.

One of the monks who was present replied on behalf of the spirit: 'I forgive you, and accept you as my lieutenant.'

After this ceremony the body was burnt on a pyre of scented woods, the full ritual of a royal cremation being used.

That Bayin Naung acted in this way is not recorded in any other history. But there are reasons which make it improbable that Pinto invented the scene. When the King's uncle was addressing the spirit, he declared that the monks, that is the Talaing monks, would not accept Bayin Naung as ruler of the Talaing country unless their late King's spirit approved. This provides a clue to the meaning. Bayin Naung was anxious to win over the Talaings and lessen the danger of future rebellions. Their monks were very influential and, if the fiction that he held from Smim Htaw satisfied them, the people would become his loyal supporters. That he arranged a ceremonial abdication in favour of the man whom he had executed may sound paradoxical, but in fact it was the act of a statesman.

The Talaings never lost their individuality as a race. They had been civilized long before the Burmese, for they were a branch of the Mon race, whose ancestors were Indian colonists and in the fifth century A.D. founded the Mon empire, which stretched from southern Burma into Siam. Their language had no connection with Burmese. After the extinction of their royal house by Bayin Naung, they remained tolerably quiet under his successors, until in the seventeen-forties, when the Toungoo dynasty was tottering, they made another bid for independence, again setting up a man called Smim Htaw as King. But the Burmese Alaungpaya dynasty, which lasted until 1885 when the British took its capital, Mandalay, reduced them as before to the position of subjects. In my time in Burma they were hardly to be distinguished from the Burmese, though they had, like our Welsh, preserved their own language. At the date of writing (1948), when Burma is showing signs of disintegrating again into racial units, the Talaings are once more raising their heads and are reported to have joined the

Karens in turning part of the old Talaing country, Thaton and Martaban, into a separate state.

This concludes what Pinto has to say about Burma. That he should have been able to grasp its politics so well, describe in his objective manner, as in a drama, its unification under Tabin Shwé-ti and Bayin Naung, and lay bare so clearly the Talaing question, the most abiding in Burmese history, is truly extraordinary when one remembers that at the time he composed the *Peregrination* nothing had been published about the country in a European language.

CHAPTER TWENTY-NINE

Pinto's second visit to Japan

The siege of Ayuthia and Bayin Naung's triumph over the Talaings have carried us ahead to the year 1552, and we must now return, as I said we would have to do, to 1546, the year that Pinto was in Siam. Between those dates he made two more journeys to Japan. They resulted in bringing him into contact with the man who was to change his life, the great Francis Xavier, the Heavenly Pilgrim.

Xavier, a Basque nobleman, was born in Navarre in 1506, and was therefore three years older than Pinto. In 1540 he assisted Ignatius Loyola to found the Society of Jesus, and in 1542 arrived in Goa as Papal Nuncio with a mission to convert the orient to Christianity. In my *The Land of the Great Image* I have described the startling impression that he made on landing by his refusal to take a palanquin to the Archbishop's palace and by going instead barefoot to the hospital, where he immediately began to wash the sores of the lepers. After a short stay in Goa he set out on his missionary travels, addressing his message particularly to the lowest classes. He went to southern India, to Malacca and the Moluccas, dressed in rags and covered with lice, but always essentially a Spanish nobleman. He had blue-grey eyes and a fair beard, and was apparently not more than five feet high. 'In his fiery passage he converted thousands, wearing himself away by his fasts and his vigils. Under the tropic sun or in the monsoon rain he would walk without umbrella or hat, at night sleeping on the bare ground of a hut, and that for not more than three hours. The enthusiasm which he aroused, the curious psychic reactions which accompanied his appearance, his fanatical single-minded-

ness, the absolute genuineness of his emotion, have been the subject of innumerable biographies, which establish beyond question
that he was that rare, uncompromising, terrific phenomenon, a
mystic and a saint.'[1] This was the personality whom Pinto was to
meet, Pinto with his conscience and his load of sin.

After his journeys in India and the Islands, Xavier began to
think of visiting Japan. As will now be told, Pinto was indirectly
instrumental in furthering that object. After he had laid out his
small capital on Siamese commodities, he returned to Malacca
and embarked for Japan in the aforesaid year of 1546 on a ship
commanded by a certain Jorge Alvarez. As on his first voyage, he
went to Bungo. But a feudal war broke out,[2] and since business
was interrupted Alvarez decided to go to Yamagawa, a port in
the gulf of Kagoshima, one hundred miles south of Bungo. There
they sold their goods at a large profit and waited for a favourable
wind to set sail. The day came, and they weighed anchor and were
standing out, when they saw two Japanese horsemen waving to
them from the shore. As some servants had recently deserted, it
was thought that perhaps the horsemen had news of them. Pinto
took a boat back to the wharf and asked them what they wanted.

One of them replied: 'Sir, I am a fugitive and my pursuers are
close behind. I beg you to save me by taking me off to your ship.'
The other appeared to be his servant.

Pinto says he was much embarrassed by the request and hesitated
to comply. Nevertheless, on recalling that he had seen the man
once or twice in Yamagawa in the company of some merchants,
he let him and his companion into the boat. They had hardly
pushed off when a body of mounted soldiers galloped up to the
wharf, shouting: 'Surrender these traitors or you are dead men!'

---

[1] My *The Land of the Great Image*, p. 37. He was also remarkable for his common sense, as was that other great mystic, St. Theresa, for hers.

[2] Pinto describes the fighting, typical of the period before Hideyoshi seized
the supreme power as Regent (Kwamboka) and suppressed the wars between
the Daimyos or feudal Dukes. It has been proved, however, by Haas in his
Geschichte des Christentums in Japan (1902) that this particular war did not take
place till four years later, an example of Pinto's proclivity to sacrifice historical
accuracy to literary convenience.

Pinto's second visit to Japan

Opining that it was safer to go on than to go back, Pinto urged the sailors to row hard and soon was out of cross-bow range. The men on shore continued to shout and threaten, but they could do nothing and the boat reached the ship in safety. Jorge Alvarez agreed to give the Japanese and his servant a passage. His name was Yajiro, and he it was who, baptized under the name of Paul of the Holy Faith, accompanied Xavier to Japan five years later, acting as his interpreter and assistant. Afterwards, when left in sole charge of a mission centre, his ardour cooled and he abandoned his post, sailing as pirate to the Chinese coast, where he was killed in a sea-fight. It seems probable that he had been a samurai and, after cutting down a man on a point of honour, had become a ronin, or masterless swordsman. His pursuers may have been, not officers of justice, but avengers. By turning pirate, he reverted to the sort of lawless existence to which he had been accustomed. Because of his romantic story and his close association with the most celebrated figure in the whole East, Paul of the Holy Faith was a man everyone had heard of at that time. We know Pinto's knack of weaving whatever was significant or sensational into his personal adventures. It is possible to check his story here, because a letter is extant written by Paul on 29 November 1548 to Loyola and other Fathers of the Society of Jesus, in which he describes his escape from Japan. There is no mention of Pinto in it, and some of the details are different, but it agrees with the *Peregrination* on the main points, that Paul was a fugitive and left on Jorge Alvarez's ship. The letter is not conclusive that the escape did not take the form it has in the *Peregrination*, though we must allow that Pinto wrote up the story, making it more dramatic and exciting, as throughout is his invariable practice.

Pinto's critics, however, catch him out in an inexactitude shortly afterwards, which causes them to view his version of Paul's escape with increased severity. He says that on the arrival of the ship at Malacca at the beginning of 1547, he and Jorge Alvarez took Paul to see Xavier, for the Japanese had shown signs during the voyage of interest in Christianity and they thought that he might prove useful to the Father in connection with his

231

projected journey to Japan. Xavier received him with pleasure, and sent him to the Jesuit house at Goa to be instructed in the faith. But Xavier's own correspondence makes it clear that he was not in Malacca at the time but on a visit to the Moluccas, and that he was not introduced to Paul until the latter part of 1547, after his return, a statement which is supported by Paul's own letter. The introduction is said to have been made by Jorge Alvarez alone, but as Pinto was in Malacca at the time, he may have been present. Paul did go to Goa, where he arrived in March 1548. Pinto has therefore antedated the interview by some nine months, which may either have been due to a lapse of memory or because he thought to make his story the clearer. The case is interesting as showing the sort of careful check which commentators have made on the *Peregrination* text and the freedom which its author used in presenting his narrative.

When all is said, the fact remains that Pinto, through having been on the same ship as Paul on his flight from Japan, began to get to know Xavier in 1547 and became his fervent admirer. He gives us a glimpse of him at this time, showing how he dominated the situation when the King of Achin raided Malacca in October 1547, an attack long anticipated, as we know. The Captain of Malacca at this time was Simão de Mello, to be distinguished from Diogo Saurez de Mello, the Burma free-lance. There had been two Captains since the death of Ruy Vaz Pereira in 1544, namely Simão Botelho and Garcia de Sá, and when Simão de Mello took over charge in November 1545 he found the fortress in a bad state. Writing to the King of Portugal, he says: 'I came to this fortress of Malacca and found it as any place must be which has had four Captains in three years, an arrangement very injurious to the service.' And he goes on to complain that travel permits had been indiscriminately issued to unsuitable persons, with the result that two hundred Portuguese were roaming about the East 'without fear of God or Your Majesty,' an interesting comment on the pirates, buccaneers, mercenaries and adventurers, of whom the pages of the *Peregrination* are so full. Though no doubt their conduct was an embarrassment to the Empire, as giving the Portuguese a bad name, Simão de Mello's chief objection was that since they and their ships never came near Malacca, he had at his disposal far less men for defence than he might be supposed to have.

The King of Achin, no doubt aware of Malacca's weakness, timed his raid accordingly. He sent a fleet of seventy galleys of various sizes with five thousand fighting men on board. They arrived at 2 a.m. on a dark and rainy night and began operations by setting fire to seven large ships in the port. The flames and the shouting of the Achins roused the garrison, but the surprise was complete and all was confusion at first. The Achins, however, did not attack the fortress. When dawn came their fleet was seen lying close in, and Simão de Mello was able to reach them with his artillery. They withdrew out of range and continued all day shouting and threatening from their decks. A fishing boat containing seven Malays from the town was captured by them, and the seven, after having their ears and noses cut off, were sent to Simão de Mello with an insulting letter, in which the Achin commander declared his intention to cruise in the Straits and seize what shipping he liked, and defied the Portuguese to interfere with him. 'The seven poor wretches,' says Pinto, 'having arrived at the town, were immediately taken into the fortress, covered with blood and disfigured as they were.'

After the letter had been read out to Simão de Mello, who was sitting at the fortress gate with his officers, Francis Xavier happened to pass by on his return from mass at Our Lady of the Mount. The Captain rose to greet him and told him of the letter. 'How would you advise me to answer such a challenge?' he asked.

'By an attack,' replied Xavier.

'I agree,' said the Captain, 'but at the moment we have only seven galleys and they are unfit to put to sea.'

'If refitting is all that is needed,' declared Xavier, 'put me in charge of it. And I volunteer to go out in the galleys when they are ready and fight against the cursed enemies of the Cross.'

These words were received with enthusiasm, and the Captain, taking Xavier by the hand, went down to the water to inspect the galleys. The master shipwright was called, but he complained that the storeroom was empty; there was hardly a nail to be had in the place. But Xavier was not to be put off. He made an impassioned speech to the officers who were present, declaring that it was their duty as Christians to sally out against the Mohammedan Achins, and that the galleys should immediately be made sea-worthy. As he spoke, he raised his eyes to Heaven, says Pinto, and his face was suffused with joy, a description of his mien which accords well with others on record. In result, seven hundred men set to work with frantic zeal to recaulk and rig the seven galleys. Meanwhile, the Achins sailed to plunder the coast and its shipping, as they had boasted in their letter.

In five days the galleys were refitted. There were only a hundred and twenty fighting Portuguese available, but these had been so animated by Xavier's speeches that they were ready to face the thousands of Achin. Unfortunately, as the galleys set sail to discover and attack the enemy, one of them immediately sank. This had a depressing effect on the spirit of the crews. They refused to proceed, declaring that they were being sacrificed in what was a foolhardy attempt. Almost a mutiny broke out, and Simão de Mello, in a panic, sent a messenger to call Xavier, who was found in the Church officiating at the mass. As the messenger entered, he had reached the words 'Domine, non sum dignus' and held the Wafer in his hands. The messenger hesitated to interrupt him, but, reflecting on the urgency of the occasion, approached the altar and opened his mouth to speak, when Xavier made him a sign to keep silence and reverently finished the service. Leaving the altar, he told the messenger to inform the Captain that he would be coming shortly and meanwhile not to be anxious, because when need was greatest the Lord was sure to be near with help. This said, he went into the sacristy to change his clothes, and was heard there to utter a prayer for divine aid.

Rising from his knees, he went to the fortress. The Captain asked him to quiet the mutineers. They were stubbornly resolved not to set sail again, and alleged that the sinking of the galley was a warning from God that they were attempting what was be-

yond their power. But Xavier had that to say which immediately calmed them. 'Put your trust in God,' he said, with a
grave and happy expression on his face. 'You have lost one
galley, but He will send you two.' And he assured them that the
two galleys would arrive that same day.

His hearers were profoundly impressed, except for a few who
laughed and gibed at him. Things being quieter, Simão de Mello
went for his dinner and Xavier paid a visit to the hospital, where,
as his practice was, he bathed the sores of the patients. When the
sun began to decline, eyes were constantly turned to the horizon
and one hour before sunset news was brought from watchers on
the top of Our Lady's Mount that two ships had been sighted.
A fast sailing boat was immediately sent out to investigate. The
reader will never guess who was in command of the ships. It was
no less a person than Diogo Saurez de Mello, the General of
Tabin Shwé-ti's mercenaries, whose death five years later has
been described further back. Apparently he had been on a trading
venture with his son Balthazar and was now returning to Burma
to join the expedition against Ayuthia.

There was great joy at the news, and the Captain hurried to
thank Xavier for his wonderful prediction. But Xavier pointed
out that it was necessary to stop Diogo Saurez, who probably had
no intention of putting into Malacca. 'I will go out and speak to
him myself,' he cried, 'if you will place a boat at my disposal.'

This was immediately done, and he set out. Diogo Saurez gave
him a great welcome. To be boarded on the high seas by so
saintly a personage was an excitement that he much appreciated.
'What can I do to serve Your Reverence?' he asked.

'I adjure you by the Five Wounds to join forces with us against
the infidels of Ach'in,' replied Xavier.

'My intention,' said Diogo Saurez, 'was not to put into Malacca, so as to avoid customs duties, but since Your Reverence
asks my help in so holy a cause, I am willing to give it, provided
that you will procure me a certificate signed by the Captain and
customs officers that they will exempt me from all dues.'

This may sound an over-businesslike reply to make to a saint who adjures you fervently to go on a crusade, but anyone who has had experience of customs rules and regulations will know that Diogo Saurez was only taking a reasonable precaution. Xavier did not rebuke him; on the contrary he immediately went back and asked for the certificate. It was sent out the following morning, and on its receipt Diogo Saurez swept into port, flying all his banners and firing salutes. In this way two heavily armed galleys, with sixty Portuguese and other soldiers on board, were added to the fleet of Malacca.

The malcontents were now fully satisfied that God wished them to seek out the Achin fleet, and professed themselves ready to embark. Dom Francisco de Sá was appointed Admiral of the fleet, with Diogo Saurez second-in-command. Before the departure Xavier addressed the Portuguese fighting men. He said: 'Always have Christ crucified in the depths of your hearts, and show in your bearing content and happiness with true valour, so that even the most cowardly of the galley-slaves may be encouraged by your example.'

Pinto proceeds to narrate first the cruise of the fleet and then what happened at Malacca during its absence. It seems that, since he remained at Malacca, he was an eye-witness of the events which took place there, but his narrative of the expedition is written in the same detailed and direct manner, and as if he had been on it, an indication of his powers as a writer and also a warning that any of his vivid stories throughout the *Peregrination* may be second-hand.

The fleet sailed up the Malay coast looking for the Achins. After passing the Sembilan isles by Perak, it anchored off the Perlis river in Kedah, the place where Pinto had had nine years before the greatest fright of his life. Dom Francisco de Sá learnt that the enemy was in the vicinity. The Sultan of Kedah had been driven out of his state, which the Achins had plundered. Their plan was to lie in ambush up the River Perlis and wait for merchantmen sailing past on their way from Bengal to Malacca.

When the Achins heard, as they shortly did, that eight Portuguese war-galleys were at the mouth of the Perlis, they decided to attack. Dom Francisco had his spies out and was warned in time. Pinto shows him to us, a gallant courteous figure, in a waist-coat of mail made of iron leaves, a red satin coat covered with gilt nails, and with a sword in his hand, going from ship to ship, animating the soldiers, smiling at his Captains, calling them brothers, and reminding all that Father Francis was praying for them that moment in Malacca.

The Achin attack, down-river and with the ebb, was a frighten-ing spectacle. They came rowing on with loud cries, beating their drums in time with the stroke, discharging their arquebuses and the cannon on their prows. Dom Francisco had taken up a posi-tion in slack water with one flank protected by a promontory and with the land close behind him. This saved him from being sur-rounded by the enemy's greater numbers. His gunnery was far better than theirs, and when the whole Achin fleet was in front of him, in some disarray owing to the swiftness of the current, he swept it again and again with a grape composed of hard pebbles. Having sunk a good many vessels in this way, he advanced, fling-ing fireballs in some ships and boarding others, while his arque-busiers kept up an accurate fire. The battle was not of long dura-tion. In half an hour the Achins were utterly defeated.

Meanwhile in Malacca there was growing anxiety, as the fleet's absence lengthened into a second month. Xavier's habit was to preach twice a week, on Friday at the small Church of the Miseri-cordia and on Sunday at Our Lady of the Mount. After his ser-mon he would ask the congregation to say a Pater Noster and an Ave Maria, as a way of praying for the success of the expedition. When the fleet had been away three weeks and no news was re-ceived, a rumour began to go round that it had been defeated. One of the Sumatran Kings heard this and crossed the Straits with a number of ships, his intention being, if the rumour were true, to lay siege to Malacca. He sent the Captain a crafty letter, in which he offered his services and suggested that he should be invited into the port. All this had so depressing an effect that one day when the Reverend Father asked the congregation as usual to repeat the two prayers, some murmured that it was no longer any use.

Others even blamed him openly, saying that he had sent the soldiers to their death, for which he and the Captain would have to account to God.

Then one Sunday as Xavier ended his sermon, he turned towards a crucifix which was beside the main altar and, with tears of emotion streaming from his eyes, began to speak of a battle, as if it was in progress, and begged God to protect his own. And, addressing himself to Jesus, he cried: 'Love of my soul, we supplicate you not to abandon us!' He seemed exhausted by the intensity of his prayer, resting his head on the edge of the pulpit, and remained so without speaking for the space of a Credo. Then suddenly he rose to his feet, his face lit up with happiness, and turning to the congregation, said in a high voice: 'Gentlemen, say a Pater Noster and an Ave Maria in thanks for the great victory which Our Lord has granted us against the enemies of the faith.' He seemed so inspired that all present were convinced that, indeed, a victory had been won, and overcome by relief and thankfulness, they broke down and wept. Six days later a fast sailing boat arrived from the Perlis river with the great news of the Achin defeat. When they compared the time it was found that the victory took place exactly at the moment when the vision of it came to Xavier in the pulpit.

With anecdotes such as this (which may well be true, for Xavier, from all we know, had psychic powers of the kind), Pinto builds up his picture of the man whom he admired so fervently.

CHAPTER THIRTY

Pinto's third visit to Japan and meeting there with Francis Xavier

The whole of 1548 went by and it was not until the middle of 1549 that Xavier, whom the Japanese, Paul, had now rejoined, was able to sail for Japan. Garcia de Sá, who had succeeded Dom João de Castro in the viceroyalty in 1548, sent orders to Pero da Silva da Gama, Simão de Mello's successor as Captain of Malacca, to provide the Father with a ship. But the only one to be had was a small junk belonging to a Chinese pirate. On this vessel the Heavenly Pilgrim embarked, and in the pirate's company set out to bring the blessings of Christianity to Japan. In spite of various mishaps which threatened to lengthen it, the voyage was unusually quick, for they reached Japan on 15 August 1549, seven weeks after they had weighed from Malacca. The place of landing was Kagoshima, the capital of the daimyo-ship of Satsuma, from which Paul had fled in 1546.

Besides Paul, Xavier had with him Father Cosmo de Torres and Brother Juan Fernandez, the first an ex-soldier and the second a one-time Spanish merchant, who had heard the call and given up his wealth. Pinto, in the course of his business, was to follow in 1551 and meet Xavier in Japan. What he precisely did between the end of 1547, after the Achin raid, and 1551 is not known for sure. The commentators make their guesses, but neither the *Peregrination* nor any other document gives definite information. It is probable that during these years his trading ventures were profitable and that by 1551 he was well off.

We must now take a glance at Xavier's experiences in Japan before the arrival there of Pinto.

Pinto's third visit and meeting with Francis Xavier

During the seven years of his mission in India and the Islands, Xavier had come to realize that it would take a very long time to evangelize the orient if one worked from the bottom upwards. Not only was it a physical impossibility to baptize more than a tiny fraction of the vast agrarian populations, but poor and ignorant people tended to lapse the moment your back was turned. The only practical method was to win over the rulers. By converting them, everyone was converted, for they would declare Christianity to be the religion of their states and see to it that their subjects worshipped accordingly. He planned, therefore, to address himself particularly to the rulers of Japan, whoever they might turn out to be. A mission to Japan had particular attractions for him, partly because the country had only very recently become known to the West, but more especially because the Japanese were reputed to be on a higher level of civilization than the Indians and the Malays among whom he had been working.

To-day we are painfully aware that this great man of heart was only deluding himself. For a hundred reasons he was no more likely to convert the state of Japan to Catholicism than would one of their ecclesiastics, arriving in Rome with an Italian for his assistant who was a renegade and a murderer, have been able to induce the Pope to abolish the Church and adopt Buddhism. It is a literal fact that the one was no more probable than the other. The most he could hope to do was to convert a few individuals, and he could not have done that if the Church of Japan had been as intolerant as the Church of Rome.

On arrival at Kagoshima on 15 August he was received in audience by the Daimyo, whose name was Shimazu Takahisa. The Daimyos at this period were, as has been said, sovereigns in fact, though in theory they were vassals of the Shogun. The word Shogun means Commander-in-Chief. The Shogun held from the Emperor, who appointed him, and his position was that of head of the administration. But this again was only theory, for the Shogun in practice was dictator. At the moment when Xavier arrived, however, the Shogunate, known as the Ashikaga, was in decline. The Shogun, a nobleman called Yashiteru, was only fifteen and, far from being a dictator and the chief of the military aristocracy, had no influence whatever over the Daimyos. Thus there were two fainéants, the Emperor at Kyoto, an old man so poor that he lived in a cottage with a bamboo fence, deserted by the hereditary Court nobles and without duties except to conduct state rituals, and the Shogun, a minor and the mere figurehead of the Daimyos, who ruled their fiefs without reference to him. As there was no effective central authority, they waged war against each other. There was always a war going on somewhere; the country was impoverished and the people famished. Such was the confusing situation into which Xavier plunged; so little did he understand it that he could not have stated the difference between the Emperor and the Shogun.

The Daimyo of Satsuma was affable to Xavier at first and gave him leave to preach freely in Kagoshima. Like most orientals, except Mohammedans, he saw no harm in a travelling holy man expounding fresh doctrines. Moreover, he had practical reasons for encouraging Xavier; very few Portuguese merchants came to Kagoshima, and he thought the presence there of a well-known priest might attract them. If he could make Kagoshima as popular as Bungo or as Hirado on the north coast, a lot of money would come his way. But the Buddhist monks saw Xavier in another light. When his preaching became annoying, as it did when he attacked them, they appealed to the Daimyo to send him away. The Daimyo refused, but tension grew so great that in September 1550 Xavier left Kagoshima and moved to Hirado. Paul stayed behind to look after the converts, and it was at this time that he turned pirate, being heartily sick of the odium in which he was held by some of the monks.

Xavier, though well received at Hirado by the local Daimyo, did not stay there. He had become convinced that if he could meet the Emperor his mission would be facilitated. He conceived of the Emperor as a sort of Pope. There was some substance for this view, for, as we have seen, the only functions that the fainéant ruler exercised were sacerdotal. But Xavier's deduction that he was head of the Buddhist Church, and so could control the monks, was totally erroneous. The Emperor's ritual functions were Shintoist; he had no official connection with Buddhism. Indeed, the monks at this time were completely out of hand, lived in castles, bore arms, kept concubines, waged war, being more like feudal lords than churchmen.

Quite uninformed on these paradoxes of the Japanese scene, Xavier set out for Kyoto, the imperial capital, which lay on the main central island at a distance of four hundred miles from Hirado. He left Cosmo de Torres behind and took with him Juan Fernandez. After crossing the strait to the main island they proceeded on foot. It was winter; snow lay thick and the winds were icy. The road was over very rough country, the inns were miserable and the fare provided scanty in the extreme, as owing to the civil wars there was famine in places. On occasions the innkeepers refused them shelter, and the people, horrified by their strange appearance, hooted at them and flung stones. To these rigours a further obstacle was added; on passing from one jurisdiction to another there were toll-gates and, since Xavier had no money, for it was his practice to carry none, he was refused permission to pass. To overcome this difficulty, he was obliged to engage himself to a travelling lord as a footman. And this entailed, says Pinto, that he had to run behind his master's horse. In this exhausting manner he and his companion, the ex-merchant, covered the immense journey to Kyoto.

He was sadly disappointed by what he found there. The city was much damaged.[1] A few years before it had been attacked by the neighbouring monks of Mount Hiei, who had sacked and burnt most of the principal houses. The Court nobility had been obliged to move out and find what quarters they could in the villages. The wretched old Emperor was living in a thatched cottage because he could not afford to rebuild the palace. His chief source of income was the sale of titles, for which, however, he got very little. He could also sell his autograph and specimens of

[1] It had a population, however, of over half a million and was therefore much larger than any European city of that date.

his calligraphy. In short, he made what he could and, of course, charged for an audience. When Xavier applied to see this strange personage he was asked to pay a very stiff fee. This he could not do, as he had no money.

Mortified and sick at heart he left Kyoto and walked back along the road by which he had come. Some months later he settled at Yamaguchi, a town on the main island not far from the strait between it and the western island, Kiu-shiu. He preached there during the spring and summer of 1551, much assisted by Juan Fernandez, who now spoke Japanese fluently. But his converts were not many and there was again friction with the monks. When in September of that year he heard that a Portuguese ship had arrived at Funai, the capital of Bungo, he decided to ask for a passage on her and return to Malacca. He had been away two years; there were matters to which he had to attend in Goa; and the prospects in Japan were not encouraging. Moreover, the project of entering China to evangelize that vast continent had begun to occupy his thoughts; if China were Christianized, Japan would follow. Accordingly, he wrote to the Captain of the ship, Duarte da Gama, expressing his wish for a passage. Da Gama sent back answer that he would be honoured and delighted to take him. On receipt of this reply, Xavier left Yamaguchi, crossed over to Kiu-shiu island and set out to walk down its east coast to Bungo.

Pinto was one of the merchants on da Gama's ship, and he describes the arrival of Xavier. One day in September 1551 three Christian Japanese arrived in Funai, and informed da Gama that Xavier had sent them on to say that he was at a village six miles away, but was ill and would have to rest there until he was better. On being questioned, they explained that his head was paining him and his feet were badly swollen from the long march of over a hundred and fifty miles. If a horse were sent to fetch him, he would probably accept it, they added. Da Gama immediately had the merchants informed. It was decided to go to the village, and a party of merchants, among whom was Pinto, started on horseback. They had hardly gone a mile before they saw the Blessed

Pinto's third visit and meeting with Francis Xavier

Father, as Pinto often calls him, coming towards them on the road, accompanied by two Japanese noblemen, whom he had recently converted. The sight disconcerted them, for he was limping along, looking tired and ill, and carrying a bundle of books and vessels for the mass, while they were well mounted and in their best clothes. Getting off their horses, they hastened to him, hat in hand, and, after profound salutations and kneeling for his blessing, begged him to make use of a led horse they had brought. But he refused to ride, though his feet were bleeding, and insisted on walking on to Funai. This obliged them to walk with him, though he told them to remount their horses.

When they reached the roadstead where their ship was anchored, a salute was fired from all the cannon aboard, a noise so loud that the Daimyo[1] sent to inquire what had happened, fearing that a pirate had put into the river. On learning that it was not a pirate but a celebrated Catholic priest who had arrived, he invited Xavier to call at the palace.

Xavier's grand reception by his compatriots astonished the Japanese because he seemed such a pauper with his rags and lice. As their own monks were mostly aristocrats and were neither poor nor badly dressed, they were not accustomed to the holy man who is an ascetic, so common in India and not unknown further east. To astonish them the more and demonstrate yet further the vast respect in which Xavier was held, the Portuguese resolved next day to conduct him in procession to the palace. Though he himself did not care for ceremony, he yielded to persuasion. Five merchants attended him, walking behind as if they were his servants. One held over him a parasol, another carried a book in a white satin bag, another a pair of black velvet slippers which somebody happened to have in his trunk, the fourth a Bengal cane chased with gold, and the fifth an image of the Blessed Virgin wrapped in a shawl of violet damask. Captain da Gama was also in attendance, holding a baton in his hand as if he

[1]This was Otomo Yoshishige, son of the Daimyo whose other son was hurt by the bursting arquebus.

244

were Xavier's steward.[1] As for the Blessed Father himself, it seems that he decided to wear his canonicals, for he had on a surplice over his black soutane and a stole of green velvet with a brocaded border. In this way he was escorted through the streets to the palace, and crowds looked on respectfully to see him pass.

So far Pinto has been giving a lively impression of what he actually saw. But now follows a more artificial passage, which purports to record the conversation which Xavier had with the Daimyo and an important abbot who was present. No doubt Pinto felt that his readers would like a peep inside a Japanese palace and want to hear how the Saint got the better of a Buddhist ecclesiastic. That Xavier was politely received by the Daimyo is certain; that he entered into an altercation with a courtier-monk is highly probable; he had already fallen foul of the monks of Kagoshima, Hirado and Yamaguchi. The little drama that Pinto weaves round these two facts is not, however, a transcript from life, but is composed of everything that he knew about the Daimyo, his palace, the ways of Japanese monks, and the doctrines of Buddhism, and so arranged as to present the Jesuit Father in a triumphant light. But Pinto, though he knew something of Buddhism, certainly far more than was generally known in Europe at that time, did not know enough to put the Buddhist case *vis-à-vis* Catholicism with any cogency.[2] The result is shallow and naïve, and would not interest the modern reader. Nevertheless, trite and tiresome though it is, it may represent well enough the sort of arguments which Xavier had with Japanese monks. Their wrangles must always have been inconclusive, since the one side can never have properly understood the full bearing of what the other alleged.

[1] It was usual in the orient for a person of importance to be attended when he went out by a troupe of servants carrying the sort of things which he might want at any moment. Xavier's escort was this custom adapted to the circumstances.

[2] The Buddhism of Japan was the Mahayana, which by then was represented by numerous sects holding quite different doctrines, some of which resembled those of Christianity. The difficulty of describing a clear-cut argument between the two religions is evident. Which sect was involved would first have had to be stated and its doctrines defined.

Pinto's third visit and meeting with Francis Xavier

When these disputations were ended Xavier embarked on da Gama's ship and set sail for Malacca.[1] During this voyage there occurred what is known as the miracle of the sloop. It is one of the most famous of Xavier's miracles and is to be found described not only in the *Peregrination* but, among other records, in the *Monumenta Xaveriana*, a collection of documents relating to Xavier, where it takes the form of a recorded statement by Captain Duarte da Gama himself. Pinto's account agrees in the main with the others. For him it was a further, and most convincing, demonstration of the Blessed Father's saintliness, whose clairvoyance in the matter of the Achin battle had already moved him to profound admiration. It brought him nearer his conversion, for the day was coming, and was not far distant, when, looking at the dead body of the Saint, he was to be carried away, and leave all, and devote himself to God.[2]

The sloop miracle is related in the *Peregrination* as follows. When the ship was in the midst of the Tung Hai or Eastern Sea, that part of the Pacific Ocean which lies between the Lu-chu Islands and the coast of China, a storm from the south blew up on the first day of the waxing of the moon. It rapidly grew worse and was accompanied by squalls of rain. They ran before it, and on the second day, the ship becoming unmanageable, they cut away a good deal of the poop-castle. It was arduous work, with the ship rolling violently, and they all helped, including Xavier. Not only did he share the labour of the common sailors, but he encouraged all and gave them heart. The ship towed a sloop, or lifeboat as

[1] On board was a Japanese envoy to the Viceroy of Goa, for the Daimyo wished to make a trade agreement with the Portuguese Government of the Indies. Trade meant a fortune, and to secure it the Daimyo of Bungo was ready, if necessary, to give Christianity every encouragement in spite of the danger of estranging the powerful Buddhist priesthood. This Daimyo eventually made enough money from Portuguese trade to pay for several campaigns against the other Daimyos of the western island, and brought half of them under his sway.

[2] Before leaving Japan, Pinto had lent Xavier money to pay for a Jesuit House and Church to be built at Bungo. This shows the close relationship that existed between them. For this point, see Pinto's letter written in 1554 to the Jesuits.

we should say, and this had to be secured as well as might be. To effect this, a crew had been put in it and, while they were at work, a sea of more than usual force snapped the cable. The ship drove on and in a moment the sloop was far behind. The Captain tried to put the ship about, but during the manœuvre laid himself broadside on to the waves and was nearly swamped. With the greatest difficulty the ship was brought again under control. By that time the sloop was no longer visible. It was at this heart-rending moment, when it seemed that they would have to abandon their comrades, that Xavier came to where the navigator was and asked him to send a man to the mast-head to try to sight the sloop. An ancient mariner standing near said gloomily: 'She will as likely turn up as we are to lose another.' (The sloop was the only boat they had.)

Xavier reproved him. 'Old Pero,' said he, 'how little faith you have! What! Do you think anything is impossible for Our Saviour? But I have confidence in Him and in His Sacred Mother, the Virgin Mary, to whom I have promised to say three masses at the Church of Our Lady of the Mount at Malacca, and am sure that They will see to it that the souls in the boat do not perish.' Old Pero was so confused by this rebuke that he did not know what to say.

To humour Xavier, the navigator sent a man to the top. But after looking in all directions for half an hour he reported that he could see nothing but the foaming crests of the waves.

'Come down then,' said Xavier; he seemed depressed, and turning to Pinto, said: 'I feel sick. Oblige me by warming some water for me to drink.'

'My sins did not allow me to render him that small service,' writes Pinto, 'because the day before, when the storm struck us, the stove had had to be thrown overboard with other things to lighten the ship.'

Xavier now admitted that his head ached dreadfully and that he felt dizzy. 'It is no wonder,' said Pinto, 'since Your Reverence has been up all night.' And seeing him yawn, he went on: 'Your Reverence would do well to lie down in my cabin.' Xavier agreed and went into the cabin. Pinto placed his Chinese servant at the door so as to be at call if the Father wanted anything. Some hours passed and Pinto asked his servant whether Xavier was asleep. 'He has not slept a wink,' answered the man. 'He has been kneeling on the bunk praying all the time.'

At sunset Xavier came out of the cabin and went up to the navigator. 'Any sign of the sloop?' he asked. 'No sight or sign,' said the navigator. 'By now, they must all be at the bottom of the sea.'

'I beg you send a man to the mast-head again,' said Xavier.

'I shall go myself,' said the navigator, to please the Father in any way he could. He and another climbed to the top. They were there awhile and shouted at last that there was nothing whatever to be seen.

On hearing this Xavier rested his head on a block of wood and seemed to be sobbing. Then, rousing himself, he lifted up his hands and began to pray fervently to Christ: 'Have pity on us and save the souls of the faithful who are astray in the boat.' This said, he leant his head again on the block, where he remained leaning for the space of two or three Credos, as if he were asleep.

'Then suddenly was heard the cry of a boy who was seated above us,' says Pinto. '"Miracle, miracle," he shouted, "here is our boat." All of us ran to the side to look, and saw about an arquebus-shot away the sloop. Everyone burst into loud crying like children, so overcome were we by the astonishing and extraordinary fact. Then we knelt to the Father, but he would not permit it and withdrew into the Captain's cabin. The crew of the sloop were received on board with a joy worthy of the occasion.'

The interpretation put on these events by Pinto, by Duarte da Gama, and indeed by everybody at the time, was that Xavier, after praying for divine aid and being granted it, had the power to draw the lost sloop back to the ship. Xavier himself, however, ascribed what had happened to Christ's action alone. While we can see merely a coincidence, we should notice that Xavier fell into what appears to have been a trance, just as he became tranced in the pulpit before predicting the naval victory. In his trances he was aware of what was happening at a distance. That the sloop's crew was in the vicinity, he sensed by some kind of telepathic sympathy. He was a strange man. His trances were matched in the other extreme by outbursts of delirious happiness. A Japanese who was baptized under the name of Bernard describes one of these outbursts, when he and Xavier were on their arduous march to Kyoto in 1550. He says: 'Sometimes he would take leaps and gambol, and would throw into the air an apple that he carried and catch it again, his face bathed in tears of joy.'[1] A sentence such as this reveals the saint to us and explains why he was so much beloved. Though an ascetic, he was full of high spirits and, like an artist, was animated at the mere fact of being alive. His adventure was complementary to those of the navigators, conquerors, free-lances and traders; in preaching Christianity on those distant coasts, he felt the same excitement that they did in battle and discovery or in making their fortunes. Indeed, he was perfectly at home in their society, knew how to be familiar with ordinary seamen, and would join rich merchants at an extravagant dinner, when their concubines would be waiting on them, and show interest in the wild games of chance they played.[2] Nevertheless, he never abated his dignity. In no circumstances, not even when running as a lackey behind a lord's pony, could he ever have been taken for anyone but a gentleman.

After the recovery of the sloop, the storm abated. They had been blown out of their course and put in to refit at the island of San-chuan, close to the mouth of the Canton river and so in the vicinity of the future Macao, to be founded a few years later. In 1551 San-chuan isle was used as a place of rendezvous by Portuguese ships trading with that part of China. But, as the season was over, only one ship lay in the road. Its commander was Diogo Pereira, and he was getting ready his sails for the voyage to Malacca.

Xavier transferred to Pereira's ship and in due course arrived

[1]Brou's *Saint François-Xavier*, II, 193, quoted by Le Gentil on p. 196 of his *Fernão Mendes Pinto*.
[2]For these details see Brou's op. cit., vol. I, 359.

safely in Malacca. But Pinto stayed in da Gama's ship and went on to Siam, for the goods which he and his fellow merchants had bought in Japan were suited to the market of Ayuthia. He remained there some months and in 1552 made his second visit to Burma, where he had the glimpse of the struggle between Bayin Naung and the Talaing pretenders, which is given further back. Later in the same year he was again in Malacca. His commercial ventures had been very successful. He had a capital of over fifteen thousand pounds and possessed a ship of his own. Contemporary writers describe him as wearing valuable jewellery and as having many slaves.[1] The idea of returning to Portugal was forming in his mind, for he was rich enough to retire in comfort. But now occurred what caused him to make far other plans.

After reaching Malacca at the end of 1551, Xavier went on to Goa, where he put his project of evangelizing China to the then Viceroy, Dom Afonso de Noronha. In May 1552 he was back in Malacca. The Viceroy had given him letters to the new Captain of the fortress, Dom Alvaro de Athaide de Gama, one of the great Vasco da Gama's sons, directing him to send the Father to China on Diogo Pereira's ship, for the latter had offered to bear some of the expenses. The plan was that Pereira should go with the title of Ambassador; that would enable Xavier to enter China, for the only foreigners allowed in by the Chinese were Ambassadors and their staff. But Dom Alvaro, who had fallen out with Diogo Pereira over a matter of money, raised every sort of difficulty. As Captain of Malacca he had powers which made his concurrence essential. Pinto, who by this time had arrived in Malacca from Burma, was a witness of Xavier's efforts to patch up the quarrel. But Dom Alvaro could not be won over, and in July 1552 Xavier had to leave without Diogo Pereira, which meant that the Chinese authorities at Canton would be likely to refuse him entry.

The ship on which he was travelling took him to the island of San-chuan, where he had already called on his way back from

[1]These details have been collected chiefly from Jesuit letters and are given on p. 101 of Schurhammer's paper in *Asia Major*, vol. III, already cited.

Japan. He had a presentiment that he was going to his death. Before embarking at Malacca, while he had one foot on the boat that was waiting to take him out to the ship, he said to the friends who came to see him off: 'I shall never meet Dom Alvaro again in this life. When next we are face to face it will be in the Valley of Jehoshaphat, a day of dreadful majesty, when Christ comes to judge the quick and the dead. On that day Dom Alvaro will have to explain why he did all he could to stop me from preaching the Gospel to the heathen. Moreover, I tell you that he will feel God's chastisement now, in his honour, in his goods, and in his very life.[1] May Our Saviour have mercy on his soul!' There and then, turning his face towards the main door of the Church across the way, he prayed Christ for Dom Alvaro's soul: 'Show God the wounds by which You redeemed us and beg Him to grant You Dom Alvaro's forgiveness.' And he took off his shoes (for sometimes he wore shoes) and struck them against a rock, as if he were shaking off the dust of Malacca for ever.

Soon after his arrival at San-chuan he tried to persuade a Chinese trader whose junk was in port to smuggle him into Canton, but the man refused to take the risk. He was casting about for other means, when he contracted dysentery. His temperature went up and he lay in his cabin, attended by the Chinese follower who on baptism had taken the name of Antonio of the Sacred Faith, a more reputable character than his former secretary, the ronin and then pirate, Paul of the Sacred Faith.

In Pinto's account of what followed he says that the Saint lost his optimism and high spirits, and began to feel a profound distaste for everything. After a fortnight it was evident that he was wasting away. When he expressed a wish to be put on shore, the sailors seem to have been relieved and landed him without delay. San-chuan, however, was merely a roadstead; there was no town, no hospital to which he could go, no inn, no decent house whose owner might have given him shelter; only, one may suppose, a

[1]Soon afterwards Don Alvaro was recalled to answer charges of maladministration. He was sent prisoner to Lisbon, his property was confiscated and he died a leper. (*Monumenta*, I, 149.)

few sheds and hovels along the waterfront. To accommodate him they built a shelter, one of those mat-and-thatch cabins that in the East can be run up in a few hours. There they left him with the faithful Antonio and two servants. There were no medicines, no comforts, nothing to relieve the misery of the final stages of his disease. He lingered thus seventeen days and at midnight on 2 December 1552, after asking Antonio and the servants to pray for his soul, for, said he, 'I have great need of your intercession,' he fixed his eyes on the crucifix and passed away. He was only forty-six years of age, though his beard had turned white, owing to his austerities and the hardships he had endured, particularly in Japan. By calling him the Blessed Father, Pinto anticipated by half a century his beatification, for he was declared by Pope Paul V in 1619 to be a person blessed in Heaven; and in 1621 Pope Gregory XV canonized him.

Xavier's most superb epitaph has been written by Paul Claudel. I quote it by permission in full because it epitomizes, in the form of a rhapsody, a view of the Saint with which the sixteenth century would have concurred, suggesting by image and splendid hyperbole far more than prose could do.

'*Après Alexandre le Grand et ce Bacchus dont parle la poésie,*
Voici François, le troisième, qui se met en route vers l'Asie,
Sans phalange et sans éléphants, sans armes et sans armées,
Et non plus roi dans le grand bond des chiens de guerre, et radieux, et
couronné,
Le plus haut parmi la haute paille de fer et le raisin d'Europe entre
les doigts,
Mais tout seul, et petit, et noir, et sale, et tenant fort la Croix!
Il s'est fait un grand silence sur la mer et le bateau vogue vers Satan.
Déjà de ce seuil maudit il sort un souffle étouffant.
Voici l'Enfer de toutes parts et ses peuples qui marchent sans bruit,
Le Paradis de désespoir qui sent bon, et qui hurle et qui tape dans la
nuit!
D'un côté l'Inde, et le Japon là-bas, et la Chine, et les grandes Iles
putrides,

Pinto's third visit and meeting with Francis Xavier

L'Inde tendue vers en bas, fumante de bûchers et de pyramides,
Dans le cri des animaux fossoyeurs et l'odeur de vache et de viande
    humaine,
(Noire damnée dans ton bourreau convulsive fondue d'une soudure
    obscène,
O secret de la torture et profondeur du blasphème!)
D'un côté les millions de l'Asie, l'hoirie du Prince de ce Monde,
(Et le trois fois infâme Bouddha tout blanc sous la terre allongé
    comme un Ver immonde!)
D'un côté l'Asie jusqu'au ciel et profonde jusqu'à l'Enfer!
(Il vient un souffle, il passe une risée sur la mer)—
De l'autre ce bateau sur la mer un point noir! et sur le pont
Sans une pensée pour le port, sans un regard pour l'horizon,
Un prêtre en gros bas troués à genoux devant le mât,
Lisant l'Office du jour et la lettre de Loyola.

Maintenant depuis Goa jusqu'à la Chine et depuis l'Éthiopie
    jusqu'au Japon,
Il a ouvert la tranchée partout et tracé la circonvallation.
Le diable n'est pas si large que Dieu, l'Enfer n'est pas si vaste que
    l'Amour,
Et Jéricho après tout n'est pas si grande que l'on n'en fasse le tour.
Il a reconnu tous les postes et levé l'enseigne obsidionale;
Son corps pour l'éternité insulte à la porte principale.
Il barre toutes les issues, il presse à toutes les entrées de Sodome;
L'immense Asie tout entière est cernée par ce petit homme.
Plus pénétrant que la trompette et plus supérieur que le tonnerre,
Il a cité la foule enfermée et proclamé la lumière.
Voici la mort de la mort et l'arme au coeur de la Géhenne,
La morsure au coeur de l'inerte Enfer pour qu'il crève et pourrisse sur
    lui-même!

François, capitaine de Dieu, a fini ses caravanes;
Il n'a plus de souliers à ses pieds et sa chair est plus usée que sa sou-
    tane.
Il a fait ce qu'on lui avait dit de faire, non point tout, mais ce qu'
    a pu:

Pinto's third visit and meeting with Francis Xavier

Qu'on le couche sur la terre, car il n'en peut plus.
Et c'est vrai que c'est la Chine qui est là, et c'est vrai qu'il n'est pas
    dedans:
Mais puisqu'il ne peut pas y entrer, il meurt devant.
Il s'étend, pose à côté de lui son bréviaire,
Dit: Jésus! pardonne à ses ennemis, fait sa prière,
Et tranquille comme un soldat, les pieds joints et le corps droit,
Ferme austèrement les yeux et se couvre du signe de la Croix.'[1]

[1]Mrs. Helen Parry Eden drew my attention to this poem, which occurs in the volume *Corona Benignitatis Anni Dei*. It is printed here by kind permission of the publishers, Gallimard, Paris. For those who may find it difficult, I give the following short paraphrase. The Saint is compared to Alexander and Bacchus as forerunners of the Christian invasion of Asia: Bacchus, traditionally supposed to have visited India with the grape for the wine of the Last Supper, but Alexander, whose cornfield of spears was composed only of straws of iron, from which no grain could grow to make the holy bread. The Saint advances alone against Asia, which is the abode of Satan, is Hell itself, the place of despair, a dark lost soul soldered to a frenzied executioner, the Devil. Vast though it is, the Saint is able to lay siege to it and to put death to death.

CHAPTER THIRTY-ONE

Pinto's conversion and fourth visit to Japan

———❦———

Xavier was buried a stone's throw from the beach. As the grave was in the open and unprotected from jackals, which abounded on the island, Antonio poured in lime, perhaps with the object of making the flesh uneatable. A member of the ship's company sent a letter to Malacca announcing the death and saying that they would bring the corpse back with them when their business was finished. In February 1553 they opened the grave and were astonished to find the body as fresh as if Xavier had just died. Though this was evidently due to the lime, which had acted as a preservative, it was hailed as a miracle. The holy body, as Pinto terms it, was taken to Malacca and re-buried in the Hermitage attached to the Church of Our Lady of the Mount on 17 March 1553. There it remained until 11 December of that year.

Pinto had again gone on business to Siam immediately after Xavier's departure to China in July 1552. He was in Ayuthia at the time of the Father's death and when his body arrived in Malacca. It was in this spring of 1553 that he began seriously to consider returning to Portugal.[1] With the wealth he now had, he could buy an estate, make a good marriage and raise the name of his family, as from the first he had planned to do. But before leaving the East should he make one more trip to Japan? He had never been very successful there. The great bulk of his fortune had been amassed in Siam, Burma, Malaya and the Islands. But

[1]The *Peregrination* is silent on what follows, which is taken from Pinto's letter of 1554, already mentioned. It is to be found, along with his letter of 1555, in Christóvão Ayres' book, *Fernão Mendes Pinto, subsidios*, etc. (Lisbon, 1904).

perhaps he would be more lucky this time; God might favour him because he had lent Xavier the money to build the first Christian church ever built in that country. On further reflection he decided not to go; there was no reason to do so; he had plenty of money. He would take ship to Goa and from there return to Portugal, which he had not seen for sixteen years.

So, in the late summer of 1553, he packed up and set out for Goa, calling at Malacca *en route*. The body of the man whom he had so much revered had been at the Church of Our Lady of the Mount since the March of that year. We may be sure that he visited the grave. He also made inquiries about his friend's death and had the story from one or more of those who were with him at San-chuan. About October or November he embarked for Goa.

Meanwhile the Viceroy, Dom Afonso de Noronha, on hearing of the events at San-chuan and Malacca, had come to the conclusion that the proper place of sepulture for Xavier was not in Malacca at Our Lady of the Mount but in Goa at the Jesuits' Chapel of St. Paul, which was attached to their House and College. Accordingly, he sent a ship to Malacca; the body was dug up a second time and was embarked for Goa in December 1553.

Pinto had reached Goa about November 1553. His intention was to get a passage for Lisbon as soon as he had settled his affairs. His frame of mind, however, was not quite that of a successful merchant on the eve of retirement. As he remembered how he had made his money, he had his uneasy moments. Then he would try to reassure himself. After all, he had done nothing so dreadfully wrong. He says in his letter: 'And I thought that so long as a man did not steal the chalice or treasure of a Church, or become a Mohammedan, there was no reason to fear Hell, and that it was enough to be a Christian, for God's mercy was great.' So he hints what was working in his mind.

It seems that he had sent letters to Xavier from Siam, addressing him at San-chuan. He had not received any answers, and it occurred to him now that perhaps the Father had written to him before he died, because they had been such good friends.[1] If so, the letter might be lying at the Jesuit headquarters, should the Father's papers have been deposited there. He decided to go to the College and inquire, though he knew nobody at the place. Apparently he went two or three times, perhaps because a clerk was making a search, and when, having been told there was no letter, he was on the point of leaving for what he supposed was the last time, a certain Brother Pero Bravo happened to come up, a priest whom he had met in Malacca. The Brother was very pleased to see him, for he knew that he was Xavier's friend and had been with him in Japan. Thinking that the other Brothers would also like to see him for the same reason and ask him questions about the famous missionary, whose body would soon be reposing in their Chapel, he took him along the veranda and introduced him to them as Xavier's great friend. 'They, hearing

---

[1]It used to be remarked by scholars as a curious fact that, if Fernão Mendes Pinto was as good a friend of Xavier's as he declared himself to be, there should be no mention of him in any of the Father's letters collected in the *Monumenta Xaveriana*. But in 1931 Maggs Bros., London, offered for sale, price one thousand pounds, a hitherto unknown manuscript letter, dated Cochin, 31 Jan. 1552, signed by Francis Xavier and addressed to the King of Portugal, Dom João III. (See item 88 in their catalogue No. 555.) The following reference to Pinto is contained in it: 'Having regard to the service of God and Your Highness, I will remind you of certain persons, of whose service it is necessary that Your Highness should know, so that you may render your thanks and they may continue to serve you: because the men who spend their all in the service of Your Highness would appreciate nothing so much as the knowledge that what they had done had been rewarded by the honour of a letter of thanks from you. . . . Fernão Mendes has served Your Highness in these parts, and lent me, when in Japan, three hundred cruzados to establish a Residence at Amanguchi (Yamaguchi). He is a wealthy man and has two brothers, Alvaro Mendes and Antonio Mendes, to induce to spend what they have and die in the service of Your Highness. You will do me a favour if you accept them as Gentlemen-in-waiting. Alvaro Mendes was present during the siege of Malacca.'

Besides the interest of this letter as a document to F. M. Pinto's relations with Xavier, it discloses, what was not otherwise known, that Pinto had two brothers in the East. That Alvaro Mendes was at the siege of Malacca may explain how Pinto was able to describe with equal vividness the pursuit of the Achin fleet and also what happened at Malacca during its absence, if we may assume that one of them was at sea and the other on shore. I am particularly obliged to Professor Boxer for bringing this letter to my attention.

me named as a friend of so blessed a Father,' says Pinto in his letter, 'came crowding round me, both Brothers and Fathers, and embarrassed me with the kind way they welcomed me and the affectionate manner in which they spoke.'

While he was the centre of a pleasant conversation, who should appear but the Provincial of the Jesuits, Father Belchior Nunez, who also seemed very glad to see him. (It were reasonable to suppose that as he was known to be a rich man, who had lent Xavier money for a church at Yamaguchi, the Provincial hoped he might make a donation.) He showed him round the College and took him into the part where the novices lived. They were in their long white cassocks and, when they saw the Provincial enter with a guest, they ranged themselves in a row and recited the *Benedicite*.

The Jesuits' cordiality and the glimpse that he had of their manner of life made a great impression on Pinto. He was at this time a man of forty-four years of age. For sixteen years he had suffered and endured in order to make money. He had money now, but he asked himself whether it was worth having. Was it worth having if you had made it by methods which put you in danger of perdition? Little avail was wealth without salvation. True, he had never been a renegade, never gone against the faith; and he had even lent money for a church, though, as Xavier had paid him back before starting for China, it could not be called a charity. But he had been a pirate and a slaver, and had done other things not to be spoken of. How happy the Fathers and Brothers were in their well-ordered existence! Such a life, free from all apprehension, how calm it was, how free from worry! Nevertheless, God was merciful, of that he was sure. He would go home, he would get honourably married. It then occurred to him that he could be very useful to the Jesuits with his experience and money. Japan, which he knew so well, was waiting to be converted, longing, like him, for the certainty of salvation. 'Our Lord made me feel,' he writes, 'how different were these truths from my lies and vain opinions. In this uncertainty I remained seven or eight days. Then the Devil, since he understood the desire which God was planting in my heart, conjured up before me money and jewels, so that I cooled and resolved finally to go to Portugal.'

There now happened the event which the inmates of the Jesuit House had been awaiting with such eager anticipation. It was February 1554 and the ship bearing the holy body of Xavier, miraculously preserved against corruption, which had left Malacca on 11 December 1553, was reported to be approaching Goa. A message was received that it had reached Cochin on the 13th of the month, but was making such slow progress up the coast, owing to the wind being in the wrong quarter, that it could not reach the city before the end of March. A proposal was made that the Jesuit Fathers should send down a galley to meet the ship and take off the body. This commended itself to them, more particularly because Holy Week began on 25 March. If the body arrived during that week, when the Church was mourning the passion and death of Christ, it would be difficult to give it the splendid reception which had been planned. Accordingly, Belchior Nunez borrowed from the Viceroy a small galley, the kind known as a foist that used both oar and sail. Pinto asked to be allowed to accompany him. Three Brothers and four acolytes were also of the party.

They found the ship becalmed off Baticala, sixty miles south. 'We boarded her,' writes Pinto, 'the boys holding branches in their hands and singing the *Gloria in excelsis Deo.*' The two Jesuit Brothers, who had accompanied the body from Malacca, took Belchior Nunez to the cabin where it lay in a coffin covered with a brocaded cloth. Pinto followed. When the cloth was removed, the body was visible, for the lid of the coffin had been taken off. Nunez turned to Pinto and said: 'Come and look at your great friend.' 'His face was covered,' writes Pinto. 'His hands were crossed and tied with his belt, which looked as new as if it had just left the shop of a leather merchant. He was wearing a very rich alb and stole and, although these had been for a long time under the lime, they looked fresh and new. He had some slippers on his feet. As I saw him thus in the attire I knew so well, I recalled the many things we had passed through together and kissed his feet with many tears. The desire I had had to serve the Lord came back at the instant, and I was greatly drawn to this Company of the name of Jesus, for I felt certain that by persevering I should obtain pardon for my sins.'

But profoundly moved though Pinto was by seeing Xavier's dead body (and so miraculously preserved), he was not yet free of his hesitations and, as we shall see, some time elapsed before he finally made up his mind and took the decisive step of joining the Society.

The bringing of Xavier's body into the city of Goa was a great religious occasion and is described both in the letter and in the *Peregrination*, though the book contains no reference to Pinto's spiritual conflict nor to its issue, for reasons which will appear later on. When the coffin was transferred at sea from the ship to the foist, a salute was fired by several ships which were in the vicinity, and the acolytes sang the *Benedictus Deus Israel*. The foist was rowed back to Goa and arrived the next night at the Church of Rebandar on the outskirts of the city. The coffin was placed in the church, and notices of the arrival were sent to the Viceroy, the Jesuit Fathers and other notables, asking them to assemble at the main quay. At dawn the coffin was replaced in the foist and rowed up to where the Viceroy was waiting, attended by his officers, and surrounded by a great crowd of people of all sorts, both Portuguese and Indian. There were also many ecclesiastics present, particularly the Fathers and Brothers of the Society. After the coffin had been landed, a procession was formed, all the notabilities bearing candles and, to the tolling of the Cathedral bells and the singing of psalms by ninety neophytes with censers lit, they all set out for the Jesuit College, the route taken being first along the main thoroughfare called the Rua Direita, which was decorated for the occasion by hanging out of the windows silks and tapestries. On arrival at the Jesuit College, the body was placed in the Chapel and a mass was sung. After mass, the notabilities were allowed to kiss the feet. The main crowd was outside the chancel grille and became so frantic to see the Saint that the iron gates gave way. The Fathers had great difficulty in restoring order. During the next three days and nights huge numbers pressed into the Chapel and kissed the feet. As it was clear that the body would be damaged by such usage, the Jesuits had to put it in a sealed coffin.[1]

After these moving events, Holy Week followed. During its course Pinto, who was now much agitated, for he wanted to become a Jesuit and yet held back, took the Sacrament, and made a full confession of his sins to Father Belchior Nunez. On 6 April 1554 Nunez, having occasion to visit the Hermitage of Our Lady of Shorao, a shrine on an island on the other side of the strait which divides Goa from the mainland, invited Pinto to accompany him. They were there two or three days, and it was then that Pinto's spiritual crisis reached its peak. He says in the letter from which I have been quoting: 'The desire of serving God grew so strong with me, that I was almost beside myself and did nothing else but sigh and moan, and beg Our Lord that He would make me feel what was most for His honour and glory, for that was the only way I could console myself.' And he describes how he knelt in the Church of the Hermitage and begged the Virgin to get Christ to cause him to save his soul, that is to say, oblige him to make up his mind. As a result of these prayers, he was at last able to come to a decision. This was not to join the Brothers at the Society's headquarters, and share their calm life of prayer and teaching, helping at the mass and attending on the Fathers. No, he would have something dramatic, for he loved drama; something adventurous, for he loved adventures. That would not only suit his character but also his sins. He would do what would oblige Christ to obtain his forgiveness. 'I left the church,' he writes, 'and went to find Father Master Belchior.'

---

[1]The extraordinary after history of Xavier's corpse is related at length in chapter III, section 7, of my *The Land of the Great Image*. It became more dry and brittle, but never decayed, and is still to be seen in Goa to-day. Xavier's ghost is also to be seen, not in Goa, but in Malacca, where it seems to have been left behind, judging by what a member of our Foreign Office told me the other day. One evening, not long ago, he went with a companion to Our Lady of the Mount and they were terrified by seeing an apparition of the Saint rising from the spot that had once been his tomb.

Pinto's conversion and fourth visit to Japan

The conversation that ensued was to this effect. Pinto declared that a triumph could be obtained for Christ in Japan, which offered by far the most hopeful missionary field in Asia. He reminded Nunez of what had just become known, that an envoy with a letter from Yoshishige, the Daimyo of Bungo, had arrived in Goa to find out whether Xavier was returning and to say that if he did come back the Daimyo would, as far as was practicable, lead the way in a general conversion; he would also enter into a trade agreement with the Viceroy, which would be very favourable to the Portuguese. 'Father Francis is dead,' went on Pinto, 'but you, Father Belchior, should take his place and reap the harvest which he has sown. If you will go now to Japan, I will go with you. Instead of retiring to Portugal as I planned, I will devote all my wealth and the rest of my life to this grand object.'

It seems that Belchior Nunez was so carried away by Pinto's enthusiasm that there and then he said that he would go.

The arrangements had to be made at once because it was already the season for a voyage to Japan. To have the advantage of favourable winds, one had to reach there by the 1st of August, which meant getting away from Malacca by the 1st of June. Goa to Malacca was a month's journey. As it was already April, there was no time to lose. Nunez and Pinto immediately left the Hermitage of Shorao and returned to the city. The first step was to see the Viceroy. He had been wondering what answer to give to the Daimyo's letter. When he heard that Nunez proposed to take Xavier's place he was delighted. On learning of what Pinto offered to do, he made a proposition. To arrange the trade agreement an Ambassador was necessary, he said. Pinto was well acquainted with Japan and with Yoshishige himself. There was no one more suitable than him for the post. Would he accept the appointment of Ambassador? Pinto replied that he was joining the Society and would be going as a novice. The Viceroy suggested that he should combine the two offices: Nunez would be his superior in all matters relating to the mission; for negotiating the treaty he would act independently. Pinto agreed and was appointed Ambassador.

Pinto's conversion and fourth visit to Japan

That settled, Pinto proceeded to divest himself of his fortune. What precisely that amounted to is difficult to determine. In the letter I have been quoting, he says: 'I thought myself very lucky and famous at being able to return to my native place with nine or ten thousand cruzados.' At this date the cruzado was worth rather more than two pounds sterling, which would give him a twenty thousand pound capital, not counting his jewels, his slaves, and goods in stock. In the sixteenth century that represented a large sum of money.

Father Schurhammer, S.J.,[1] the great authority on the *Peregrination*, refers in this connection to a statement by a Jesuit Brother called Luis Fróis, who was in Goa at the time and who joined the expedition to Japan. Fróis says that Pinto, before joining the Society, sent two thousand cruzados home to his relations and gave a charity of fifty to the Church of Our Lady of Shorao. With the balance, four thousand cruzados or more, he bought presents for the Japanese Daimyos, paid the expenses of the voyage to Japan, and reserved the balance for building a Jesuit House there and financing the mission's further activities. The point here is that he did not make over his fortune to the Jesuits, but took with him to Japan about four thousand cruzados with the intention of expending them on the Society's behalf. It seems clear that he left a balance in Goa, which, if his figure of ten thousand cruzados is taken for his total liquid capital, was about four thousand cruzados. To that must be added the value of his stock of goods, 'a great capital of spices.'[2]

After disposing of his fortune in this fashion, Pinto freed his slaves. 'He had many slaves,' wrote Father Aires Brandão, S.J., in a letter dated Goa, 23 December 1554, 'whom he freed forthwith, telling them that in future they should acknowledge only God as their master. Amongst these were three slaves who, seeing his resolve, threw themselves at his feet, crying that they wished

---

[1] See note on p. 27 of Schurhammer's op. cit.

[2] This definite statement as to the nature of Pinto's business occurs in Father Francisco de Sousa's *Oriente Conquistado* (Lisbon, 1710), where, on p. 106, he describes the scene in the Church of Shorao which follows here.

to go and die with him in Japan. He left another three in this College, so that after they had been taught and instructed in the Faith they could follow what calling they chose, and he dismissed the remainder in comparable manner. . . . What this man did astonished everyone in India, for he was regarded as having the most coined money in ready cash of any merchant in the place.'[1]

The date of departure was fixed for 15 April 1554, and the preparations for the voyage were hurried on. 'The Lord gave us strength to arrange so many things in so short a time,' writes Pinto. 'Day and night everyone in the house was busily occupied. Many of the nobility showed such zeal for the work that they gave us rich presents for the Japanese lords who might be converted.' Indeed, such was the fervour that many fidalgos and noble ladies professed themselves ready to join the mission.

Pinto had not yet been received into the Society, for Nunez was opposed to his taking the vows in a hurry. The embarkation being very close, Nunez and the Jesuits who were to sail with him to Japan went one night to the Hermitage of Our Lady of Shorao, there to renew their vows, as was the custom before starting on a journey. Pinto accompanied them, as did many other lay persons. It was a stifling night, the height of the hot season, and the church was filled to suffocation. Pinto watched the Jesuits go and kneel before the image of the Virgin, renew their vows and with tears embrace each other. At sight of this he was overwhelmed with emotion, and weeping copiously, with flushed face, began himself to take the vows, his voice rising as he promised perpetual chastity, poverty and obedience, though he did not know the correct wording of the vows. The Jesuits heard him with surprise, and one of their number tried to stop him. But nothing could stop him. Speaking louder yet, he cried that he would live and die in the Company of Jesus and spend all he possessed to spread the Gospel in Japan.

When he ceased, Belchior Nunez addressed him kindly, begging him to take thought again of the sort of life it was that he

[1]*Monumenta Xaveriana*, II, Fasc. VI, Annus 21.

was choosing. But Pinto, asserting violently that he understood well the choice he had made, demanded to be accepted there and then as a novice. Nunez could not refuse, and calling for a cassock, dressed him in it.

So dramatic was this scene, and such was the intense emotion aroused, that a pandemonium of hysterical weeping broke out. The old Pilot-Major of India, who was among those present, could not contain himself, and fell to the ground, sobbing convulsively. When Pinto descended from the chancel where Nunez had invested him, he was embraced by all in turn with demonstrations of joy. Presently the Jesuits left the church, but he remained behind, and going before the Virgin, took off his rings, which were studded with great gems, and slipped them on to the fingers of the Son on her lap.[1]

Though Pinto was now a novice in the Society, he was also an Ambassador, and it was thought more suitable that he should not wear ecclesiastical dress. Indeed, he had ordered a very expensive suit, which he put on when the mission embarked, though he declared that when his official duties were over he would present it to one of the Japanese lords, 'who are not less vain in their dress than are the Portuguese,' observes Father Brandão.

The missionaries made a rather slower voyage than they had calculated, and did not reach Malacca until 6 June. On board also was Dom Antonio de Noronha, who had been appointed to succeed Dom Alvaro de Athaide de Gama, the Captain who had been so obstructive to Xavier in 1552. On Dom Antonio's arrival, Dom Alvaro was arrested and sent home, where, as already stated, he died of leprosy. But he had his partisans and they gave trouble. Indeed, for a time Malacca was turned upside-down. As a result of these disturbances, Pinto and Belchior Nunez found it impossible to get a ship to take them on to Japan and missed the season. The mission had to wait in Malacca the rest of 1554 and did not leave till April 1555.

It was during this wait that Pinto wrote the letter giving the

---

[1]This scene is taken from Father Brandão's letter already cited and from Father Francisco de Sousa's op. cit.

account of his conversion from which I have been quoting. It was addressed to the Jesuit Fathers in Portugal, who found it so edifying that they ordered it to be read out to the members of the Society at meal-times. Besides what related to his becoming a novice, it contained some chatty information about what he had seen in Burma and Siam.

Apart from the letter, we have another intimate glimpse of Pinto at Malacca. He will have felt it very trying that the mission should have had to wait ten months. To find himself detained in the town where he had been so well known and where, no doubt, he had many worldly connections, such as former servants, old slaves, women, native acquaintances, other merchants, and a house where he had entertained less than a year ago, must have embarrassed him, particularly as he will have known that he was the talk of the place and that every eye was on him as he walked the streets. But he did not shrink or hide himself. On the contrary, he did what will have greatly increased the talk. When the Jesuits, obeying their vow of poverty, went from door to door begging their bread, he went begging with them, dressed in ragged clothes like a mendicant friar, waiving for the time being his ambassadorial dignity. What his former friends and acquaintances thought of this is not recorded, but in a letter of Belchior Nunez's, which describes the begging, it is declared that Hindus and Mohammedans were profoundly impressed and looked with more respect on Christianity than ever before. It is probably wrong to think that he suffered embarrassment for long. He had all the fervour of the recent convert and went about in a dream of devotional excitement.

They left for Japan on 1 April 1555. The route taken was the same as that followed by Pinto in 1539 when he cruised with the corsair, Antonio de Faria; first the Singapore Strait, then up the east Malay coast to Patani, across to the delta of the Mekong in Cambodia, along the east coast of Champa and Cochin-China, over the mouth of the Gulf of Tong-king to Hainan island, and on to the estuary of the Canton river, the usual route between Malacca and China. Thence the journey would lie through the Formosa Strait, past the Lu-chu group, and so to Japan. With the monsoon wind blowing from April to July in those seas, the section to China generally took a month, and from China to Japan a fortnight. But the mission, instead of arriving in China by 1 May and so having ample time to reach Japan before the end of July, did not get to China until 3 August, too late in the season to continue the journey. We possess a second letter written by Pinto in November of this year, 1555, which explains how they came to be so delayed. The *Peregrination* gives the same story, though less vividly and continuing to suppress all reference to the fact that Pinto was a novice as well as an Ambassador. Letters by Belchior Nunez and by Luis Fróis are also extant and support Pinto's in every detail. This part of the *Peregrination* is therefore proved to be pure autobiography and does not contain the usual admixture of facts taken from other contexts. It may be argued that in describing what was already well known to the Jesuits, Pinto was obliged to keep strictly to the plain truth, though for the special reasons which will appear he suppressed his own part as a Jesuit novice. Perhaps, however, the best explanation is that from a literary point of view the story required no arrangement, because it fell naturally into a dramatic form. Startling though his earlier adventures had been, this final one of inspiring the Society of Jesus to follow up Francis Xavier's exploratory mission to Japan, and financing it to make a sustained effort to bring that country into the Christian fold, was the most extraordinary thing he ever did. For him, to begin with, it was far more exciting than making a fortune by commerce, piracy and slaving, or fighting for loot as a King's mercenary, because its aim was to win his soul's salvation, an aim which, could we be as clear as was he how to accomplish it, would engage our hearts and minds as madly as it did his.

The ship carrying the mission was a caravel, a light sailing vessel, which belonged to the King of Portugal. The first stage, as I have said, was the Singapore Strait; this they entered on 9 April. The Captain, who was a weak and incompetent man, here ran the ship on to a coral reef. The crew was terrified, and he was unable to restore their confidence. The frightened men turned to the Jesuits. Pinto and Nunez offered to take a lifeboat and get help from a ship which had passed them in the morning and was now becalmed twelve miles further on. The boat was got ready and they climbed down into her with one of the Brothers and a soldier. The channel used by shipping wound at this point among a number of small islands where sea-gypsies lived, dangerous petty marauders of the sea-lanes, who used blow-pipes and poisoned arrows, and would attack a stray boat or a disabled ship. The hot tropic night had fallen when Pinto and his companions set out. By what glimmer of stars there was they soon saw prahus of Saleeters[1] moving about, and told their oarsmen to pull harder. After they had been rowing for some time and the slaves were very exhausted, they ran in the darkness on a shelf of rock close to the headland of an island. 'The Lord knows how we escaped,' writes Pinto in his letter. 'They shouted to us from the hill, which was very dark, calling to know who we were and where we were going. But we got the boat off and answered nothing.'

With the boat leaking and having to be bailed, they rowed to sea as fast as they could. About midnight, two prahus came out from an island and began following them. When the prahus were close enough, their occupants called on them to stop. Pinto shouted back in Malay that they were harmless Portuguese from Malacca on the way back to their ship. The Saleeters took no notice and continued to pursue. At last they desisted, but soon afterwards the boat rounded a point and Pinto sighted a little fleet of Saleeters anchored under the lee of the shore. As soon as the boat was noticed, the Saleeters manned their oars, and with

---

[1]Pinto calls them Salates. Writers of the seventeenth century called them Saleeters. They are now called Salons. Still sea-gypsies, they live in boats of a peculiar construction which, though small, are exceptionally seaworthy and can withstand the waves of the monsoon. No longer pirates of the isles, they make their living by collecting pearls and ambergris. They are shy, slinking creatures, who seek solace in opium, their former fierceness all gone. Sometimes they build huts on very tall posts in the foreshore mud of a little port. There was a settlement of them below my house at Mergui, when in 1932 I was Deputy Commissioner there. Cf. my *Siamese White*, p. 21.

loud cries made an attempt to surround the Portuguese. It seems that, as the boat was now using a small sail, the savages could not row fast enough to enclose it. They followed, however, very close. A waning moon was rising and they could be clearly seen. Their intention was evidently to board. Pinto warned them to come no nearer or he would let them have his lead. Two arquebuses were in the boat, his own and the soldier's, and to make it seem that there were three he cut off a piece of his match, lit it and put it in Nunez's hand. The Provincial of the Jesuits was a brave man, and Pinto says that he would have envied him his courage more than his scholarship even if that had been ten times greater than it was.

The Saleeters were undaunted by the sight of the three matches and pressed after them as doggedly as before. Had they caught up sufficiently to board, nothing could have saved the Portuguese, who were greatly outnumbered. But at this moment the light of the moon disclosed the ship which they were seeking. The Saleeters saw it too and, noting the new confidence in Pinto's voice as he urged his men to a final spurt, rested on their oars. As we have seen, Pinto had many escapes from death; this was his last and it was also perhaps his narrowest.

The Captain of the ship, Luis Dalmeida, did all he could to help, sending Pinto and Nunez back to their caravel in a boat large enough to take off its crew, if necessary. But when dawn broke, they saw the caravel had floated off the reef and was sailing towards them. Re-embarking, they continued on their voyage, rounded the Malay peninsula and began to ascend its eastern coast. On 14 April they reached the island of Tuman off Pahang, and anchored to take on water and repair damage. Here five of the crew deserted, fled into the jungle and could not be found. The inhabitants were hostile and the Captain, who had quite lost his nerve, begged Nunez to appoint another in his place. The Father soothed him with tact and patience. Had Xavier been there, says Pinto, he could not have done more to console and hearten them.

On 20 April they left Tuman and on 6 May reached Patani. Pinto, who knew the Sultan well, having, as we know, been to

Patani before (and latterly, as he tells us, in a ship of his own),
went ashore to the palace with a present of two flasks of rose-
water and a coif, a cap of white silk as worn by Portuguese grandees at that date. The Sultan received him as an old friend. He was
a Malay Mohammedan, but an ally of Malacca's, a man with
a broad sense of humour. It evidently amused him to see Pinto in
his new guise. On learning that he was off to Japan to convert
them there, he turned to his courtiers and observed with a laugh:
'How much more sensible to make a fat profit in China, than to
go spreading lies in such distant parts!' However, he called the
Superintendent of the Port and said: 'Be careful to let these people
have what they want, and remember that it is not my custom to
give an order twice.' It was just as well that the Sultan was so
friendly, because Luis Dalmeida, whose ship had arrived two days
before, attacked a Siamese junk in the river, an act which so an-
noyed a section of the population that it was not safe for any
Portuguese to go about the streets.

After buying provisions at Patani, they set sail and crossed the
Gulf of Siam to Pulo Condor, off the mouths of the Menam. Here
a storm struck them and left them so battered that the cowardly
Captain refused to go on, and went all the way back to Tuman
island.

A galleon commanded by Francisco Toscano came in two days
later. To cut short a long story of mishaps and delays, the mission
transferred itself to the galleon and on her left Tuman for China,
but not until 24 June. After working up the Cochin-China coast,
they anchored to take water at an island, which Pinto calls Pulo
Champilo, somewhere in the entrance to the Gulf of Tongking.
It was uninhabited. First they noticed a cross carved on a rock,
under which was engraved the date 1518 and the name Duarte
Coelho, an early voyager whom Pinto says was then in Brazil.
But on going further ashore they saw what was less pleasant and
must have reminded Pinto of his pirate days. Hanging from trees
were sixty-two corpses, and others were on the ground half-
eaten by wild animals. Near-by was a banner on which was written
in Chinese: 'Let any crew of ship or junk which puts in here to

take on water leave at once after having done so, under penalty, if they linger, of suffering the same fate as these wretches who have incurred the anger of the Son of Heaven.'

Pinto's interpretation of this sinister find was that some Chinese Admiral, cruising with his warships, had surprised a vessel watering at the island and, after making a prize of her, had hung her crew, thereby pretending that his own piracy was an act of justice, a device, he says, which corsairs sometimes were in the habit of using.

Sailing from this island they crossed over to Hainan and on 20 July reached the isle of San-chuan. Here the first thing they did was to visit the grave in which Xavier had lain from December 1552 to February 1553, and which had been the scene of the miracle of his body's incorruptibility. They walked there in procession, the Jesuits in full canonicals and all with candles lit, to find the grave overgrown with bushes, only the points of the cross being visible. After pulling up the bushes and the many weeds, they enclosed the place with a palisade of stout wood, surrounded by a ditch, and planted a tall handsome cross at the entrance. When this pious work was done, an altar was brought and a full mass sung by the orphans whom they had with them. The solemnity ended with a sermon in which Nunez recalled the main incidents of Xavier's life and how he came to his death on that lonely isle, far from his friends and with no one to comfort him. Preached thus on the scene of the Saint's last agony, and to persons who themselves had suffered many vicissitudes and for whom, perhaps, like Xavier, there would be no returning home, the Jesuit's words, echoing over the waste, were so moving that many were reduced to tears.

Leaving San-chuan they covered the short distance to Lampacau, on Bullock Horn Island, a short distance west of the Canton estuary and, so, close to the future Macao. Lampacau was in 1555 what San-chuan had been in 1552, the rendezvous for Portuguese ships trading to China. Macao was to become their base two years later by arrangement with the Chinese. The prosperous settlement of Ningpo up north near the Yang-tse mouth, which Pinto has described so vividly, had been closed, and perhaps destroyed, by the Chinese in 1544 as a punishment for the lawless behaviour of its inhabitants, who, it is said, attacked the neighbouring villages.

It was now, as I have said, August 1555, and the mission had missed the monsoon again. To proceed was impossible until the following May. But the Father was never idle during their long wait. He built a little chapel on shore, celebrated mass there, and heard the confessions of the Portuguese from the ships in the roadstead. He also made, by permission of the Chinese authorities, an expedition up the Pearl river to Canton. In its prison a certain Mateo de Brito had been confined for five years with several companions. Nunez managed to effect their release by paying a substantial sum, which was subscribed by the Portuguese at Lampacau.[1]

Pinto himself visited Canton in November 1555 to make some purchases. On his way there he landed at Macao, then a Chinese village, and put that address at the head of the letter[2] from which I have just been quoting. It is the earliest surviving letter written by a European from Macao. (Pinto had an extraordinary flair for always being first on any scene.) In this same letter he says that Nunez wanted Brother Luis Fróis to learn Chinese in case later a China mission should be possible, and adds with truth, for the Jesuits were afterwards grievously disappointed by their failure to win over the Chinese Emperors and so be able to effect a grand conversion: 'It seems to me that there is no greater mistake than for anyone to believe that it is at any time possible to convert the Chinese by natural means; it would require a miracle by God to do it.' Here speaks the man who had knocked about those coasts for twenty years, not the enthusiastic novice who, fired by Xavier's example, had set out to convert Japan. The sentence is

[1]The commentators point out that de Brito could have supplied Pinto with the sort of information he used in the account of his own alleged imprisonment in China after the robbery of the royal tombs. But no doubt Pinto had many sources available, if, in fact, his story of the imprisonment was a literary device to enable him to describe what Chinese jails were like.

[2]Cf. pp. 255 note and 267.

evidence that he had started to cool. It was not in his nature to feel interest in missionary labours that led to no more than a few baptisms. Only the sudden dramatic conversion of a whole nation could fire his imagination. And he was beginning to doubt whether that was possible.[1]

May 1556 came round at last and the mission sailed on the 7th for Japan in a ship whose captain was Dom Francisco Mascarenhas. In a fortnight they sighted Tanegashima, the island where the arquebus was first introduced to the Japanese, and continuing on to Bungo, reached it safely after the vexatious delay of another fortnight, due to a miscalculation by the pilot, who overshot his port by one hundred and eighty miles, with the result that they had to beat back that distance against the wind.

What happened at Bungo can be shortly stated: it was exactly what might have been expected. The Daimyo, Yoshishige, when pressed by Nunez to become a Christian and lead his subjects into the Catholic fold, excused himself on the ground that such a move on his part would be too impolitic, particularly at a moment when the country was already much disturbed; but in the matter of the embassy he asked Pinto to convey his friendliest sentiments towards the King of Portugal and the Viceroy.

Pinto's account of his negotiations makes lively reading. On arrival at Funai, the capital, he learnt that Yoshishige had very recently unmasked a conspiracy by some of his lords to overthrow him and, marching on their castles, had defeated and executed them. It was said that the Buddhist monks (themselves, it should be recalled, lords with armed retainers) had instigated the plot, angered and alarmed by the spread of Christianity.

---

[1]Nunez himself was doubtful whether to go on. He received while at Lampacau a letter from Loyola, the head of the Society of Jesus, saying that the Provincial of the Jesuits in Asia should not go to regions so distant that he could not quickly return to his headquarters. He also got letters from Goa complaining that he had already been away too long. But encouraging letters were received from Japan. The Daimyo of Hirado invited him to stay, adding that several of his retainers had been baptized by Xavier's lieutenant, Fernandez, who had continued to reside in Japan. This letter decided him to go on. These facts show that Pinto very nearly gave up the project at this point.

Pinto's conversion and fourth visit to Japan

Though Yoshishige had managed to crush the rebellion, the whole of Bungo was in an uproar, and he had thought it safer to retire to a castle on the coast at a distance from the city.

Pinto was anxious to see him at once, though this meant going to the castle, a dangerous journey when the countryside was so unsettled. However, he landed and asked the Japanese Admiral to provide him with horses and an escort. This was readily accorded him and next morning he set out and by noon reached a village a mile from the castle. There he halted, and sent ahead one of his Japanese escort to announce his arrival and tell the Daimyo that he came this time as an Ambassador.

Yoshishige replied by letter that he was out fishing on an island a couple of miles from the castle. It was no ordinary fish that he was after, he said. A whale, a creature that he had never seen before in his life, had got lodged in a narrow and he had surrounded it. 'Come and join me,' he wrote, 'and see the sport. I am sending a boat to fetch you.'

Pinto was delighted and embarked with his suite. Within the hour they reached the island and found Yoshishige with two hundred men in boats trying to dispatch the whale with spears. It was not an easy task, but at last the monster rolled over dead. Yoshishige was in the highest spirits. So pleased was he with the fishermen who had assisted him that there and then he said that he would remit their taxes and raise them a step in rank.[1] When he greeted Pinto, it was with a laughing face; he was downright glad to see him again in Bungo, for he wanted to corner the Portuguese trade, even though that meant encouraging Christianity with all the risks entailed thereby. The Daimyo of Hirado was competing for the monopoly, and must be circumvented at all costs.

By now it was getting dark, and Yoshishige returned to his castle, after giving his Treasurer instructions to put up Pinto and his suite for the night. But later he sent a message inviting them

---

[1] This way of rewarding the common people for special services was a very old Japanese and Chinese practice. I have come across frequent mention of it in Pan Ku's *History of the Former Han*, a book written in the first century A.D. Its exact significance is not clear, but no doubt the promotion carried privileges.

to dinner. By the time they arrived he had finished eating and was, it seems, a little drunk and in a very merry mood. 'As you love me,' he cried, 'let me see you eat with your hands.'

Only his wife and daughters with their ladies were present. 'Do show us how you eat,' they echoed, as if it would be fun to see.[1]

As requested, Pinto and his suite, to the vast amusement of their hosts, helped themselves with their fingers to the food in the neat little bowls which were set before them. 'The ladies' jokes at our expense amused the Daimyo more than could have any comedy,' he writes. When they had finished eating, one of Yoshishige's daughters, extremely pretty and about fifteen, asked her mother's permission to act a charade or little farce, having to do with what they had just seen. She and some companions went out of the room. Meanwhile the jokes went on. 'It was a little vexatious,' says Pinto, 'but we put the best face on it we could, for it was all to the good for the Daimyo to be so amused.'

Presently the daughter came into the room again. She was dressed as an old pedlar. Kneeling before her father, she said: 'I am a very poor man with many children. Borrowing some money I laid it out on goods, which I have been trying to sell all over Japan, but cannot find a single purchaser. They told me at Kyoto that Your Highness would be able to do something for me. Though I know it is an impertinence to come in like this, my white hair, my feebleness, my poverty and huge family will, I hope, be accepted in excuse. Foreigners from the West have just arrived, they say. What I have for sale is certain to please them.'

The pretty child said this with so funny a face, and posed so amusingly as a decrepit old man, that everyone was convulsed with mirth. 'What have you got for sale?' asked the Daimyo, trying to keep a level face. The ladies were nudging each other and tittering. What had she got, what was it going to be?

Now her companions entered the room, dressed to look like

[1]It has been pointed out that spoons and forks were rare in fifteenth-century Europe. Certainly Portuguese adventurers in Asia did not bother to carry them. Nor had Pinto, for all his experience of China, mastered the chopstick.

the pedlar's assistants, and carrying parcels on their shoulders. These were opened before Yoshishige. Inside were hands, wooden hands they looked like to the Portuguese, who, mystified, could not see the point.

The little Princess now said demurely: 'These hands will be found very convenient by people who eat with their hands, for they can use them when their own go to the wash.'

The Daimyo nearly split himself laughing. Pinto says he felt abashed; there was no denying the Japanese superiority in table manners. But Yoshishige did not want him to take it so seriously. 'You must forgive me,' he said. 'My daughter only played this joke because she knew we were all friends together.' To which Pinto replied that it was a great honour to have been made fun of by His Highness.

The Princess, pleased at the hit she had made, tried to raise another laugh. 'If your God would take me on as his servant,' she said to Pinto, 'I have plenty of farces that I could act for him, better than this one and which would please him better.'

Pinto had a gallant answer to this sally: 'We indeed hope that Your Ladyship will become his servant and then we shall see you Queen of Portugal.'

More playful conversation followed. At a very late hour the party broke up. Not a word of business had been said. However, the next morning the Daimyo sent a messenger to Pinto asking for precise information about the Jesuits' intentions and what the embassy could offer. On being fully informed, he declared that he would give formal audience to Pinto next week in the city, and after him to Father Nunez.

What are we to think of this episode? Pinto is never artless. The story has been inserted where it stands for a purpose. He is saying something with it; it states, or hints at, what he does not care to say directly. Let us consider the facts. Here was a merchant-adventurer who, two years and four months previously, had experienced a sudden and violently emotional conversion. He should have stepped ashore in Japan like Xavier, burning with zeal, and immediately, by some striking action, as he had done in

Malacca, have demonstrated to the Japanese that he was a changed man and that Christianity had changed him. Instead of giving us some indication of such a state of mind, of the gravity of the occasion, of his own deep seriousness under the cloak of an Ambassador, he regales us with a comedy, one of the most amusing in his book, the point of which is that the Japanese found the Portuguese ridiculous, rather barbarous people, and which concludes with a flippant remark about the Christian God, put into the mouth of a charming young lady, to which he represents himself as giving a jocular answer. His meaning is clear. The story is a way of saying that when he reached Japan he realized that the mission had come out under a complete misapprehension, and the idea that the Japanese, led by their rulers, would abandon their own religion, and suddenly, humbly, and admiringly embrace Christianity, was rubbish. The influence of Xavier's fervid character had worn off. The Blessed Father was, of course, a great and good man, but had attempted the impossible. Though Pinto certainly wanted the Japanese, the Chinese, and all other Asiatics to become Christians, he saw that it could not be done in the way he supposed when he had financed the mission, at a moment when his judgment was weakened by the horrid fear of his own personal damnation. Missionaries in Japan would have to strive patiently, undergo hardships, brave dangers and be satisfied with converting a fraction of the natives. Pinto admired such missionaries, but he knew that he himself could never settle down to a life which paid such low dividends.

With this in mind, the reader is briefed to get a clear notion of the meaning of what followed.

As he had promised, Yoshishige returned to the capital and sent for Pinto. It must have been about the first week of June 1556. Pinto walked to the palace with his suite, for that was the custom. Behind him were carried the presents, which he had paid for out of his own money; they included two Spanish genets caparisoned for jousting and with the other appurtenances for that sport. The Daimyo received the embassy, seated on a dais in an outer courtyard. He had his army paraded, which consisted of four hundred horsemen and one thousand arquebusiers, by now a regular part of his forces. Pinto presented the Viceroy's letter, which was read out in translation.

Yoshishige now asked some questions about the size of the King of Portugal's army. How many men in full armour and mounted on caparisoned horses could His Majesty put into the field? Pinto writes: 'I must admit that I was embarrassed how to answer this question, and afraid I might blush through having to tell a lie. One of my suite, noticing this, took it upon himself to answer for me. "Our King," said he, "could muster a hundred or even a hundred and twenty thousand cavaliers so armed," a remark which astonished the Daimyo and me also!'

At the conclusion of what was a most satisfactory audience the Daimyo, after saying good-bye to Pinto, added: 'And by the way, when you judge it suitable, you can tell the Father to come to see me.' The main object of the mission was thus relegated to a secondary place.

As soon as Pinto got back to his lodgings, he told Belchior Nunez that he advised him to go at once to the palace, as everybody was dressed and ready. Accordingly the Father started off, accompanied by Brother Juan Fernandez, Xavier's assistant, whose Japanese was now so good that he could act as an interpreter, and by four small orphans dressed in cassocks and caps of white taffeta with silk crosses on their breasts. Yoshishige received them politely in the courtyard. He said to Nunez: 'You remind me of Father Francis, whom I was very fond of.' And he took him aside into a room and made him sit down by him. The orphans attracted his attention, for he had never seen European children, and he made much of them.

Nunez, after expressing his thanks, explained the object of his visit. The Viceroy, he said, had sent him for the express purpose of saving His Highness's soul from damnation. The Daimyo intimated his gratitude for His Excellency's kind thought. Thus encouraged, the Father launched into a 'sacred harangue or sermon,' which he had prepared especially for the occasion and showed the Daimyo what was necessary to do to be saved.

Pinto's conversion and fourth visit to Japan

At its conclusion the Daimyo said: 'I cannot say how delighted I am to have you with me and to hear what you have been telling me. But you will appreciate that I cannot give you an immediate answer, on account of the conditions in my territory, which are such as you will already have observed. I suggest that Your Reverence now take a good rest after your very arduous journey. The situation requires a great deal of tact. Were my subjects to notice any sudden change in me, they might side against me with the monks. But no doubt the Fathers here have pointed out to you the dangers that I run. A deplorable outbreak occurred only the other day, and I was obliged to execute thirteen lords. I must therefore defer consideration of what the Viceroy has been good enough to advise.'

Said Nunez in reply: 'Your Highness should consider that men are mortal and that death may come at any time. Were Your Highness to die before taking the step which the Viceroy recommends, what will become of your soul?'

'God knows,' replied Yoshishige, with a smile.

Seeing that it was useless to press the matter, the Father changed the subject and began talking of what he knew would interest the Daimyo, such as details about Western manners, methods of government, ships and money.

During the days that followed he had other conversations with Yoshishige, who, however, was careful not to commit himself. When pressed, he always evaded the point and never gave a straight answer. Discussions with learned monks were arranged, but these led to no practical result. After a while the Daimyo returned to his castle, saying affably to Nunez before he left: 'You must come to see me in a day or so, for I have much enjoyed my talks with you.'

When not a word was heard from him, Nunez decided to follow Xavier's example and make a tour through the villages, taking Brother Fernandez to translate. But he had not Xavier's physique. He wrote afterwards: 'I fell ill on account of the food and the beds; one has to sleep on a mat with a piece of wood for a pillow, and rice without butter or anything to give it a taste is all you get to eat. I was so gravely ill that I had to be carried back to Bungo on a beast of burden, where for the next three months I had continual bouts of fever and shivering. What with my health, the disturbed state of the country, and the fact that my duties as Provincial obliged me to return, I had to embark for Goa.'[1]

We should remark here that Pinto did not accompany Nunez on his preaching tour, but remained at the capital in his capacity as Ambassador. In short, he took no part whatever in the evangelic side of the mission which he had inspired and financed. The apprehension which we have seen growing in his mind, that he had made a mistake in thinking that the Daimyo of Bungo would embrace Christianity and induce his subjects to do likewise, had become a conviction. Certain now that what he had planned was impossible, he had to decide what he himself should do. He was a novice in the Society of Jesus. On his return to Goa, when he laid down his office as Ambassador, he would come wholly under the orders of Belchior Nunez, Provincial and Rector of all the Society's activities in Asia. He might be sent to any place, to some part of India, to Abyssinia, to China, anywhere at all that it pleased his superior to direct. He might find himself as a Brother in some small town, acting under the orders of a Father, perhaps his junior in years and certainly in knowledge of the East, his whole duty to preach to rustic audiences and rescue ploughmen or sweepers from Hell, a very different prospect from the spectacular conversion of all Japan, which would have made him in one stroke as famous an apostle as had been St. Augustine in England, St. Columba in Scotland, St. Boniface in Germany, or St. Patrick in Ireland. To have become St. Pinto, or whatever name in religion he might have taken, that would have been worth while, more than worth while, a wonderful crown. He would have gone down to history as the man who had sacrificed a great fortune and evangelized a great nation. In some ways he would have eclipsed Francis Xavier, a saint, no doubt, though in

[1]This letter is on p. 99 of Christóvão Ayres's *Fernão Mendes Pinto e o Japão, Pontos controversos* (Lisbon, 1906), and is quoted by Le Gentil on p. 204 of his op. cit.

fact a failure, for had he not left Japan in disappointment and died before he could enter China? But to become a drudging, preaching, struggling missionary—he could not face it and resolved to leave the Society. His resignation would not endanger his soul, for by giving away so much of his fortune and helping the mission for two years he had done enough to insure his salvation. Nor would he be left destitute, for he still had unexpended the money which he would have allotted to the upkeep of the mission and the building of the church, had he remained. That sum, though much less than he had intended to retire on, would yet suffice to support him in comfort at home. How much more profitable to live even in a cottage in Portugal, married, with children, than to be ordered here and there into swamp and jungle, to die young, perhaps, on a lonely island, of dysentery or some other painful disease, unknown and forgotten, for no miracle would happen at his grave! He was only a novice; he had not taken the full vows as a Brother. His resignation would be nothing unusual; the rules of the Society provided for just such a case as his. What he must do now was to round off the ambassadorial side of the mission by getting from Yoshishige a suitable letter and present for the Viceroy. If he returned to Goa as a diplomat, who had successfully arranged the first trade treaty between the Portuguese empire and the Daimyo of Bungo, he could claim a reward for his services, a reward which ought to indemnify him for what he had given away, so that in the end this last trip to Japan would not have been unprofitable, for with the appointments and honours he might reasonably expect, he would have got what money alone would not have bought him.

Judging from what happened afterwards, this is how Pinto thought at this time. In November 1556, when the ship was ready which was to take them all back to Goa, he sought a final audience with the Daimyo, who was still in his castle. This was granted, and Yoshishige gave him a letter to the Viceroy with a present of two swords and a hundred fans. The letter was extremely civil and amounted to a guarantee of friendly relations. Pinto was quite satisfied; his embassy could be called successful and the Viceroy would be obliged to reward him. He and Nunez embarked and set sail on 14 November 1556, after a visit which had lasted about six months.[1] On 4 December they reached Lampacau at Canton and on 17 February 1557 arrived safely at Goa. Of all Pinto's voyages it was the fastest and the least eventful. In the course of its three months he will have explained to Nunez, if he had not already done so, his intention to leave the Society. He cannot very well have given all the reasons which I have sketched, but he may well have given some of them. Nunez was a clever man and no doubt divined much of the rest. In any case, common sense will have told him that Pinto was not the sort of man likely to make a satisfactory Brother. There is nothing to show that any ill-feeling existed between them. In the *Peregrination* Pinto's references to Nunez are invariably correct, nor do any of Nunez's letters contain disagreeable reflections on Pinto.

[1]To satisfy the curiosity of the reader, I append here a short note on the fortunes of Christianity in Japan after the departure of Nunez and Pinto. More Jesuits came out and made some headway in the island of Kiu-shiu and in Kyoto. In their efforts to enrich themselves by Western trade, several of the Kiu-shiu barons became Christians, at least in name. In 1578, twenty-seven years after Xavier's visit, Yoshishige himself was baptized, having retired two years earlier from the headship of his state. In 1582 the Jesuits officially reported that there were one hundred and fifty thousand converts, all in Kiu-shiu except twenty-five thousand scattered on the main island in the neighbourhoods of Kyoto and Yamaguchi. This was the favourable period. It corresponded with the rise of the Baron Nobunaga to supreme power as *de facto* Shogun in 1568. Besides the Daimyos he had to reduce the militant Buddhist monks, and it therefore suited him to favour the Christians. But with his successor Hideyoshi (1582) the tide turned against Christianity. In 1587 Hideyoshi issued a decree of banishment against the Jesuits, because he regarded them as a political danger. Gradually pressure was increased and Japanese Christians were proscribed. A series of persecutions took place, each more severe than the last, from 1597 until 1636, which resulted in the suppression of the religion. The persecutions were part of a larger policy of closing Japan against all Europeans. In 1637 it was decreed that no Japanese should leave the country. Foreign trade was abolished except for a few Chinese and Dutch ships which were allowed to visit Nagasaki. Japan remained cut off from the rest of the world until 1868. On the reopening of the country, a few families who had remained Christian were discovered by the missionaries who re-entered with the merchants. Pinto's considered estimate of the Jesuits' future in Japan thus turned out to be sound.

CHAPTER THIRTY-TWO

Pinto returns to Portugal

———————————❖———————————

O n Pinto's arrival at Goa on 17 February 1557, he immediately called on the Viceroy, then Francisco Barreto,
and delivered Yoshishige's letter and presents. The Viceroy was very satisfied with the results of the embassy; an official
trade could now be inaugurated with that part of Japan in place of
the unregulated visits of independent adventurers. Since Pinto had
borne the expenses, the Viceroy was under an obligation to him
and made him the offer of some unspecified appointment or com-
mission which, had Pinto accepted it, would have put a good deal
of money into his pocket. But he was not willing to accept an
appointment in Goa. He had wanted to go home in 1553, and
now in 1557 he was the more inclined to depart. His spectacular
entry as a novice into the Society had been widely discussed and
his resignation therefrom, after such a display of piety at Malacca
and the extravagant hopes which he had voiced, was likely to be
debated by the Jesuits with disapproval and by the public with
amusement. It was not, he thought, a moment to linger. True, to
recoup himself for the very heavy expenses which he had incurred
was a temptation. But there was another way of doing that. He
would ask the Viceroy to set out his services in an official paper and
recommend him for suitable reward to the Crown of Portugal.
In every respect this was more sensible. He was nearing fifty, and
had been in the tropics for twenty years.

The Viceroy made no difficulty whatever in signing the cer-
tificates and attestations which Pinto required of him; we may
well suppose that he was relieved, for thereby he shifted his
obligations on to other shoulders. And he gave him a letter

addressed directly to the King of Portugal 'in which,' says Pinto, 'he made so honourable a mention of me and of my services that relying on my hopes, founded as they were on the most solid grounds, I embarked for home as contented with the papers which I carried with me as if they had been the major part of my fortune, as indeed I believed them to be.'

He does not mention the date of his departure, which may either have been before or after the monsoon of 1557. It is more likely to have been after it, say in November or December 1557, in which case he will have spent some eight months in Goa. That will have given him time to realize all his assets and even perhaps to do a little more business. It is impossible to calculate the sum of money with which he went home, because we do not know how much went in the expenses of the mission, but if, as I estimated further back, he had left a credit of four thousand cruzados in Goa before starting for Japan, and if he still had two thousand of the four thousand cruzados he took with him, the sum will have been six thousand cruzados, or, say, twelve thousand pounds, equal to eighty thousand pounds nowadays. In short, though half his fortune was gone, he retired a rich man.

He reached Lisbon on 22 September 1558. King John III had died the previous year and had been succeeded by his grandson, Sebastian, a child of three years, whose grandmother, Queen Catherine, was acting as Regent. She received Pinto and he presented the Viceroy's letter of recommendation and all the papers of his case. In reply to her questions he gave an account of his adventures, 'in so far as they were likely to further my hopes,' he says. She listened graciously, expressed much interest and made him promises of her favour. At the conclusion of the audience, she handed his papers to one of her ministers, directing him to consider what award should be made. Pinto left her presence quite confident that he soon would be summoned again. But the minister could not be induced to make a recommendation. Four and a half years passed and, though Pinto used all the interest he commanded, he got nothing at the end. 'In pressing my case,' he says, 'I suffered more fatigue than in the worst of my voyages.'

Pinto returns to Portugal

We do not know whether he was asking the Crown to reimburse him for the expenses he had incurred as Ambassador, or petitioning for some title or appointment on the ground of his discovery of Japan, his greatest feat, as he claimed. In the *Peregrination* he declares that he wasted a good deal of money in pushing his claims. I am inclined to think that he wanted an appointment, for he will have known that the Crown was unlikely to accept responsibility for a debt which lay between him and the Viceroy.

That he did not get a post was good fortune in disguise, for had his leisure been occupied he would not have filled it by writing the *Peregrination*. As it was, abandoning his solicitations, he settled down quietly at Almada, opposite Lisbon across the Tagus, married, had children and started to write his famous book, an adventure as extraordinary as any that he had experienced.

It is not easy to describe this last adventure, which occupied him from 1562 until his death in 1583, for it was not just a case of a retired merchant writing a book. Nothing could have been more natural than that he should have wanted to write; he had such new and exciting things to tell. But it was the way he said them that was so unexpected. Most men of his type, when they wrote, did not compose, but jotted down what befell them as in a diary, adding without arrangement useful facts about the products of the countries they had visited, their geography, zoology, manners and customs. Such books are generally short, concise, rather dry and baldly phrased; and they lack form, they are not welded into a unity. But Pinto wrote a book of immense length, over three hundred thousand words, which is an artistic whole. He evolved a style and sustained it; he designed a machinery which was compact and yet allowed him scope, each episode being at once an independent drama and yet a part of the whole picture; he managed his transitions with ease, and did not leave his descriptions in the air, with the result that tension is maintained equally throughout; and though he gives a quantity of information, all his facts are digested by the composition. The *Peregrination* is not a travel book, an autobiography, a history or a romance, for it does not conform to the convention of any one of the four. The author presumes to take an absolute freedom, governed only by the rules of art. His book is the greatest baroque masterpiece in the Portuguese language, and he was one of the literary geniuses of that nation. What could be more extraordinary than this? For twenty years he had devoted all his energies to making money, and, consorting with rough men, far from books, never meeting literary people, kept his eyes turned outward upon a vast panorama of Kings, massacres, shipwrecks, battles, not for an instant realizing that in reality he was a great artist in the act of providing himself with a subject. He comes home with an enormous documentation in his head and, the urge to create presenting itself to him as a happy occupation, he looks inward and, without any assistance or example to guide him, finds in himself, where it had always been, the knowledge of how a work of art is produced. Even then, I surmise, he remained largely in ignorance of his identity, for though he must have felt a profound satisfaction at the release of his powers and the creation that grew under his pen, he could not know how good it was, for the book was not published during his lifetime and so he never had the support of other opinions, the public approbation without which no artist becomes fully conscious of himself. Therefore, the answer to the question—why did Pinto write the *Peregrination* in the way he did?—is that he worked under the dictates of a sense of artistic form which was the essence of his being. He did not know how to write it in any other way. When he took up his pen, he fell naturally into that form; one perceives a glimpse of it even in his two extant letters, where some of the literary devices he afterwards used are to be detected in embryo. To have gone against his prompting as an artist would have only confused him; he would have written badly and painfully, and probably soon have abandoned the effort. What he did was the natural movement of his mind. He could not have known that he was breaking the rules of history, autobiography, travel literature and fiction, because he did not know what the rules were. He just wrote and a work of art gradually took shape. He did not bother to polish; his surface is often rough and the whole lacks the finish of professional writing. But the form, with its balances and tensions, is as strong as a rock and could not be bettered.

The passages where he speaks of his book bear out this interpretation. After saying that God had spared his life to write the *Peregrination*, a rude and unpolished production, but suitable for his children to learn to read in, and hold as a memorial of him and an inheritance, he goes on: 'I have written in my own rough manner, the way I knew how to do it, and without taking pains beyond that. For I thought the best course in dealing with my subject was to treat it as nature has taught me, without searching for circumlocutions or words borrowed to strengthen my poor native talent,' and adds that they would only have laughed at him if he had.

As we have seen, Pinto's way of writing is to present each episode as a drama (tragedy, comedy, melodrama or satire), and arrange the facts, conversations and background accordingly. To add verisimilitude, a quantity of detail is marshalled. If history fits, well and good; if not, dates are transposed. Very little is invented outright, but all is arranged to suit his conception of form. The object of the book is to provide a general impression of Asia between 1538 and 1557, and to give the author opportunity, within the framework, of stating his view, as a man of sensibility, on any matter that arises. No episode can be wholly taken as a direct source for history, but the whole enormously vivifies our apprehension of history.

One question remains to be answered: why did Pinto omit from the *Peregrination* all mention of the religious crisis which led to his entering the Society of Jesus and financing a mission to Japan? The main facts were known to many people in the East and a few at least will have known them in Portugal. His letter of 1554, wherein he describes his conversion in moving terms, had been widely read in Jesuit circles. Why did he suppress the episode in his book, when it was already public property? And if, as I have argued further back, the *Peregrination* has running through it the theme of the sinful man who by expiation comes to enlightenment, surely an account of the enlightenment would have crowned the argument?

But Pinto did not want to discuss this crisis and its denouement. If the interpretation given further back is correct, and he left the Society because he saw that his idea of an immediate and dramatic conversion of Japan was baseless, we can well understand that for him to say so was impossible in a book. To explain how he came to believe that he could do what Xavier had laboured to do, to write that he once pictured himself as effecting an evangelization that would have made him the equal of the great missionary saints of the past, and to declare how in the end he discerned that he had only been dreaming, would have brought him directly into conflict with the Church. The Japan mission was going on; as I have mentioned in the note on page 282, it had some success at first. For Pinto to write that he had left the Society because he perceived that Japan would never submit to Rome would have been to express a most dangerous opinion. In alternative, to have told of his entry into the Society and given an untrue reason for his resignation would have been pointless; why relate the story, if he falsified it? Moreover, what other reason could he give? Living as he had done in close companionship for two years with Belchior Nunez, he must have told the Father the truth. His only course was to omit the episode altogether. His decision in this did not, however, hurt the *Peregrination* as a work of art. Indeed, the balance of its form, which is its great literary excellence, would have been upset had he inserted at this point and nowhere else a long and heartfelt account of a private crisis. Had he been writing an autobiography the omission would have been fatal. But the *Peregrination* has none of the introspection of that kind of writing and has a coherency of another sort. To have implanted a piece of burning introspection would have disrupted its surface. To have included it, a different sort of book altogether would have been required.

The years passed and Pinto lived on at Almada, slowly putting the book into shape. He had his friends, and he talked to them freely of what he was doing, entertaining them by reading out parts or verbally recounting to them his adventures. He remained on good terms with the Society of Jesus. In 1569, when he may have been nearing the end of his task, a certain Father Cipriano Soares, S.J., of the University of Coimbra, who had been to see him, wrote on 22 February of that year to Father Diogo Miron, S.J., in Rome. In the letter he speaks of João de Barros, for a time head of the India House at Lisbon, but now retired to his country seat to finish his history, called *Decadas*, three volumes of which had already been published. He says that Barros was a friend of Pinto's and was often at his house collecting information from him, particularly about Japan. But, he goes on, when the letters written by the Jesuit missionaries in Japan became available, Barros realized that they were a better source for history than what Pinto had read to him from the *Peregrination*. 'Pinto, who has a most happy memory, told me,' he adds, 'that he was a captive eighteen times in various kingdoms. He has written a Commentary on the things which he saw, a book whose publication the public awaits with great interest.'[1]

Barros was an official historian, and has been called the Livy of Portugal. Though to term him so is to overpraise, nevertheless, he was one of the most distinguished men of letters then alive. The heroic achievements of the Portuguese in Asia, crowded into the seventy years which separated Vasco da Gama's first voyage from the date of Soares' letter, had stimulated literature in Portugal, as did a little later in England the exploits of the Elizabethans. For instance, the poet Camoens was living in Lisbon at this very time, and in 1572 published his *Os Lusiadas*, the most celebrated epic poem in the language, and whose subject was his countrymen's conquests in Asia. Besides Barros, two other historians of merit had been writing on Asia, Fernão Lopez de Castanheda and Gaspar Correa. The *Peregrination* was therefore not a solitary phenomenon, but the product of a literary movement, perhaps its

[1]This letter was discovered by Schurhammer in the Jesuit archives in Rome, and is given on p. 140 of his essay *O Descobrimento de Japão pelos Portugueses no ano de 1543*, published in the Annals of the Portuguese Historical Academy in 1946. I am much indebted to Professor Boxer for providing me with it.

greatest product, since it remains to-day more generally readable than any other Portuguese book of the sixteenth century, including *Os Lusiadas*, which, though more polished, is less well constructed, and being dehumanized by a bogus classical mythology, is so tedious and stylized in a vogue now long dead that the modern mind cannot take it seriously.

During the fifteen-seventies Pinto continued to live at Almada, a man known to have written a book on his experiences in Asia which was likely to be interesting, but totally unrecognized for what he was, the greatest living writer in Portugal, if you allow that he has outdistanced Camoens in the contest for immortality. The last date mentioned in the *Peregrination* is 1578, which indicates that he was at least retouching it until that year. Now in 1578 there occurred the most dreadful disaster in Portuguese history. Sebastian had become King at the age of fourteen in 1568. He can only be described as an idiotic youth. In 1578 he led a crusade against the Moors of Morocco, an enterprise several centuries out of date, and was killed along with many of his nobles at the battle of Alcazar. He had no children and his great-uncle, the Cardinal Henrique, who was sixty-six, succeeded. But Philip II of Spain argued that he was the rightful heir as the son-in-law and nephew of John III of Portugal. The Cardinal Henrique died in January 1580, and in December of that year Philip II crossed into Portugal and obtained the requisite Portuguese backing for his claim. Portugal became part of Spain for sixty years, and, as her interests were subordinated to those of her senior partner, her prosperity declined and her empire in Asia began to slip from her grasp.

These events touched Pinto indirectly. One of the things which the Cardinal Henrique did during his brief reign was to ask a Father Maffei, S.J., to write a history in Latin of Portuguese rule in Asia, with special reference to its missionary side. Maffei accepted and, leaving Rome, arrived in Lisbon in the late autumn of 1579. He began at once to collect material in the royal archives. A few months later the Cardinal died and Philip II appeared on the scene. On being informed what Father Maffei was doing, he expressed approval and ordered that every facility should continue to be given him. Maffei went on with his researches and, in order to supplement the papers he found in the archives, decided to make inquiries from persons who had been to Japan. He was advised to consult Pinto, who had already given Barros information and was so well known to the Society as a former novice. In October 1582 Pinto, by now a man of seventy-three, was invited to Valderosal, an estate near Almada which belonged to the Jesuits. There he was received by Maffei's assistant, Father Rebello, and another Jesuit called Father Gonçalvez. Rebello made a note for Maffei[1] of what Pinto said, and that note has recently been discovered by Schurhammer[2] among Maffei's papers in the Jesuit archives. It is a document of importance in Pinto's biography.

The *Peregrination* was finished, but not published, before Pinto went to Valderosal; we do not know whether he had tried to find a publisher or not. He may have been afraid to do so, for it contained political and religious opinions which might have offended both the Crown and the Inquisition. What is most likely, however, is that he could not find a publisher. As far back as 1569 Father Soares, S.J., as we have seen, knew of the book's existence, and what he said of it suggests that its publication was expected. That Maffei, though he must have heard of it, had not at that time read it in manuscript is clear from the fact that he invited Pinto to Valderosal and questioned him on what was to be found set out there at length.

Let us consider Pinto's position in regard to his interview with the Jesuits, which I shall discuss in detail in a minute. He had written a book which he hoped to get published, or knew was likely to be published eventually. This book was an artistic creation, a wonderful unity in which information of all kinds was transmuted into a style, a book which transcended history, autobiography and romance, for it was all three, and yet none of the three, a unique book, unlike any other, which he had evolved

[1] It is not clear whether Maffei was present, but it would seem likely that he was.
[2] See p. 34 *seq.* of his op. cit.

out of his consciousness as an original artist. He was not a critic. He had no means of telling how it would be received and how it would be classified; nor whether it would be held to contain the essential truth even if, driven by his feeling for form, he had been compelled to arrange his narrative. But he will have known instinctively that the Jesuits were the wrong people to discuss it with; they were not interested in that kind of writing, being annalists and propagandists. How should he answer their questions? Common sense told him that his replies must coincide with what he had written. Were he to make statements differing from the *Peregrination*, without being able to explain to them why the differences existed, his book, which contained much that was difficult to believe, though true, would receive no credence at all when it came out. Everything in it, to his mind, was true in a large sense; it was the most authentic and complete picture of sixteenth-century Asia that had been written, that would ever be written. But it was a picture as seen by an artist, not by a chronicler. For him to qualify it in advance would be a stupidity. This, we may be sure, was the line he had already taken with Barros; he would take it again with Father Maffei.

We can now understand his answers to the Jesuits' questions, which were confined to China and Japan. He began by relating a piece of legendary Chinese history about the origin of that kingdom, a story that someone had told him in China. He described Peking with fair accuracy, as its main features had been reported to him, adding information about Chinese law, their appellate system, their punishments, their prisons, their prison libraries and their prisoners' welfare societies, and intimating that he was speaking from personal experience. Instinctively he used his device of adding verisimilitude by means of intimate detail, and informed them that in Peking restaurants the waiter brought you a menu with the names of the dishes and their prices, a custom then unknown in Europe. He said that the chief Chinese religion was Buddhism, similar to the religion of Burma and Siam, and in a parenthesis minutely described the Burmese pagodas, and spoke of the jewelled umbrella that crowns their summits. The

Tartar invasion is mentioned and, in reply to a question about the Christianity already in China, he told them about a Christian missionary, the descendants of whose converts were still to be found, a story that appears to be an echo that had reached him of the Nestorians of the seventh century and the Franciscan Friars of the thirteenth. The episode of Ines de Leiria, daughter of the Ambassador, Tomé Pires, who showed him the cross on her arm, is duly recounted. When they asked him about Japan, he declared that he with two other Portuguese was its first discoverer, and added another of his detailed statements, a curious one not mentioned in the *Peregrination*, relating to the storm that drove them to Japan. Rebello's record of it is as follows: 'They experienced, he said, great hardships on the high seas, especially in regard to water. The way it was rationed was as follows: a handkerchief was moistened in the water and, as soon as a man had sucked it, it was dipped again and given to another.' There follows the story of the burst arquebus and how Pinto healed the young Prince's hand. The return to Ningpo, the rush of the merchants to Japan, and Pinto's shipwreck on Okinawa are included, as is his second visit to Japan and the flight of Antonio of the Sacred Faith. In short, all he told them came out of the *Peregrination* with the exception of a few extra details.

The sequel to the visit is interesting as an indication of what was later to follow. Maffei published his book, *Historia Indica*, in 1589, seven years later. He does not mention Pinto nor the *Peregrination*, though, as we shall see, he had read it in the meantime. He adopted other sources for the discovery of Japan, and, though he made some use of the *Peregrination* where it deals with Xavier, he does not acknowledge this. In short, for the precise annalistic record which he was compiling, he rejected Pinto as an authority.

Philip II, as stated, crossed into Portugal in October 1580 and took up his residence in Almada in July 1581, not far from Pinto's house, later crossing the river to Lisbon, where he remained until February 1583. In the course of these twenty months he heard of Pinto as a man who had had unusual adventures in the East and had written a book about them. It is thought he may have been told this by Maffei, whose acquaintance he made, as we know. But from whatever source the information came, he was interested and sent for Pinto. We have the spectacle of the great Spanish King taking a fancy to the extraordinary adventurer, who was also a great artist. He invited him more than once to come to see him and tell him stories about the Far East. 'The King loved to listen to him by the hour.'[1]

Now that Pinto at last had the ear of royalty, it would seem probable that he told Philip how the Regent, Queen Catherine, on his retirement twenty-two years before, had promised on the Viceroy's recommendation to do something for him but had never done anything. At any rate, Philip felt he deserved some official recognition and on 15 January 1583 granted him 'for his services in India', as the document says, an annual rental of two hogsheads of corn, i.e. one thousand pounds' weight, equivalent to three loaves of bread a day.

But Pinto had come to the end of his life. He died the same year on the third day of May.

---

[1]So says Francisco de Herrera in the preface to his Spanish translation of the *Peregrination* (published 1620). He adds: 'Pinto told King Philip the same story which is now before me. What was good enough for His Majesty is good enough for the public.'

CHAPTER THIRTY-THREE

The Peregrination

T he story of what happened to the *Peregrination* is the last adventure I have to record. Pinto died before finding a publisher. But he gave instructions about the disposal of the manuscript. In its text he had left it to his children as a memorial and an inheritance; now he decided to dispose of it differently, as if, in default of publication, he desired that it should be read at least by some people. The Casa Pia das Penitentes was an institution in Lisbon for fallen women. He was interested in it, and may have been one of its visitors. The *Peregrination*, he thought, would be suitable reading for these women, and he directed that it was to be made over to the Governor of the Casa Pia on condition that it should be read out to them. After his death his daughters—for apparently his children were daughters —respected his wish, which was apparently not in testamentary form, and delivered the manuscript, thereby abandoning it as a personal inheritance. Perhaps they despaired that it would ever be published.

It seems that the Jesuits were also visitors of the Casa Pia. When they heard that the Governor had a book which they had long heard of but never read, and which was reputed to contain passages relating to Xavier, they borrowed it. It was then that Maffei, S.J., read it, and drew on it for his *Historia Indica* of 1589. It was also read by João de Lucena, S.J., who incorporated into his *Historia da vida do Padre Francisco de Xavier*, published in 1600, those parts of it which describe the Saint's journeys in the Far

East, though without acknowledgment.[1] Fernão Guerreiro, S.J., did the same, as is proved by an examination of his *Relaçam Anual* (1602-1612), and so did Tursellini, S.J., in his *De vita Francisci Xaverii* (1594).

This interest in the book from so high a quarter eventually led the Governor of the Casa Pia to think of publication; no doubt, he and those of his friends who had read it saw its possibilities and liked it as much as, I am sure, the fallen women did. But there were delays and difficulties. One of the difficulties was that Pinto had not left the manuscript ready for publication. It was an immense work and required careful revision. The dates and names were confused in places, there were no chapter divisions, the curious place-names were hard to read, some passages required cutting or modification. But who was competent to prepare it for the press? And who would give the time, who was trustworthy? In the end they got the best man they could, a certain Francisco de Andrada, who had the official post of Chief Chronicler to the government. (The Spanish translator, Herrera, had a poor opinion of Andrada, who, he says in the preface to his edition of 1620, damaged the book by confusing rather than correcting the arrangement. But since the Spanish edition is from the first Portuguese edition and not from the manuscript, it sounds as if Herrera had insufficient grounds for this criticism. The real criticism to my mind is that Andrada did nothing to clear away the obvious blemishes in the text.)

Application was made for permission to publish in 1603. The Inquisition's licence is dated 25 May of that year, and declares the book to contain nothing 'contrary to the sacred faith and good morals'. Indeed, the censor, Brother Manoel Coelho, who was, I assume, a Dominican, evidently enjoyed the book, for he added

---

[1] It was not customary at that date to make acknowledgments. Pinto himself takes from Gaspar da Cruz's *Tractato . . . da China* (1569) without acknowledgment. Some have argued that the Jesuits never forgave Pinto for leaving the Society and wanted to suppress his name. But I see no proof of any animus; cf. Soares' letter, Maffei's consultation and recommendation to Philip II, their eagerness to read his book, and, finally, the fact that they used no pressure to prevent it being published.

to the formal authorization: 'It is a very good history, full of novelties and variety which ought to please everyone.' This was the first written criticism of a work which was to continue to be a subject of critical discussion from that date until the present time.

In spite of Brother Coelho's little puff, no publisher could be found willing to bring out a book of such length and dealing with such unusual subjects. Official historians, like Barros, and the Jesuit writers had funds behind them, but the *Peregrination* came up strictly as a commercial proposition. For ten years the search for a publisher continued. At last a certain Pedro Crasbeeck accepted it, and it was published in 1614.

Thirty-one years had elapsed since Pinto's death, and between sixty to eighty years since the events described in the book. In that interval much had happened to make its contents less extra-ordinary and new. Barros, Camoens, Castanheda, Correa, Maffei and the biographers of Xavier had published their books. The situation in the orient had also much changed, for the English and the Dutch East India Companies had been founded, and their ships ranged over the Portuguese preserves. The *Peregrination*, from being a topical book, had become a description of a period that was ended.

But all this made no difference to its success, which was enor-mous. It ran into nineteen editions in six languages between 1614 and 1700. There were two Portuguese editions, seven Spanish, three French, two Dutch, two German and three English. (The English translation by Henry Cogan was not complete, for it left out, among other passages, the chapters relating to Xavier, as its Commonwealth readers would not have been interested in a Papist missionary.) How enormous was the success is not fully conveyed by the number of editions. In the seventeenth century, the reading public was small and confined to the top. The figures, in fact, indicate that most educated people in Europe had read it before 1700. By that date Pinto had as many readers as Cervantes, whose *Don Quixote* was published in 1604 (first part) and 1615 (second part).

But Pinto was read for entertainment, not for truth. Few people believed him, for the same reason that no one in the centuries that followed Marco Polo's death believed the Venetian traveller. His stories sounded too extraordinary to be true. As the century went on, his reputation as a liar increased. When in 1695, Congreve made Foresight in his *Love for Love* abuse another character by saying: 'Ferdinand Mendes Pinto was but a type of thee, thou liar of the first magnitude,' he was making an allusion which everyone in the audience perfectly understood. This common repute, as reflected in the play, is explained by the incredulity of ignorance. It was not that the public had examined the text against other sources and found it mendacious. On the contrary, Cogan had prefaced his translation by a long argument, founded on what authorities he could marshall, that the *Peregrination* was reliable history. The reason was simply that people could not believe in Pinto's adventures.[1]

Nevertheless, it is possible that some whisper, originating in Jesuit circles, had gone round. The Jesuit point of view at this date was curious. What Pinto had written of Xavier, they believed or at any rate used for propaganda. But their missionaries in Japan had told them flatly that in their opinion the *Peregrination* was not an historical document. A certain João Rodriguez Tçuzzu, S.J., who was in Japan and Macao from 1577 to 1634, wrote in his *Historia da Ingreja do Japão*: 'Fernão Mendes Pinto in his book of fictions seeks to present himself as one of the three men (who discovered Japan). But that is false, as are many other allegations in his work, which he seems to have composed more to amuse than to convey the truth, for there is not a kingdom or an event with which he does not pretend to have had to do.'[2] Though this over-

[1]In one of Dorothy Osborne's letters to Sir Willam Temple we have the seventeenth-century view of Pinto and his book amusingly expressed: "'Tis as diverting a book of the kind as ever I read and as handsomely written. You must allow him the privilege of a traveller, and he does not abuse it. His lies are as pleasant harmless ones as lies can be, and in no great number, considering the scope he has for them. There is one in Dublin now, that ne'er saw much farther, has told me twice as many (I dare swear) of Ireland.' Professor C. R. Boxer drew my attention to this passage.

[2]See p. 33 of Le Gentil's op. cit. and Schurhammer's *D. P. Johann Rodriguez Tçuzzu als Geschichtschreiber Japans* (Rome, 1932). The word Tçuzzu is a rendering of the Japanese word for interpreter and was given this Rodriguez as a nickname to distinguish him from another Jesuit also called Rodriguez.

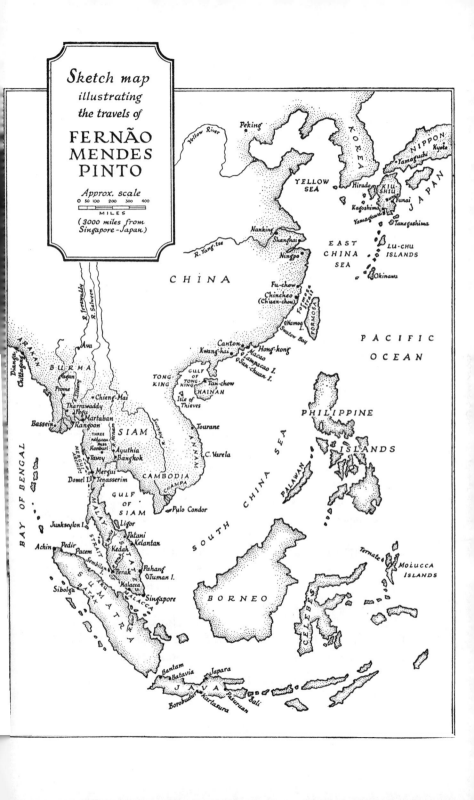

Sketch map
illustrating
the travels of

FERNÃO
MENDES
PINTO

Approx. scale
0 50 100 200 300 400
MILES
(3000 miles from
Singapore – Japan.)

sharp criticism was not known outside the headquarters of the Society, for Tçuzzu's history was not published,[1] it and others like it from missionaries on the spot will have given the Jesuits a measured opinion of the *Peregrination*, totally different from the blank incredulity of the general public, yet contributing to it if their criticisms were whispered round. But they had to be careful, for if they openly criticized Pinto they would be doing the memory of their Saint Francis Xavier no good.

While everybody read Pinto in the seventeenth century, general interest in him died down in the eighteenth, because in the clear light of that century his book seemed too Catholic and old-fashioned. In fact, it was only reprinted for the devout. This neglect continued through the greater part of the nineteenth century.

But a change was coming that was to bring him again to the fore. When modern historians turned their attention to oriental history, they were astonished to find that the *Peregrination* was concerned with real events. To take an example: Arthur Phayre published in 1883 his *History of Burma*, the first ever written from original sources. In it Tabin Shwé-ti and Bayin Naung figured as important historical personages, though for nearly three centuries it had been assumed that Pinto had invented them. It was the same all the way along the line. A strong reaction in Pinto's favour now set in. He had been wronged, wronged by people who thought they were smart but were merely ignorant. Professor H. Külb, in his *Ferdinand Mendes Pinto's abenteuerliche Reise* of 1868, said: 'At first, when Pinto alone described these distant lands, one regarded his narrative as an adventurer's fabulous story, but we have learnt from recent books of travel that even the more unlikely parts are based on fact. Though one is prepared to admit that particulars are embellished, in general the book gives a truthful picture.'

This was the period when justice was also being done to Marco Polo, who had lain under a cloud for six hundred years. In 1871 Henry Yule published his elaborate edition of the *Travels* and

---

[1]It did not appear until 1900, when J. M. Cros, S.J., included part of it in his *Life and Letters of St. Francis Xavier*.

proved that Polo was a conscientious reporter, who had never intentionally uttered a falsehood. Many scholars began to study Pinto with care, their first impulse being to clear his memory and show that the *Peregrination* was a unique document for the history of the years 1537 to 1557 in Asia. As time went on, the book was put under a microscope, and articles, notes, papers and commentaries in Portuguese, French, German and Japanese were published one after the other, *vide* those enumerated in Schurhammer's pamphlet in *Asia Major*, Vol. III, pp. 3–33 (Leipzig, 1927). The examination of the text is not yet complete, and is still being carried on with unabated zest by Schurhammer himself and a host of others. In 1930 Jordão de Freitas brought out a new Portuguese edition with notes and a biographical introduction. Professor Charles Boxer of the University of London has told me that at one time he contemplated editing an English edition, but abandoned the project, deterred by his conviction that the book was not an historical source proper and that its examination in that sense would be a waste of time. Indeed, if my view is correct that it is a work of art of an original kind, a scholar, in attempting to assess its historical value in a critical edition, would sink in a morass of speculations. Nearly every statement in it has a degree of historical value, but that degree varies from the plain statement of a fact to the statement (in the form of a drama, a description or a dialogue) which is an amalgam of things seen or heard somewhere and arranged to bring out a point, relevant to the understanding of the period but not precisely a statement of a particular happening. An editor of a fully annotated *Peregrination* would be obliged to disentangle the various degrees of historical value and make a pronouncement upon each, a task which would be limitless in a book of the *Peregrination's* size. Moreover, since each of these pronouncements would be a matter of opinion, no agreement would be possible on the whole range of them. The scholars who have examined the *Peregrination* with a view to distilling from it an historical essence have come to opposite conclusions on particular passages. By the exercise of sufficient ingenuity it is possible to give an identification for every place-name in the book, but no two scholars would agree on the list; it is also feasible to date every event but not in a way to carry general conviction. The more the book is dissected with such objects in view, the more inextricably tangled does the commentary become. A point is reached when the scholar inevitably asks himself the question: 'Am I applying to this extraordinary work a method unsuited to its nature and incapable of wringing from it anything definite?'

The historical method, however, has yielded certain very definite results. In the seventeenth century the public thought Pinto was a liar, a man of the most fertile imagination, who had invented a whole world of Asiatic adventure. As a result of the investigations of the twentieth century it is now known that he invented nothing; his description of sixteenth-century Asia is authentic to the last detail. But he did not set it down, as I have said, in any one of the manners generally used for conveying information of the sort, that of the reporter or the historian, the autobiographer or memoir writer, the traveller or novelist. His temperament dictated to him a different manner and he threw his total impressions of twenty years into an artistic form, which has no clear definition, but which pleased him, satisfied his sense of what was fitting, had a certain roundness and uniformity allied to the baroque, and which he alone knew how to manage with success.

He had no master and he has had no disciples; no book composed like the *Peregrination* was written before him, nor has any been written since. Among the great host of those who have subsequently made Asia familiar to us, the historians, the travellers, philosophers and novelists, the scholars, journalists, the residents and soldiers, not one has modelled himself on the *Peregrination*, which has never been recognized for what it is, a masterpiece which enlarges, by transcending, truth.

Bibliography

Alvares, Franciso, *Viaggio nella Ethiopia* (Venice, 1563).

Ayres, Christóvão, *Fernão Mendes Pinto, subsidios para a sua biografia e para o estudo da sua obra* (Lisbon, 1904).
Fernão Mendes Pinto e o Japão, Pontos controversos (Lisbon, 1906).

Barbosa, Duarte, *Livro em que dá relação do que viu e ouviu no Oriente* (1516).
The Book of Duarte Barbosa (Hakluyt Society, 1918–21).

Barros, João de, *Decadas da Asia de João de Barros e de Diogo do Couto* (Lisbon, 1778–1788).

Bellessort, André, *L'apôtre des Indes et du Japon, saint François Xavier* (Paris, 1917).

Botero, Giovanni, *Relationi universali* (Brescia, 1598).

Bonhours, Le P., *Vie de saint François-Xavier* (Avignon, 1828).

Boxer, Charles Ralph, *Some aspects of Portuguese influence in Japan, 1542–1640* (The Transactions of the Japan Society, vol. XXXIII, London, 1936).
Notes on Early European Military Influence in Japan (The Transactions of the Asiatic Society of Japan, Tokyo, 1932).
Three Historians of Portuguese Asia (Barros, Couto and Bocarro) (Macao, 1948).
Fidalgos in the Far East, 1550–1770 (The Hague, 1948).

Brou, *Saint François-Xavier, 1506–1548* (Paris, 1922).

Camoëns, Luis de, *Os Lusiadas* (Lisbon, 1572).

Campos, J. J. A., *History of the Portuguese in Bengal* (Calcutta, 1919).
Early Portuguese Accounts of Thailand (1940).

Bibliography

Cartas que os padres e irmãos da Companhia de Jesus, que andão nos reynos de Japão, escreverão aos da mesma companhia da India e Europa desd'o anno de 1549 até o de 66 (Coimbra, 1570).

Cartas que los padres y hermanos de la Compañia de Jesus, que andan en los reinos de Japon escrivieron a los de la misma compañia desde el año de 1549 hasta el de 1575 (Alcalá, 1575).

Cary, Otis, A History of Christianity in Japan (London, 1909).

Castanheda, Fernão Lopes de, O terceiro livro da historia do descobrimento e conquista da India (Coimbra, 1552).

Castanhoso, Miguel, História das cousas que o mui esforçado capitão D. Cristóvão da Gama fêz nos reinos do Preste João (Lisbon, 1936).

Castilho, António Feliciano de, Fernão Mendes Pinto excerptos seguidos de uma noticia sobre sua vida e obra (Rio de Janeiro, 1865–1875).

Charignon, A. J. H., A propos des voyages aventureux de Fernand Mendes Pinto, notes de A. J. H. Charignon recueillies et complétées par Mlle. M. Médard (Peking, 1936).

Cogan, Henry, The Voyages and Adventures of Ferdinand Mendez Pinto, a Portugal. During his Travels for the space of one and twenty years in the Kingdoms of Ethiopia, China, Tartaria, Cauchin-china, Calaminham, Siam, Pegu, Japan, and a great part of the East Indies. With a relation and description of most of the places thereof; their Religion, Laws, Riches, Customs, and Government in the time of Peace and War. Where he five times suffered Shipwrack, was sixteen times sold, and thirteen times made a slave. Written originally by himself in the Portugal Tongue, and Dedicated to the Majesty of Philip King of Spain. Done into English by H. C. Gent (London, 1653).

Collet, O. J. A., Terres et peuples de Sumatra (Amsterdam, 1925).

Conquista de Reyno de Pegu, feyta pelos portuguezes sendo visorrey da India Ayres de Saldanha no anno de 1600 (Peregrination, edition of 1711).

Correa, Gaspar, Lendas da India (Lisbon, 1858–1861).

Bibliography

Cortesão, Armando, *The Suma Oriental of Tomé Pires* (Hakluyt Society, 1944).

Couto, Diogo do, see Barros.

Cros, S.J., José-Marie, *Saint François-Xavier* (Toulouse, 1900).

Cruz, Gaspar da, *Tractado em que se contam muito por extenso as cousas da China, com suas particularidades e assi de reyno Dormuz, Composto por el. R. Padre Frey Gaspar da Cruz da orden de Sam Domingos* (Evora, 1569).

Danvers, F. C., *The Portuguese in India* (London, 1894).

Delplage, L., *Le catholicisme au Japon, saint François-Xavier et ses premiers successeurs, 1540–1593* (Brussels, 1909).

Du Jarric, Pierre, *Histoire des choses mémorables advenues tant ez Indes orientales que autres païs de la descouverte des Portugais* (Bordeaux, 1608).

Esquemeling, John, *The Buccaneers of America* (London, 1684).

Fergusson, Donald, *Letters from Portuguese captives in Canton, written in 1534 and 1536, with an introduction on Portuguese intercourse with China in the first half of the sixteenth century* (Bombay, 1901).

Figuier, Bernard, *Les voyages adventureux de Fernand Mendes Pinto, fidellement traduits de portugais en français par le sieur Bernard Figuier, gentil-homme portugais* (Paris, 1645).

Freitas, Jordão de, *Peregrinação, nova edição conforme à de 1614, precedida de una noticia bio-bibliografica* (Lisbon, 1930).
F. Mendes Pinto, Literatura portuguesa ilustrada.

Frois, P. Luis, *Die Geschichte Japans 1549–1578*, translation of G. Schurhammer and E. A. Voretzsch (Leipzig, 1926).

Galvão, Antonio, *Tratado dos descobrimentos antigos e modernos, feitos até a era de 1550, com os nomes particulares das pessoas que os fizerão: e em que tempos e as suas alturas, e dos desvairados caminhos por onde a pimenta e especiaria veyo da India às nossas partes* (Lisbon, 1781).

Bibliography

Guzman, Luiz de, *Historia de las misiones que han hecho los religiosos de la Compañia de Jesus para predicar el Santo evangelio en la India oriental y en los reinos de la China y Japon* (Alcazar, 1601)

Haas, Hans, *Geschichte des Christentums in Japan,* t. I: *Erste Einführung des Christentums in Japan durch Franz Xavier* (Tokyo, 1902) t. II: *Fortschritte des Christentums unter der Superiorat des P. Cosme de Torres* (Tokyo, 1904).

Harvey, G. E., *History of Burma* (London, 1925).

História trágico-marítima (Oporto, 1936–1937); partial translation, *Tragiques histoires de mer au XVIe siècle* (Le Gentil, Paris, 1939).

Kammerer, A., *Le problématique voyage en Abyssinie de Fernand Mendes Pinto, 1537.*

Le Gentil, G., *Fernão Mendes Pinto, un précurseur de l'èxotisme au XVIe siècle* (Paris, 1947).

Lucena, João de, *Historia da vida do Padre Francisco de Xavier e do que fizerão na India os mais religiosos da Companhia de Jesu* (Lisbon, 1600).

Maffei, *Histoire des Indes de Jean-Pierre Maffei, bergamesque, de la Société de Jésus* (Lyons, 1603).
   Historiarum indicarum libri XVI (Anvers, 1605).

Marsden, William, *The History of Sumatra* (London, 1783).

McLeod, John, *Voyage of His Majesty's Ship Alceste along the coast of Corea to the island of Lewchew* (London, 1818).

Mendoça, Joan Gonzalez de, *Historia de las cosas mar notables, ritos y costumbres del Gran Reyno de la China* (Rome, 1585).

Monumenta Xaveriana, t. I, Madrid, 1899–1900 (*Monumenta historica societatis Jesu*) t. II, *Processus varii de vita, virtutibus et miraculis sancti Francisci Xaverii* (Madrid, 1912).

Murdoch, James, and Isoh Yamagata, *A history of Japan during the century of early foreign intercourse (1542-1651)* (Kobe, 1903).

Nagaoka, H., *Histoire des relations de Japon avec l'Europe aux XVIe et XVIIe siècles* (Paris, 1905).

Bibliography

Orlandino, Nicolão, *Historiae societatis Jesu pars prima sive Ignatius.* (Anvers, 1620).

Parmentier, *Le discours de la navigation de Jean et Raoul Parmentier de Dieppe* (Paris, 1883).

Phayre, Arthur, *History of Burma* (London, 1883).

Pinto, Fernão Mendes, *Peregrinaçam de Fernam Mendez Pinto em que da conta de muytas e muyto estranhas cousas que vio e ouvio no reyno da China, no da Tartaria, no de Sornau, que vulgarmente se chama Sião, no do Calaminham, no de Pegu, no de Martavão, e em outros muytos reynos e senhorios das partes orientais, de que nestas nossas do occidente ha muyto pouca ou nenhũa noticia, e tambem da conta de muytos casos particulares que acontecerão assi a elle como a outras muytas pessoas. E no fim della trata brevemente de algũas cousas e da morte do Santo Padre mestre Francisco Xavier unica luz e resplandor daquellas partes do Oriente e reytor nellas universal da Companhia de Jesus, escrita pelo mesmo Fernão Mendez Pinto, dirigido à Catholica Real Majestade del Rey Dom Felippe o III deste nome nosso senhor. Com licença do Santo Officio, Ordinario e Paço, Em Lisboa por Pedro Crasbeec anno 1614.*

Ricci, Matteo, *I commentarii* (Macerata, 1911); *Le lettere della China* (Macerata, 1913).

Sadler, A. L., *A Short History of Japan* (London, 1946).

San Roman, Antonio, *Historia General de la India oriental compuesta por Fray Antonio San Roman, monge de San Benito* (Valladolid, 1603).

Sansom, G. B., *Japan, a short cultural history* (London, 1931).

Schnitger, F. M., *Forgotten Kingdoms in Sumatra* (Leiden, 1939).

Schurhammer, P. Georg, *Der Heilige Franz Xaver, der Apostel von Indien und Japan* (Freiburg, 1925).

    Fernão Mendez Pinto und seine Peregrinaçam (*Asia Major*, Leipzig, 1926).

    P. Johann Rodriguez Tçuzzu als Geschichtschreiber Japans (Rome, 1932).

Bibliography

O Descobrimento do Japão pelos Portugueses no ano de 1543, translated into Portuguese by P. Francesco Rodriguez, S.J., in Anais II série, vol. I, 1946, of Academia Portuguesa da Historia.

Sousa, Francisco de, *Oriente Conquistado* (Lisbon, 1710).

Steichen, M., *Les daimyô chrétiens ou un siècle de l'histoire religieuse et politique du Japon 1549-1650* (Hong Kong, 1904).

Thomas, Henry (in collaboration with Armando Cortesão), *The discovery of Abyssinia by the Portuguese in 1520* (London, 1938).
Carta das Novas que Vieram a El Rei Nosso Senhor do Descobrimento de Preste João (Lisbon, 1521) (Lisbon, 1938).

Trigault, Nicolas, *Histoire de l'expédition chrestienne en la Chine entreprise par les P.P. de la Compagnie de Jésus, tirée des commentaires du P. Mathieu par le P. Nicolas Trigault, de la même Compagnie* (Paris, 1618).

Tursellini, *De vita Francisci Xaverii* (Rome, 1594).

Whiteway, R. W., *The Rise of the Portuguese Power in India 1497-1550* (London, 1899).

Winstedt, Sir Richard, *Malaya and its History* (London, 1948).

Wood, W. A. R., *A History of Siam from the earliest times to the year A.D. 1781* (London, 1926).

Index

Index

Index

Index